HURON COUNTY LIBRARY

HURON COUNTY LIBRARY

3 6492 00346563

D0856276

31482

6768

823
.8
Stoke
-H

Haining, Peter.
  The un-dead : the legend of Bram Stoker and
Dracula / Peter Haining and Peter Tremayne.
--London : Constable, 1997.
  199 p., [12] p. of plates : ill. --

Includes bibliographical references (p. 185-191) and
index.
833896   ISBN:0094754306

(SEE NEXT CARD)
439   97DEC04   3559/he   1-496342

THE
UN-DEAD

The Legend of
Bram Stoker and Dracula

THE
UN-DEAD

The Legend of
Bram Stoker and Dracula

PETER HAINING
AND
PETER TREMAYNE

CONSTABLE · LONDON

DEC 1 6 '97

First published in Great Britain 1997
by Constable and Company Limited
3 The Lanchesters, 162 Fulham Palace Road
London W6 9ER
Copyright © Peter Tremayne and Peter Haining 1997
The right of Peter Tremayne and Peter Haining to be
identified as the authors of this work has been asserted by
them in accordance with the Copyright, Designs and
Patents Act 1988
ISBN 0 09 475430 6
Set in Linotron Ehrhardt 10½ by
CentraCet Ltd, Cambridge
Printed in Great Britain by
St Edmundsbury Press Ltd
Bury St Edmunds, Suffolk

A CIP catalogue record for this book
is available from the British Library

For
'The Bloofer Ladies'
– Philippa and Dorothy

CONTENTS

ILLUSTRATIONS

between pages 96 and 97

Sir Henry Irving as Mephistopheles, in Goethe's *Faust* (*Courtesy of James Carew*)

Whitby Harbour and Church Steps (*Authors' collection*)

Slain's Castle, the inspiration for Dracula's castle (*Courtesy Aberdeen City Council*)

The model of Dracula's Castle built for the 1979 film version of *Dracula* (*National Film Archive, London*)

PREFACE

One hundred years ago, in June 1897, Constable and Company of London published a novel entitled *Dracula* by Bram Stoker. It has became part of world folklore for it was not just another Gothic horror tale. Like its literary predecessor, Mary Shelley's *Frankenstein*, it was seen as a moral myth, replete with allegorical implications, whose appeal has not only passed from one generation to another but has transcended nationality and differing cultures, having succeeded in harnessing haunting and powerful imagery which impinges on the universality of the subconscious. *Dracula* has been one of the most extraordinary literary creations of any age.

This volume is not just another biography of Bram Stoker. Neither is it a critical dissertation on the novel. *Dracula* has, in fact, promoted more researches, literary studies and legend-making concerning its origins and compositions than most major works of fiction. Psychologists and would-be psychologists have also had a field day as they stumble around seeking signs and symbols in the text. But the current volume is simply an attempt to present the realities behind the numerous fables which have sprung up about Stoker and the influences which led to the writing of the novel which he initially entitled 'The Un-Dead'.

In this celebration of the centenary of the original publication of the world's most enduring weird fantasy will be found much new biographical material concerning Stoker's first thirty-one years in Ireland and, therefore, the formative influences on his writing career. To date there have been no fewer than four full-length biographies of Stoker – two English, one American and one French – and doubtless others may appear in this

11

centenary year. Sadly, in our opinion, those so far published have perpetuated many errors of fact. Stoker's early years and family background seem to have been badly researched. That area of his life strangely, has apparently not been considered relevant to his work. This, we feel, is like trying to propose the argument that James Joyce's *Ulysses* can be understood without an appreciation of the fact that James Joyce was a product of a particular Irish cultural background. Stoker's own Irish cultural consciousness is an integral part of his masterpiece.

The countless studies on the supposed influences behind Stoker's creation have, curiously, tended to ignore this background and set off in search of the exotic and bizarre in Transylvania. Stoker never went there. His influences were more immediate and were to be found in Ireland, in London and Whitby in England, in Cruden Bay in Scotland, and among his family and friends.

It is our intention to bring Stoker back from the realms of misinformation, speculative fantasy and legend, to the reality of his background and those immediate influences which caused him to create one of the most enduring, terrifying stories ever written – a tale which has become one of our most lasting twentieth-century myths.

CHAPTER ONE

The Making of a Legend

On the morning of Thursday, 20 May 1897, a hansom cab rounded London's Parliament Square and rattled along Parliament Street towards Whitehall. It was a bright, warm day. The white roofs of many of the hansoms were proof that the cab drivers had taken notice of the heat wave which had begun on Tuesday and already changed into their summer colours. The *Daily Mail* had observed that morning: 'The summer of 1897 has dawned for the eighth time, and everyone declares it has now come to stay'. On the previous two days the temperature had varied between 64°F and 76°F.

Along Whitehall, women in summer frocks and parasols, more in order to be seen than with a fixed destination in mind, strolled up and down while ice-cream vendors and fruit-sellers enjoyed a brisk trade. The open-top horse-drawn omnibuses clattered along with their upper decks crowded with people trying to avoid the stuffy interiors. 'To wait for a 'bus with a vacant top is like waiting for the Jubilee,' commented the *Daily Mail* correspondent drily. Queen Victoria's Diamond Jubilee celebrations, scheduled to be held on 22 June, had long been in the planning and were the subject of much speculation and frustration. Many business houses had already put their porters and messengers in white summer uniforms, and the appearance of water-carts in residential streets was another sign of the onset of the hot weather.

The hansom clattered into the broad Whitehall thoroughfare, in the direction of Trafalgar Square, but then slowed to make a right-hand turn into a small side road which led into a cool, tree-lined cul-de-sac; a square

which enclosed a luxuriant garden, a country-style oasis in the middle of
the city. Whitehall Gardens consisted of a row of seven elegant terraced
Georgian houses. Alas, these buildings no longer exist, neither does
Whitehall Gardens. They are now replaced by the imposing Ministry of
Defence building. The gardens had once been the Privy Gardens of
Whitehall Palace at the rear of the Banqueting House where Charles I had
stepped to his execution. Residential houses were first built there in the
eighteenth century, their back lawns stretching down to the banks of
the sedately flowing Thames. During the nineteenth century Whitehall
Gardens, as the Privy Gardens were renamed, became one of the most
fashionable residential streets in London. The new terraced houses were
erected during the first decade of the century. No. 4 had been the home of
Sir Robert Peel, who died there on 2 July 1850 as a result of a fall from his
horse, while Benjamin Disraeli moved into No. 2 two years before Victoria
made him Earl of Beaconsfield. He lived there until 1878.

It was outside No. 2 Whitehall Gardens that the hansom cab drew to a
halt that warm May morning. No. 2 consisted of four storeys with a
basement and an attic, but it was no longer a family house. It had been
turned into offices. The basement and the first two floors were the offices
of the publishers, Archibald Constable and Company. Three other firms
used the remaining floors. All these companies held the premises by
leasehold.

Although the firm of Archibald Constable and Company had been in
business in London for only seven years, the name had long been respected
in the world of literature and publishing. Archibald Constable (1774–1827)
from Carnbee, Fife, had become an apprentice to an Edinburgh bookseller
named Peter Hill. In 1795 Constable had opened his own shop and, in
1798, began publishing books for himself. In 1801 he had purchased the
Scots Magazine and the following year launched the *Edinburgh Review*.
The *Edinburgh Review* was Europe's most influential literary review in its
heyday. Sir Walter Scott began publishing his novels with Constable from
1803 and also invested heavily in the company. In 1812 Constable
purchased the rights to publish the *Encyclopaedia Britannica*. However, in
1827, Constable's London agents, Hurst and Robinson, financially collapsed. This had a domino effect, bringing on the failure and bankruptcy
of Constable. The firm folded with a staggering debt, for those days, of a
quarter of a million pounds. This, in turn, brought about the bankruptcy
of another famous Edinburgh publisher in which Constable had an interest
– the firm of James and John Ballantyne, uncles of the writer R. M.

Ballantyne. The *Edinburgh Observer* called the collapse of Constable 'nothing less than a national calamity. It is a stab in the very vitals of the literature of the land.' *The Scotsman* claimed it was 'a calamity to Scotland'.

The bankruptcy brought about Archibald Constable's early death. However, his son Thomas started his own business and by 1869 had become printer to Queen Victoria in Scotland. His son, also named Archibald after his grandfather, decided to move south to England and in 1890 established a small publishing company in Newgate. Soon afterwards, he moved into more prestigious offices at 14 Parliament Street. But his interest was orientalism; in fact his first books were reprints of oriental travel titles, and he did not long remain active in the firm he founded. In 1893 he handed over the chairmanship of the company to his nephew H. Arthur Doubleday, also a relative of Nelson Doubleday, the founder of the American publishers. In 1895 Doubleday was joined by William Maxsee Meredith, son of the novelist George Meredith (1828–1909), and by Otto Kyllmann of Macmillan and Company, who became partners in the firm. The company then moved office from Parliament Street along to No. 2 Whitehall Gardens towards the latter part of 1896.

On that May morning of 1897, when the hansom cab drew to a halt outside Constable's offices, a tall, well-built man in his late forties, with bright red hair, a trim beard and close-set light blue eyes, descended from the cab, paid the driver, and turned into the building. He was carrying a manuscript-sized package under his arm.

He presented his card to the office clerk and asked, in a well-modulated Dublin accent, to see Mr Otto Kyllmann. The visitor's card read: 'Bram Stoker MA, Barrister-at-Law'.

The Irishman was shown into the reception room while the clerk went to see if Mr Kyllmann was ready to receive him. Some of the daily newspapers had been left in the room to occupy visitors while they were waiting. The headlines were all concerned with news of the crushing defeat of Crown Prince Constantine's Greek army by the Turks of Edhem Pasha at Domokós in Thessaly which had culminated in the bloody end of the thirty-day war that had started on 17 April between the two neighbours. The newspapers that day were commenting on the opening of armistice negotiations and had given much space to reports of the final battle on the previous day in which all correspondents observed that the Greeks had carried themselves well, striving to turn back three Turkish army divisions with less than half of their enemy's strength. Greece was now devastated. Two of its richest provinces, Larissa and Trikala, had been ravaged by the Turks and some 130,000 refugees had fled from Thessaly. Epirus was also ravaged. The Turks were blaming the Greeks for starting the war and demanding £10 million in indemnity; they also insisted that the Greeks agree to Turkish garrisons in Thessaly and withdraw their army from Crete. It was not until 1913 that Crete joined the Greek state. There was no doubt that most newspapers supported Greece.

Bram Stoker probably reflected on what his young brother George, whom he would be meeting shortly, would make of the news. George had served as a surgeon in the Imperial Ottoman Army during the Russo-Turkish War of 1877–78 and had been Chief of Ambulance of the Red Crescent. He had even received a medal from the Turks for his services when in charge of transporting the Turkish wounded to safety after the battle of Shipka Pass in the Balkans. The Turks had then lost 4000 killed and wounded and 36,000 prisoners. George had written a memoir of the war, *With 'The Unspeakables', or two years campaigning in European and Asiatic Turkey*, published in Dublin in 1878.

Certainly the reports had more than a passing interest for Bram Stoker, particularly as the reason why he was at Constable that day was to sign a contract for a novel in which his main character was based on an historical figure who had fought for Wallachian independence against the Turks of the Ottoman empire: this same empire that had now brought its former possession of Greece to its knees once again.

But there was an item of news of even more personal interest for Bram that day; this was the report that Oscar Wilde had been released from gaol after serving two years' hard labour. Bram had been a friend of Oscar's parents in Dublin and knew Oscar and his elder brother Willie very well. In fact, Bram's wife, Florence, had been Oscar's first serious love but she had rejected the young poet to marry Bram. This had not prevented Bram and Florence continuing a friendship with Oscar who had, a few years before, presented Florence with a copy of his *Salomé*. Bram and Oscar, and Oscar's elder brother, Willie, had all belonged to the Irish Literary Society in London which had been formed by another young Dublin poet named William Butler Yeats and some friends in 1892. Oscar's mother, Lady Jane Wilde, had been a neighbour in Chelsea until her death on 3 February the previous year, while Oscar had been in prison.

Although most newspapers, such as the *Daily Telegraph*, that day devoted only three lines to Oscar's release, the *Pall Mall Gazette*, to which both Oscar and Bram had been contributors, had featured a full column on the previous day. It appeared that at 8.15 p.m. on Tuesday, Oscar had been escorted to Pentonville from Reading Gaol, where he had completed his full two-year sentence, sewing coal sacks. 'Shortly after nine o'clock this morning an unobstrusive private brougham drew in to the principal entrance of the Metropolitan House of Detention, and some five minutes later it left with Oscar Wilde – a free man. There was no one with him and there were but a couple of people who witnessed his departure. Mr Wilde has declined to make any statement for publication beyond the fact that he is "mentally tired".' In fact his old friend from university days, Robert Ross, had met him and they went directly to the house of the Revd Stewart Headham, the clergyman who had put up a bail bond for Oscar during his trial. More friends, Ernest and Ada Leverson, were waiting to welcome him. That evening, the evening of 19 May, with his two friends, Robert Ross and Reginald Turner, Oscar boarded the ferry steamer to Dieppe. Three years later, on 30 November 1900, Oscar Wilde died in Paris of 'cerebral meningitis'. It would be claimed that Bram's own early death, allegedly from a sexually transmitted disease, in 1912 was a result of his visits to Parisian brothels while engaged in taking money to Oscar.

In spite of Oscar's bankruptcy and desperate need for money, the *Pall Mall Gazette* was able to report: 'It may be of interest to the gatherers of ill-considered trifles to learn that one of the first things Mr Oscar Wilde did on regaining his freedom was to refuse an offer of £1000 for a short description of his prison experiences.' Indeed, Wilde had something of more literary worth in his head than a journalistic description of life in Reading Gaol. He was shortly to write what is considered his greatest and most celebrated poem, 'The Ballad of Reading Gaol'.

One wonders what thoughts passed through Bram Stoker's mind as he sat meditating on the release of the son of his former Dublin mentors who had so helped in his own artistic development.

A short time passed before the imposing Irishman was shown to the first-floor back room – the office of Otto Kyllmann, Constable's chief editor. It was an impressive room, treated in the French style, with wall panels containing oil paintings of rural and still life subjects. The ceiling had a central panel with a painted floreated wreath and an ornate glass chandelier. The mantelpiece was carved marble with a pier of glass above.

Kyllmann, 'O.K.' to his friends, was twenty-seven years old. He had been born in Manchester of a family of German origin. He was a protégé of the publisher Sir Frederick Macmillan and had worked for Macmillan and Company in New York and then in London before joining Constable.

Although only two years with the firm, Kyllmann had just made a reputation among publishers by persuading his colleagues at Constable to pay the unheard-of and sensational sum of £10,000 to secure the publishing rights of a book entitled *Farthest North* by the Norwegian scientist and explorer Fridtjof Nansen. Nansen, during 1893–96, had attempted to reach the North Pole through the pack ice in a crush-resistant ship. Constable, in spite of paying such an enormous advance for the book, had their investment fully justified when it was published later that year. On the day of publication it was reported that Whitehall Gardens became completely blocked by wholesalers' and booksellers' carriages.

Now Otto Kyllmann was about to bring off yet another publishing coup: the tall, red-haired Irishman was delivering the corrected proofs of a novel which Kyllmann had accepted earlier that year. Stoker had already signed a handwritten contract some months before but now, with the proofs corrected and approved, a typewritten contract had been drawn up for signature. Bram's latest biographer, Professor Barbara Belford (*Bram Stoker: A Biography of the Author of Dracula*), was unaware of the existence of this previous contract when reflecting on the signing of a contract so close to publication day. She suggests that a verbal agreement had been previously made. However, the earlier contract was witnessed by Charles E. Howson, who signs himself as a librarian of 53 Battersea Rise, SW11. Curiously, Professor Belford does refer to Howson in her work, describing him as 'a near destitute old actor forced to eke out a living copying hand parts at sixpence a time' who was employed as an accountant at the Lyceum. She says 'he was extremely jealous of Bram'. It is strange, if this is so, that Bram asked him to witness the initial contract for his vampire novel.

The novel was entitled 'The Un-Dead'; a weird Gothic tale of terror. Kyllmann had realised that the novel was unconventional and bizarre even by the standards of the day when strange tales were in popular demand. *The Invisible Man* by Herbert G. Wells was being serialised that month in *Pearson's Magazine*. The Victorian public were in the mood for such exotic and supernatural tales. 'The Un-Dead' was certainly a *tour de force*, much better than the two previous books that Stoker had published with Constable. Even so, Kyllmann was not entirely satisfied with the title.

It was the author who suggested the alteration to *Dracula, or The Un-Dead*. Two days before, on Tuesday, 18 May, on the very day Oscar Wilde was being released from Reading Gaol, Bram had produced a four-hour reading of his own dramatic adaptation of the book at the Royal Lyceum

Theatre, under that title. The reading was merely designed to ensure dramatic copyright of the work and not meant as a serious theatrical production. Indeed, the Lord Chamberlain granted the requisite copyright licence on 1 June. However, the contract was already typed with 'The Un-Dead' as the title and so it remained. When the book appeared in a six shilling edition a month later, the title page carried the simple title *Dracula*. Kyllmann had decided to do away with a subtitle.

The author was accommodating and had also agreed to Kyllmann's suggestion that the very first chapter of the book be deleted. It has been suggested by Dr Belford that this was in fact the second chapter, but the deleted chapter refers to events which took place before those in the eventual first chapter. It was Kyllmann who pointed out that this chapter had a distinct echo of a short story by Stoker's fellow Dubliner, Joseph Sheridan Le Fanu. The story was 'Carmilla', published two years after Stoker had graduated from Trinity College, Dublin, where Le Fanu had also been a distinguished alumnus. Stoker accepted the deletion of the chapter although this had been his way of acknowledging his inspirational debt to Le Fanu.

In no way would that chapter have been considered plagiarism but a 'literary compliment'. Even so, Kyllmann thought that using the sequence at the beginning of the novel would create a prejudice among critics. The chapter was duly deleted only to be found after Stoker's death by his widow, Florence, who published it as a short story in its own right. She believed 'it was originally excised owing to the length of the book, and may prove of interest to the many readers of what is considered my husband's most remarkable work'. This reason for the excision was demonstrably not correct; a few thousand words here or there would have made little difference to the length of the publication.

Kyllmann had offered the author no financial advance, as he had done for Nansen's epic, and, indeed, only after the book had sold 1000 copies would Constable pay the sum of 1s. 6d. on subsequent copies sold. The first printing would be 3000 copies. It was a safe investment from the publisher's viewpoint. Indeed, during the next ten years, Constable would print eight editions of the book, with several impressions, including a sixpenny paperback edition in April 1901. After Bram's death, in 1912, William Rider and Son took over publication and published five more different editions with various impressions, selling, so they claimed, an impressive one million copies by 1919.

It is fascinating to note that a clause in the initial contract states: 'The

publishers shall print, bind, advertise and publish the work at their sole
cost and shall publish it during the year 1897 but not until the rights have
been secured in the United States of America to the author.' *Dracula* was
not published in the United States until 1899 when Doubleday issued it
following a serialisation in the *New York Sun*.

Dracula would become part of world folklore. There has never been a
time when it has not been in print in Britain – indeed, during the 1970s
there were three different UK paperback editions vying for sales from
Arrow, Signet and Sphere. The book has been translated into nearly fifty
languages, and has spawned countless sequels and prequels and 'spin-offs'
in vampiric literature. Dramatisations have been staged constantly
throughout the world, since 1928, and at least fifty films have been based
on the novel. A veritable 'Dracula industry' grew up from the 1930s
onwards.

On 20 May 1897, Constable and Company had erected a milestone along
the road of popular fiction; *Dracula* became a book, so it was once claimed
in the 1970s, to have been outsold only by the Bible and the Collected
Works of Shakespeare.

It did not seem such a momentous occasion as Bram scrawled his
signature on the typed contract, under the approving eye of the young
'O.K.', while a clerk named H. Robeday witnessed it. Bram had other
things on his mind as he asked the porter to find him a hansom to take
him on to the Royal Lyceum Theatre in Bow Street. He had to meet his
employer, Sir Henry Irving, the actor-manager of the Lyceum, for, in
spite of his being called to the Bar of London's Inner Temple, Bram's
main career was as manager and treasurer of the Royal Lyceum Theatre
Company Ltd. It was nearly noon, and Bram had to pick Irving up from
the theatre; they were both due in Fitzroy Square where, at twelve-thirty,
Her Royal Highness the Princess Louise, Marchioness of Lorne, was to
open the 'Oxygen Home' and hear of the method of treating wounds and
chronic ulcers by an oxygen gas process.

The 'Oxygen Home' was to become the Fitzroy Clinic and it seemed an
unlikely port of call for Bram Stoker, not to mention Sir Henry Irving, but
the fact was that the new process was the invention of the clinic's director
who was Bram's youngest brother, Dr George Stoker. In fact, the reception
would also launch a small booklet by George on *The Oxygen Treatment for
Wounds, Ulcers & etc.*, published by Messrs Baillière of London.

George specialised in wounds; as well as his services in the Turkish
army as a surgeon, he had also been awarded a medal for his medical work

in the Zulu War of 1879–80. In two years' time he would follow the British Army in their war against the Boers and be mentioned in despatches, being awarded the Queen's South African medal and three clasps.

The report of the official opening of the 'Oxygen Home', with which George Stoker remained linked until his death on 23 April 1920, was carried on the front page of the *Evening Standard* later that day. It failed to mention Bram's attendance, mentioning only Sir Henry Irving, but the theatrical magazine *Era* corrected the oversight two days later. The 'Oxygen Home' housed thirty-six patients. The president of the clinic was W. Burdett-Coutts MP; he explained the new treatment which, it was pointed out, had been discovered and carried out solely by Dr Stoker. Patients undergoing the treatment, said the *Standard* reporter, were showing the most extraordinary progress after nine months of monitoring.

Following the reception Bram and Sir Henry were to hasten back to the Lyceum to continue with the day's performances.

It was a long and busy day for Bram Stoker. In all the hustle and bustle, perhaps the significance of the agreement which he had signed with Constable was lost on him. Did he have any idea that his book would become such a bestseller, be one of the most translated literary works, or that it would become part of world folklore, having a profound effect on the genre of weird supernatural literature and ranking alongside Mary Shelley's *Frankenstein*? Could he know that the change he had made in title from 'The Un-Dead' to *Dracula* would cause the name Dracula to become a byword for vampiric horror stories? As he made his way home to his house in St Leonard's Terrace, Chelsea, after the final curtain at the Lyceum that evening, the forthcoming publication of *Dracula* was probably the last thing on his mind.

CHAPTER TWO

The Secret of the Trunks

Almost a century after Bram Stoker had signed the contract at Constable's offices and approved the corrected proofs, an extraordinary event occurred in America. The original manuscript which he had taken to Otto Kyllmann in Whitehall Gardens was rediscovered in an old trunk where it had been stored, forgotten, since the dying days of the nineteenth century. Long believed to have been lost, the manuscript was initially thought by those who unearthed it to be a completely different work, although it was undeniably by Bram Stoker because his name was scrawled in ink beneath the title 'The Un-Dead'. The real mystery began once it had been established that the manuscript was, indeed, the original of *Dracula*. For *how* had it got into a trunk in an American barn? The answer to this question, so we have discovered, is as surprising as it is intriguing.

The precise date and location of the finding of Stoker's manuscript have remained a secret kept by its present owner and, although we believe we have unravelled the mystery of its origins, we propose to honour his decision. What we can reveal is the extraordinary, not to mention gruesome, nature of the find. The manuscript was discovered in an old barn on a Pennsylvanian homestead not far from Philadelphia. The barn had belonged to the same family since the end of the last century, and during much of this time was used purely for storage. In recent years, however, the building had fallen into a state of disrepair. When some members of the family were foraging around in the debris for anything that might be worth saving, they came across three old storage trunks, battered and grimy, which had clearly not been touched for years. The searchers decided to remove them for cleaning and perhaps using in the house.

The trunks were hauled into the daylight and prised open. In the first was an assortment of old clothes; in the second, some jumble and a large brown paper package. In the third, the searchers were horrified to find, were the corpses of several withered and dried-out dead rats! What these rodents were doing in the trunk and how they had got there was beyond anyone's immediate imagination and it was hastily shut. Not surprisingly, it was a little while before the unsettled group could bring themselves to go through the remaining two trunks.

They started by rummaging through the trunk containing the brown paper package.

Unwrapping the bundle revealed a bulky manuscript bearing the words 'THE UN-DEAD By Bram Stoker' with a list of the author's other titles and the words 'Copyright 1897'. When the new owners of one of the most fabulous manuscripts in literary history realised what they had found, the mystery of the dead rats took on an even more grisly fascination. But how they got into the trunk has defied all explanation, beyond the possibility that they might just have been nesting there when the trunk was last shut. Any direct connection with the manuscript about a vampire count seems unthinkable . . .

That 'The Un-Dead' was, in fact, *Dracula* was confirmed for the family first by a local autograph dealer and then by another expert who compared the handwriting on the pages of the document with that on Bram Stoker's working papers which fortuitously happened to belong to the Rosenbach Foundation Library in nearby Philadelphia. These papers, which had originally been sold in a file box belonging to Stoker by auction at Sotheby's in London on 7 July 1913, where they fetched the princely sum of two guineas (£2.10) from a Mr Drake, were bought by the library sixty years later, on 25 February 1970, for rather more. They were part of a collection of documents, signed copies of books and other items belonging to Bram which his widow had put up for auction and which raised £400. We shall be discussing these revealing documents and the light they throw on the writing of *Dracula* later in this book.

The manuscript of 'The Un-Dead' was sold by the Pennsylvanian family to a dealer and changed hands again before reaching its final destination, in private hands, in Orange County, California, where it now resides. In 1984, when it was suggested the manuscript might be available for sale once more, offers of between $50,000 and $1 million were reportedly made, although the owner decided not to part with his highly valuable possession.

That the bulky 529 pages of typed manuscript, which vary in width between 8½ and 10 inches and are 14½ inches deep, are genuine is beyond doubt. Although the thought of a manuscript of Stoker's time being typewritten may initially give rise to some scepticism, the typewriter had in fact already been in existence for more than a decade, and it is really no surprise that a writer with such an appalling hand as Stoker should have typed his novel before submitting it to Constable. Interestingly, of course, Stoker obliquely paid tribute to the invention of the typewriter by having Mina Harker type one of her final Journals in *Dracula* on a 'Traveller's typewriter'. Although the Blickensderfer typewriter is considered the first real portable typewriter, it is more likely that Bram would have Mina use the 'Columbia Type-writer', in production from 1885, weighing six pounds and priced at five guineas (£5.25).

The manuscript itself had been extensively revised and annotated in a hand that is clearly Stoker's, with further additions in blue pencil that may be those of Kyllmann or an assistant editor at Constable. A great many of the pages have been cut up and repasted together in a different order – some with lengthy handwritten paragraphs and sentences linking the text – all indicating that a considerable amount of work was done on the book before it was sent from Constable's offices to their printers, Harrison and Sons in St Martin's Lane, 'Printers in ordinary to Her Majesty, Queen Victoria'.

Aside from numerous grammatical, stylistic and factual corrections and the renumbering of the pages from the original typewritten numerals to handwritten figures, it is fascinating to discover that the title itself might well have been slimmed down to the even shorter 'Un-Dead', until the final choice of *Dracula* was arrived at. Crucially, too, although Stoker had settled on the names for most of his major characters during his earlier research, several were still unnamed when the manuscript was being typed, including Van Helsing, who was represented by a blank space or the word 'The Professor', and Renfield, referred to as 'The Flyman'. The very fact that these crucial names had not been decided upon when Stoker typed the novel is a clear indication that it represents the only draft of the book made from the researches and notes he had assembled in Whitby, Cruden Bay and London, to which we shall be returning later.

The deletion of one episode from the published book seems to us inexplicable. This is the destruction of Dracula's castle. On page 388 of *Dracula*, as published, appears the paragraph:

> The Castle of Dracula now stood out against the red sky, and every stone of its broken battlements was articulated against the light of the setting sun.

But in Stoker's manuscript, the following three paragraphs are typed and then crossed out:

> As we looked there came a terrible convulsion of the earth so that we seemed to rock to and fro and fell to our knees. At the same moment, with a roar that seemed to shake the very heavens, the whole castle and the rock and even the hill on which it stood seemed to rise into the air and scatter in fragments while a mighty cloud of black and yellow smoke, volume on volume, in rolling grandeur, was shot upwards with inconceivable rapidity.
>
> Then there was a stillness in nature as the echoes of that thunderous report seemed to come as with the hollow boom of a thunder-clap – the long reverberating roll which seems as though the floors of heaven shook. Then down in a mighty rain falling whence they rose came the fragments that had been tossed skyward in the cataclysm.
>
> From where we stood it seemed as though the once fierce volcano burst had satisfied the need of nature and that the castle and the structure of the hill had sunk again into the void. We were so appalled with the suddenness and the grandeur that we forgot to think of ourselves.

We can only hazard a guess as to who decided to delete this spectacular climactic moment. Did Kyllmann or his assistant editor feel it was unnecessary or inappropriate? Or did Stoker, perhaps, remove the sentences with a half-formed thought in his mind that perhaps one day he might write a sequel to *Dracula*? We shall never know. But certainly no other writer or film-maker has ever attempted anything quite so destructive to the Dracula legend!

Final confirmation that the manuscript found in America *was* the Constable setting copy has been effected by a line-by-line comparison of the much-edited text with the first published edition of *Dracula*. But the biggest question still remains: *How* did it get there?

The answer, as with so many things to do with the life and work of Bram Stoker, begins in Ireland, and in Dublin specifically, during his days as a student at Trinity College.

The seventeen-year-old who entered university had overcome a sickly childhood to grow into a burly, muscular youth who threw himself tenaciously into the social and sporting sides of undergraduate life. He excelled at walking – taking no fewer than four silver goblets for winning the Dublin University Foot Races between 1866 and 1868 – and also proved himself a formidable debater, eventually becoming President of the Philosophical Society. But it was as the champion of a reviled American poet that Bram Stoker showed a special brand of courage.

In 1868, William Michael Rossetti (1829–1919), the Inland Revenue official turned translator of Dante's *Inferno*, and one of the seven pre-Raphaelite 'brothers', published *The Selected Poems of Walt Whitman*. Whitman (1819–1892) was already a highly controversial figure in his native America, where his tackling of taboo subjects such as the 'beautiful affection of man for men' caused him to be accused of publishing immoral and indecent material and to be labelled as a lecherous old man. When Rossetti's collection of his work appeared on this side of the Atlantic, Whitman was again the object of ferocious attack. Eventually, his realistic approach to the life of man, glorifying the emergence of the masses, was to profoundly change the course of modern poetry. His single most influential work was *Leaves of Grass*, first published in July 1855. It was then only ninety-five pages in length, published at the author's own expense. Between then and 1892 Whitman published nine separate editions, all different in content and in the arrangement of the poems. After 1881 he simply added new poems to the book. Today *Leaves of Grass* is almost universally recognised as one of the masterpieces of world literature, but it was greeted at the time with abuse and ridicule by many critics.

Indeed, the publication of *Selected Poems* raised a storm in British literary circles, critics seizing on those parts which they considered offensive to morals and good taste to lambast Whitman who was then working in Washington as a government clerk. In 1873 he suffered from a paralytic stroke. His mother died that year and he was forced to live on the charity of his brother George, who had been wounded in the Civil War and whom Walt had nursed back to health. He went to live with George in Camden, New Jersey. Lonely and depressed, Whitman longed for death. The carping of the critics did not help. In Trinity College, Dublin, Whitman's poetry was greeted with 'Homeric laughter', according to a later account by Stoker – especially by students seeking the 'more noxious passages'. For days the book was the subject of endless scorn, until finally, Bram decided to find out for himself and secured a copy which another student was on the point of throwing away. The effect on the twenty-one-year-old student was cathartic.

'I took the book with me into the Park and in the shade of an elm tree began to read it,' he wrote in *Personal Reminiscences of Henry Irving*. 'Very shortly my own opinion began to form; it was diametrically opposed to that which I had been hearing. From that hour I became a lover of Walt Whitman.'

Stoker was glad to find that a few other brave souls shared his view; in particular Edward Dowden, the Professor of English Literature at Trinity, who, in Bram's words, 'took the large and liberal view of *Leaves of Grass*.' He and Dowden led the counter-attack, and when the professor addressed the Philosophical Society on 'Walt Whitman and the Poetry of Democracy' on the evening of 4 May 1871, Bram was delighted to have the opportunity of introducing the speaker to the packed audience.

Later, when working as a government clerk, as Whitman had, Bram continued his unrelenting defence of the poet, winning a number of others over to the side of the 'Walt Whitmanites'. He even plucked up the courage, on 18 February 1872, to write a personal letter to Whitman. The copy, which survives in the Whitman archives, is almost overpoweringly emotional.

If you are the man I take you to be, you will like this letter. If you are not I don't care whether you like it or not and only ask you to put it into the fire without reading any farther. I don't think there is a man living, even you, who are above the prejudice of the class of small-minded men, who wouldn't like to get a letter from a younger man, a stranger, across the world – a man living in an atmosphere prejudiced to the truths you sing and your manner of singing them. You are a true man, and I would like to be one myself, and so I would be towards you as a brother and as a pupil to his master . . .

Shelley wrote to William Godwin and they became friends. I am not Shelley and you are not Godwin and so I will only hope that sometime I may meet you face to face and perhaps shake hands with you. If I ever do, it will be one of the greatest pleasures of my life. If

you care to know who it is that writes this, my name is Abraham
Stoker (Junior). My friends call me Bram. I live at 43 Harcourt St.,
Dublin. I am a clerk in the service of the Crown on a small salary. I
am twenty-four years old. I am six feet two inches high and twelve
stones weight naked and used to be forty-one or forty-two inches
round the chest. I am ugly but strong and determined and have a
large bump over my eyebrows. I have a heavy jaw and a big mouth
and thick lips – sensitive nostrils – a snubnose and straight hair. I am
equal in temper and cool in disposition and have a large amount of
self control and am naturally secretive to the world. I take a delight
in letting people I don't like – people of mean or cruel or sneaking or
cowardly disposition – see the worst side of me. Now I have told you
all I know about myself . . .

Be assured of this, Walt Whitman, that a man of less than half your
own age, reared a conservative in a conservative country, and who has
always heard your name cried down by the great mass of people who
mention it, here felt his heart leap towards you across the Atlantic
and his soul swelling at the words or rather the thoughts. It is vain
for me to try and quote any instances of what thoughts of yours I like
best – for I like them all and you must feel that you are reading the
true words of one who feels with you. I have been more candid with
you – have said more about myself to you than I have ever said to
anyone before. How sweet a thing it is for a strong healthy man with
a woman's eyes and a child's wishes to feel that he can speak so to a
man who can be if he wishes, father and brother and wife to his soul.
I don't think you will laugh, Walt Whitman, nor despise me, but at
all events I thank you for all the love and sympathy you have given
me in common with my kind.

Having poured out his soul in this extraordinary 'fan letter' – which
certainly reveals more about his nature than has heretofore been suspected
– Bram Stoker decided against posting it; perhaps out of a mixture of
embarrassment and diffidence. Instead, the sheets went into his desk
drawer in Harcourt Street where they remained for four years. Then, after
another particularly bruising debate about Whitman at the Fortnightly
Club in Dublin on 14 February 1876, Bram wrote to Whitman again,
enclosing a copy of the earlier letter and adding: 'It speaks for itself and
needs no comment; it is truly what I wanted to say as that light is light.'

Just over a month later, to his amazement and delight, Bram received a reply from his mentor. It was dated 6 March 1876, and he read it with a mounting sense of pleasure.

My dear young man [the letter began in Whitman's flourishing hand], Your letters have been most welcome to me – welcome to me as a person and then as Author – I don't know which most. You did well to write to me so unconventionally, so fresh, so manly, and so affectionately, too. I, too, hope (though it is not probable) that we shall one day personally meet each other. Meantime I send you my friendship and thanks.

Whitman added that he would soon dispatch copies of the new edition (1876) of his poems to Dowden and Stoker and ended with a reference to his physical condition which was already causing concern among his admirers on both sides of the Atlantic:

My physique is entirely shatter'd, doubtless permanently – from paralysis and other ailments. But I am up and dress'd, and get out every day a little, live here quite lonesome, but hearty, and in good spirits – Write to me again.

To someone of Stoker's experience, who had overcome the ill health of childhood to achieve vibrant good health, these words must have been particularly affecting and made him all the more determined to prove Whitman wrong and meet him face to face. Efforts by a group of the poet's admirers to get him to come to England in 1873 had failed when he had his paralytic stroke. The opportunity for Stoker to meet Whitman did not arise until ten years later when Stoker, by then Henry Irving's manager, crossed the Atlantic with the actor's company on an American tour which took them to Philadelphia.

On the night of Wednesday, 19 March 1884, during a dinner held in Irving's honour at the Clover Club in Philadelphia, Bram met their host, Thomas Donaldson (1840–1922), a lawyer, occasional poet and close friend of Walt Whitman. He had been conducting the poet's affairs since his move from Washington to Camden in 1873. On hearing of his two guests' great admiration for Whitman, Donaldson invited them to meet the poet at his home on the following day. In the early afternoon, the English actor

and his Irish manager were driven to the lawyer's home at 326 North 40th
Street. Bram could hardly contain his excitement when they entered the
house.

> On the opposite side of the room [Stoker wrote later], sat an old man
> of leonine appearance. He was burly, with a large head and high
> forehead slightly bald. Great shaggy masses of grey-white hair fell
> over his collar. His moustache was large and thick and fell over his
> mouth so as to mingle with the top of the mass of his bushy, flowing
> beard. I knew at once who it was. When Donaldson said, 'Bram
> Stoker', Walt Whitman leaned forward suddenly and held out his
> hand eagerly as he said, 'Bram Stoker – Abraham Stoker is it?' I
> acquiesced and we shook hands as old friends – as indeed we were.

The meeting proved to be, as Stoker had hoped it would be all those years
before, one of the great moments of his life.

Thomas Donaldson, who was the go-between at that meeting and all the
subsequent meetings of Stoker and the poet which took place at his small,
ramshackle home at 328 Mickle Street, later wrote in his biography of
Walt Whitman: The Man that it was normally very difficult to get Whitman
to give an opinion about any of his visitors. But not in the case of the red-
bearded Irishman.

> I also recall a visit I made to Mr Whitman accompanied by Bram
> Stoker, A. M. of London, in 1885. It was a cold, raw day, but Mr
> Whitman lighted the sheet-iron stove and made us comfortable. Mr
> Stoker, a man of intelligence and cultivation, having had the advantage
> of association with the most cultivated in all walks of contemporary
> English intellectual life, was at his best. Mr Whitman was captivated.
> Mr Stoker had previously met Mr Whitman at my house in
> Philadelphia in 1884. We remained an hour, and then left in spite of
> his protest. Many days after this visit, he referred to it by saying:
> 'And friend Stoker; where is he now?' I replied, 'In Chicago.' 'Well,
> well; what a broth of a boy he is! My gracious, he knows enough for
> four or five ordinary men; and what tact! Henry Irving knows a good
> thing when he tries it, eh? Stoker is an adroit lad, and many think
> that he made Mr Irving's path, in a business way, a smooth one over
> here.' I replied, 'Indeed!' 'I should say so,' was his answer. 'See that

he comes over again to see me before he leaves the country. He's like a breath of good, healthy, breezy sea air.'

Bram, for his part, had taken an instant liking to Donaldson, and not just because he had arranged the meeting with Whitman. He found the calm, assured lawyer a man after his own heart; interested in literature and the arts and devoted to the ailing poet. With Stoker's encouragement, Henry Irving made a donation of $50 to Donaldson to help Whitman, Bram adding $25 himself.

Subsequent meetings between Stoker and Whitman, arranged by Donaldson, confirmed for Bram that the poet was 'all that I had ever dreamed of, or wished for in him; large-minded, broad-viewed, tolerant to the last degree; incarnate sympathy; understanding with an insight that seemed more than human.' Whitman, for his part was equally pleased with the relationship, confiding to Horace Traubel, another biographer, who would later publish *With Walt Whitman in Camden*: 'The English theatrical people have always seemed to like me – Irving has been here; then there is Bram Stoker – he has treated me like a best son.'

In October 1886, Whitman appeared frailer, but nonetheless 'genuinely glad to see me', noted Stoker, 'and asked much about London and its people, especially those of the literary world'. The two men also talked about the assassination of Abraham Lincoln – Whitman having been close to Ford's Theatre in Washington on 14 April 1865, when the President was shot by the actor John Wilkes Booth. Bram never forgot the words that the poet used to describe the grief and rage which gripped Lincoln's entourage after the murder. 'It might have been that the old sagas had been enacted again when amongst the Vikings a Chief went to the Valhalla with a legion of spirits around him.'

Stoker and Donaldson returned to Mickle Street on 22 December 1887, during Irving's winter tour of the States. Whitman now 'resembled King Lear' and at the end of their conversation, he presented Bram with a copy of the very rare 1872 edition of *Leaves of Grass*, which he autographed in indelible blue pencil. Although Stoker did not know it at the time, this was to be the last time he would ever see 'the man who for nearly twenty years I had held in my heart as a dear friend'.

In 1888, Whitman suffered another crippling stroke, and though well cared for and supported by a small circle of friends including the absent Bram, he eventually died on 26 March 1892. It was not until two years later, in February 1894, that the Irishman was in Philadelphia again and could renew his friendship with William Donaldson. There was much talk about the dead poet until Donaldson suddenly stood up and left the room. He returned a minute later carrying a large brown envelope which he handed to Bram. 'This is for you from Walt Whitman,' he said. 'I have been keeping it till I should see you.'

Bram opened the package nervously and found inside several pages of notes in Whitman's unmistakable handwriting. They were the original notes for a lecture on Abraham Lincoln which he had delivered at the Chestnut Street Opera House in Philadelphia on 15 April 1886. With the pages was a letter to Donaldson with the addendum: 'Enclosed I send a full report of my Lincoln Lecture for our friend Bram Stoker.' It was, as Bram later wrote, 'my Message from the Dead'. Bram, himself fascinated by the life and work of Lincoln, had given lectures on him in England and also at the Chickering Hall, New York, on 25 November 1887, after which the *New York Times* critic sourly observed that Stoker had 'delivered this lecture with great acceptance before unenlightened English audiences, and his utterances have been highly commended by the semi-educated English press. On this side of the water, however, where Abraham Lincoln lived and died, and where American history is taught in public schools, a historical review of the life and times of the martyr President, even when presented by Mr Henry Irving's manager, is apt to fall flat.'

However, Donaldson's kindness in passing Whitman's invaluable manuscript to him was something Bram Stoker never forgot during the ensuing years when the two men remained in touch, although they only met on three more occasions. After one of these, the American gave his Irish friend a newly minted copy of his *Walt Whitman: The Man*. Stoker knew that Donaldson's other great passion in life – according to Harrison S. Morris in his *Walt Whitman: A Brief Biography with Reminiscences* (Harvard University Press, 1929) – was as 'a collector of all that was odd but often not valuable'. He sensed just how much Donaldson would have liked the Lincoln notes for himself and admired him all the more for his honesty in handing them over. He determined to offer the American collector something by way of return.

The 'something' was the setting copy of *Dracula* which was to make Bram Stoker world-famous in the years following its publication in 1897.

The location of its eventual discovery, the rumours that it had belonged to a minor poet, and the association with Walt Whitman, all point to Thomas Donaldson having been the original recipient of one of the most famous manuscripts of the nineteenth century. It is tempting to think that if Whitman had still been alive, Bram might have contemplated making a presentation of it to his mentor – but such an eventuality never arose. After Donaldson's death the manuscript went into the hands of relatives and thereafter remained forgotten in that old trunk until rediscovered by pure chance.

What Bram Stoker did do, though, in memory of Walt Whitman, was to dedicate his only known published item of poetry to him. This, too, has been overlooked by his biographers and is further evidence of his admiration for the American poet. Called 'The One Thing Needful', it appeared in *Youth's Companion* of 1885, not long after he had first met Whitman, and it is actually a thinly disguised portrait of Whitman himself as the 'weary Master' who is nearing death. The final verse reads:

> One thing alone we lack. Our souls, indeed,
> Have fiercer hunger than the body's need.
> Ah happy they that look in loving eyes.
> The harsh world round them fades. The Master's voice
> In sweetest music bids their souls rejoice
> And wakes an echo there that never dies.

Bram Stoker had paid his last respects to the inspirer of his youth – and in presenting *Dracula* to Thomas Donaldson repaid his debt for their meeting.

CHAPTER THREE

Was Dracula Irish?

THE ENTRY IN HARPER AND ROW'S *The Reader's Encyclopedia* 3rd ed., 1988 claims that Bram Stoker was English. It is not, alas, an unusual error and the *Collins Gem Dictionary of Biography* (1971) makes a similar claim. Stoker is not the only Irish writer whose origins have been transformed into either English or, more frequently, British. Even when Ireland was politically part of the United Kingdom, between 1801 and 1922, it was never part of Britain – the state was called the United Kingdom of Great Britain *and* Ireland. From 1922 the name of the UK state has been the United Kingdom of Great Britain *and* Northern Ireland. When Samuel Beckett was awarded the Nobel Prize for Literature in 1969, some London newspapers actually described him as a 'British writer'. Beckett was born in Dublin, took his degree at Trinity College, Dublin, and worked in Paris for two years before becoming a lecturer at Trinity College, Dublin. He finally settled in Paris in 1932. Even more bizarre was *The Reader's Encyclopedia*'s listing of Dubliner George Bernard Shaw as 'English' for his 1925 Nobel Prize for Literature.

When discussing the vampire literary tradition, Anthony Masters, in *The Natural History of the Vampire*, says of another Irish writer: 'whilst back in England in 1872 Sheridan Le Fanu produced his exquisite *Camilla* [*sic*] – whose descriptive passages are amongst the very finest in English vampire-literature'. 'Carmilla', while its first known publication was in a three-volume collection, *In a Glass Darkly*, published in London, was actually written in Ireland. Its author was Irish-born and educated and had never lived in England at all.

We have to start out with what many English people might confuse as a 'political point' in order to present a cultural point. Although these Irish writers chose to write in English, and not in the Irish language, this fact cannot be a 'catch-all' for describing them as English or British, any more than Canadians, Americans, New Zealanders or South Africans using the English language can be designated as English writers. With the case of Irish writers, their Irishness leaps off every page. It is not jingoism to make the point that a particular, non-English cultural expression permeates their work.

For example, it has often been demonstrated that James Joyce's *Ulysses* could not have been other than the work of an Irishman. Henry Levin, editor of *The Essential James Joyce* (Cape, 1948), observed: 'The first consideration with an Irishman is nationality. Joyce . . . was "all too Irish" – all the more Irish because he was a "wildgoose", because he resided in foreign countries . . .' Analysing the man credited with starting the school of weird Gothic writing in Ireland, Robert E. Lougy says in *Charles Robert Maturin*: 'But Maturin is neither English, Italian, nor Spanish: he is Irish, and his work must finally be judged in terms of the Irish tradition.' The same, therefore, must be argued of Bram Stoker. It is obvious that the culture one is born and brought up with, or, indeed, spends the first decades or so of one's working life with, is going to have a profound influence on one's literary endeavours wherever one is subsequently based. Even Joyce, in attempting to 'escape' from Ireland, was being essentially Irish. To attempt to understand Joyce or Samuel Beckett without admitting their Irish background would be an exercise in futility.

In a reverse situation one can imagine the scorn that most English critics would pour on Ireland if the Irish decided to claim William Blake, England's great poet, painter, engraver and mystic, as 'Irish'. Yet there is more cause to do so than to claim Stoker or Shaw for England. William's father James Blake had emigrated to London from Dublin. W. B. Yeats, writing on Blake in 1910, had interviewed Dr Carter Blake from Fuengirola, near Malaga, who revealed that a John O'Neill of Dublin escaped some political and financial trouble by marrying an Ellen Blake, who kept a shebeen at Rathmines, and took her name. His eldest son was James, the father of the poet: another son entered the wine trade and settled in Malaga where the family was still in business when Yeats interviewed Dr Blake. Yet it would be ludicrous to claim Blake for Ireland; even more farcical to claim Stoker for England.

The Irish actor, Ivan Stokes Dixon, himself a descendant of the Stoker family, once said: 'The creator of *Dracula* was born, raised and died as an Irishman. To separate him from his culture is impossible.' Even the authors of *Ireland: The Rough Guide* (1990) claim to see Stoker's *Dracula* as essentially Irish. '. . . Its concerns – the nature of the soul versus the bestial allure of the body, for instance – are curiously Irish.' The essential question, perhaps, is, could Bram Stoker's *Dracula* have been written by anyone other than an Irishman? Stoker did not leave his native country and settle in London until he was thirty-one years old. How much, then, did Ireland and things Irish shape his powerful creation? We can even go further and ask whether the Irish critic and author, Aodh De Blacam, was correct when he maintained, in *A First Book of Irish Literature*, that Bram Stoker was one of a particular school of Irish writers which he designated 'The Maturin School', naming it after the Dublin writer Charles Robert Maturin (1780–1824).

Maturin, who, like Stoker, was an alumnus of Trinity College, Dublin, wrote many Gothic novels and plays. Today his fame rests on his classic and complex vision of Gothic fiction – *Melmoth the Wanderer* (1820). Coincidentally, it was the first Archibald Constable who gave Maturin an amazing, for its day, advance of £500 for this novel because of Sir Walter Scott's high praise of Maturin's work.

According to De Blacam, Maturin himself was 'manifestly in the tradition of Swift'. Jonathan Swift (1667–1745), another Dubliner, was the creator of the fantasy now best known under its shortened title of *Gulliver's Travels*. At the same time, however, De Blacam believed that Maturin went further to be the first in a new school of horror fantasy writing because, in his work, 'we see a definite vein of Irish genius, an horrific imagination which dramatizes the insane universe of the sceptic'. One of his biographers, Robert E. Lougy, says: 'it is difficult to speak of Maturin as other than an Irish novelist.' Following closely in Maturin's footsteps, according to De Blacam, was Fitzjames O'Brien (1828–1862), the Limerick man who, after graduating from Trinity College, became a journalist and poet, went to London but then migrated to the USA where he joined the Union Army and was killed in the Civil War. O'Brien's short stories place him firmly in the tradition of the 'weird'. 'The Diamond Lens' (1858), his best-known tale, is about life on a microscopic world in a drop of water. 'What Was It?' (1859) is more horrific, with the threat of a malevolent, invisible creature now claimed as the prototype of Guy de Maupassant's 'Horla'. H. P. Lovecraft, in his *Supernatural Horror in Literature*, says: 'O'Brien's early death undoubtedly deprived us of some masterful tales of strangeness and terror . . .' De Blacam places next in this 'school' the incomparable Joseph Sheridan Le Fanu, to whom we shall return later. Bram Stoker is considered as the next generation in the school after Sheridan Le Fanu.

We might also add that Oscar Wilde himself has a claim to be related to this school for, had it not been for Maturin, *The Picture of Dorian Gray* (1891) might not have been written. In *Melmoth the Wanderer* there is a portrait of 'J. Melmoth, 1648' hanging in an obscure closet in the ancient Melmoth mansion in Co. Wicklow. The portrait is a hidden reminder that Melmoth has lived two centuries. Wilde took this theme and imbued it with his own poetic genius to write his vivid contribution to weird literature. Indeed, Oscar Wilde paid Maturin an unusual tribute in the fact that, during his last, sad days in exile in France, he chose the name 'Sebastian Melmoth' as a pseudonym. Even Lovecraft recognised that 'Oscar Wilde may likewise be given a place amongst the weird writers' not only for *Dorian Gray*, but for his exquisite fairy tales.

De Blacam could well have made a reference to Lafcadio Hearn, who has often been wrongly designated as an American. In fact, Patrick Lafcadio Hearn was born on the Greek island of Levkos in 1850, the son of an Irish father and a Greek mother. By the age of three, Pat Hearn was brought to his father's home in Dublin where he was raised by some strange and influential aunts. At the age of twenty, in the year Bram graduated, Pat Hearn took himself off to the United States to begin a journalistic career. He began to achieve a reputation for macabre stories. In 1890 his travelling took him to Japan where he married a Japanese woman, became a Japanese citizen, took the name Koizumi Kokoro and was appointed Professor of English Literature at the Imperial University of Tokyo. It is, however, under the name Lafcadio Hearn that he published his books on the weird ghost stories and macabre legends of various countries, achieving international fame.

Prominently missing from this school of writers, because De Blacam contents himself with prose writers only, is the work of the Dubliner James Clarence Mangan (1803–1849). Mangan was a legendary figure in Dublin in the decade before Bram was born. 'The figure in broad-brimmed hat and flowing cloak, the figure lost in meditation upon a high ladder in the long hall of the Trinity College Library, the tortured soul who consumed liquor and opium and died at forty-six; all add up to the Edgar Allan Poe variation on a theme from Byron.' So says William Irwin Thompson in his study *The Imagination of an Insurrection; Dublin, Easter,*

1916 (Harper and Row, 1967). While intemperance did play a part in Mangan's early death it was malnutrition that finished him off; a death attributed to the 'Great Hunger' which was causing the death of countless thousands in Ireland at that time. The weird and supernatural of Irish folk-tales permeate Mangan's poetry, as in 'The Nameless One':

> Tell how this Nameless, condemned for years long
>   To herd with demons from Hell beneath,
> Saw things that made him, with groans and tears, long
>   For even death.

And Mangan's powerful imagery is revealed in 'Shapes and Signs':

> I see black dragons mount the sky,
>   I see earth yawn beneath my feet –
>   I feel within the asp, the worm
> That will not sleep and cannot die,
>   Fair though may show the winding-sheet!
>   I hear all night as through a storm
> Hoarse voices calling, calling
>   My name upon the wind –
> All omens monstrous and appalling
>   Affright my guilty mind.

Mangan made many translations from Irish, of poems from the eighth to the eighteenth centuries, which had a profound influence on those that followed him. He also translated from German, from the works of Heine, Rückert, Goethe and others. It is interesting to observe that Goethe himself had given substance to the vampire legend in his *Braut Von Korinth* (1797), and Mangan was well acquainted with it. Goethe, incidentally, believed that *The Vampyre* (1819), which appeared under Lord Byron's name, 'was the best thing Byron had written'. We shall deal with this later. But the weird, dark side of Mangan's poetry, his constant references to the supernatural elements and those who cannot die, certainly give him a place in the macabre school of literature.

Mangan was only twenty-one years old when Maturin died. Nevertheless, the young Mangan had become acquainted with Maturin and was an admirer of his work. Maturin's death, on 30 October 1824, from poverty and ill health, presaged Mangan's own early death from similar causes.

Watching Maturin conduct a funeral service at St Peter's, Dublin, where he had been a curate since 1804, Mangan once wrote:

> His long, pale, melancholy, Don Quixote, out-of-the-world face would have inclined you to believe that Dante, Bajazet and the Cid had risen together from their sepulchres, and clubbed their features for the production of an effect. But ... the great Irishman, like Hamlet, had that within him which passed show ... He bore the 'thunder-scars' about him, but they were graven, not on his brow, but on his heart.

When Maturin died, Mangan wrote:

> He – in his own dark way – understood many people; but nobody understood him in *any* way. And therefore it was that he, this man of the highest genius, Charles Robert Maturin, lived unappreciated – and died unsympathized with, uncared for, unenquired after – and not only forgotten, because he had never been thought about.

According to De Blacam, Mangan himself had a direct influence on the poetry of his American contemporary, Edgar Allan Poe. And interestingly enough, while discussing the 'Maturin School', De Blacam adds: 'Before leaving Maturin and Sheridan Le Fanu, it is worthy of note that the American master of the short story, Edgar Allan Poe (1809–49), who excelled in tales of horror, was of Anglo-Irish stock.' De Blacam was not the first critic to claim some Irish cultural themes in Poe's work. The Irish playwright, novelist and poet, Pádraic Colum (1881–1972), wrote in 1908, in an introduction to Poe's stories: 'Certain peculiarities in his work have been put down to racial tendencies, for his father, though American born, was of Irish descent.' Poe himself wrote that he was 'a descendant of a race whose imaginative and easily excitable temperament has at all times rendered them remarkable'. While it would be unreasonable to claim Poe for Ireland, it is nevertheless fascinating to note that his paternal grandfather was born in Co. Tipperary and that Irish links permeated Poe's life.

Does Bram Stoker really have a place in this 'Maturin School' of *Irish* writers of the macabre, as De Blacam claims?

As we have explained in the Preface, it is necessary to understand his early life and the cultural influences upon him before we can attempt to put *Dracula* in a critical context. The following pages contain new

information about Stoker's life and some necessary correctives to previous
biographies which would appear to have relied heavily on family memories,
particularly on information supplied by Bram's only son, Irving Noel
Thornley Stoker (1880–1961). Professor Barbara Belford's *Bram Stoker: A
Biography of the Author of Dracula* has diligently attempted to go further
than mere family oral tradition, and succeeds in correcting many previous
errors, but still fails to deal adequately with Bram's first thirty-one years
in Ireland.

Because of this, the authors of this study make no apology for dwelling
in detail on the Irish period.

Abraham Stoker, henceforth called 'Bram' to differentiate him from his
father, Abraham senior, was born on 8 November at 15 Marino Crescent,
Clontarf, just north of Dublin. It was the year when the horrific 'Irish
Famine' was at its height – a period when Ireland lost a million of its
population by death from malnutrition and attendant diseases and a further
million-and-a-half through forced migration. 'The great Hunger' still
rankles in Irish folk memory for it was an artificially induced famine: the
absentee English landlords refused to allow the Irish rural workers a
redistribution of the wealth they produced. Some 6000 absentee landlords,
living in London and Paris, owned 8 million acres of Irish land. One
contemporary observer pointed out that Ireland, in spite of the potato
blight, was producing enough grain, barley, oats, meat, wool and flax to
feed and clothe twice its population. Even *The Times* of 26 June 1845
confessed:

> They are suffering a real though artificial famine. Nature does her
> duty; the land is fruitful enough, nor can it be fairly said that man is
> wanting ... the island is full and overflowing with human food. But
> something ever intervenes between the hungry mouths and the ample
> banquet.

That 'something' was the landlords. For every famine relief ship
entering Cork harbour, says one eyewitness, three ships loaded with cattle,
sheep and grain were leaving for England. The Oxford-based historian,
Professor Roy Foster, has referred to it as 'Ireland's Holocaust'. Bram was
six months old when these conditions led to the abortive Irish uprising of
1848.

Clontarf, where the Stoker family lived until Bram was about eighteen
months old, is the Anglicised form of the Irish Cluain Tarbh, the pasture

of bulls, where, on 23 April 1014, the High King of Ireland, Brían Bóroimhe, broke the strength of the armies of the Viking invaders for all time. Here, in 1172, the invading Anglo-Normans started to build a castle to dominate the native Irish. Here, in 1843, Daniel O'Connell ('The Liberator') planned a massive demonstration calling for the dissolution of the Union with England. Here, when Bram was nineteen years old, the head of the revolutionary Fenian movement, the Irish Republican Brotherhood, James Stephens, known by his shadowy sobriquet '*An Seabhac Siúlach*' (the wandering hawk), lay in hiding with a £3000 reward on his head. Stephens had been captured and gaoled in Richmond Gaol in Dublin but the IRB had effected his escape from this high security prison; he had made his way to Clontarf where a local businessman named Weldon smuggled him out of the country on a ship called the *Concord* to exile in France.

Indeed, it was in Clontarf town hall, in January 1916, that the Supreme Council of the Irish Republican Brotherhood met and decided to call for a general insurrection in Ireland which led down the irrevocable path to Ireland's emergence as an independent country once more.

Bram's father, Abraham, had been born in Dublin during the year of another major Irish uprising, that of 1798. The Stoker family was, however, mainly Unionist in their politics. The family attended the Anglican Church of Ireland and were part of the 'Protestant Ascendancy' which ruled Ireland for the British empire. They had an underground family burial vault at St Michan's Church in Church Street, just north of the Four Courts. Built in 1095, it is the oldest building on the North Side of the city.

Significantly, the church is renowned for an unexplained atmospheric freak, perhaps caused by the presence of magnesium lime, or tannic acid, or even, some argue, a combination of dry air and methane gas secreted by rotting vegetation beneath the church. Whatever the reasons, conditions have preserved corpses intact as in natural mummification. Today the ruined church is open to tourists who can see the mummified corpses, some 300 years old, with skin, fingernails and hair all clearly identifiable. Perhaps this macabre phenomenon had a far-reaching effect on young Bram in shaping his later fiction. Probably less important to the young boy was the fact that the eighteenth-century church organ was the one which George Frideric Handel played during his stay in Dublin in 1742 when he presented the world première of his oratorio *Messiah*.

It has been claimed, at various times, that the Stoker family were either English or Flemish settlers in Ireland. Someone called Stoker is certainly

listed in the 'Adventurers for Lands in Ireland' under the Act of 17
Charles I, chapt. 33, 1642. These Stockers, who had financed Cromwell's
army on the basis of receiving land from the dispossessed natives, were
found mainly in the parish of St John the Evangelist, Dublin, from 1654.
The English name is said to have derived from the town of Stoke. But the
Flemish claimants say this is a corruption of the name Stock. Professor
Belford, picking up a family oral tradition, believed that the Stokers had
arrived in Ireland in the person of Bram's great-grandfather in 1690 with
William of Orange. She says that this great-grandfather, Richard Stoker,
was a quartermaster of the 'Old Green Horse Dragoons', and came from
Morpeth, Northumberland. The 'Green House' was actually an eight-
eenth-century nickname for the 5th Dragoon Guards (Princess Charlotte's
Own). Its earlier regimental designation was the 2nd Horse (Regiment)
but, admittedly, dragoon regiments did serve in William's army.

Yet the mathematics of this claim do not appear to add up. Even if we
make this claimed 'great-grandfather' twenty years old (exceedingly young
to be a quartermaster of a regiment) in 1690, and remembering that Bram's
father was the eldest of his family, born in 1798 with the youngest being
born in 1821, we would have to put the great-grandfather in his nineties
when he became father to Bram's grandfather.

The fact is that Bram's family seems to have been related to neither
English nor Flemish lines. They had moved to Dublin from Co. Down, in
Ulster, during the first decade of 1700, where they had descended from
one of the initial settlements from Scotland about 1608–10. The name was
an Anglicisation of the Gaelic Mac an Stocaire (son of the trumpeter).
This family were a sept of the Mac Pharlain (McFarlane) clan. As they
were initially Presbyterians the move to Dublin and subsequent appearance
as Anglicans is significant. An Act of 1704 had excluded all Presbyterians
in Ireland from holding office in the law, the armed forces, Customs and
Excise, and local government. In 1713 even Presbyterian schoolmasters
were given three months' gaol if found pursuing their profession, and
ministers were forbidden to conduct services. Marriages by Presbyterian
ministers were deemed illegal and mixed marriages between Presbyterians
and Anglicans were forbidden. This persecution of all Dissenting Protestant religions, as well as Catholics, following in the wake of the Williamite
conquest of Ireland (whose laws recognised only the Anglican religion)
caused a quarter of a million Ulster Presbyterians to emigrate to the New
World in search of religious freedom between 1717 and 1776 alone. Some
Presbyterians, however, simply converted to the Anglican religion, as did

some Catholics. The first recorded member of the Stoker family to enter Trinity College, Dublin, was an Edward in 1732, son of 'Mr Stoker formerly of Lismahon, Co. Down'.

The Dublin Stoker family had a strong medical tradition. William Stoker, Bram's grandfather, was connected with the Dublin House of Recovery and later the Cork Street Fever Hospital in Dublin. He had written a *Treatise on Fever* in 1815. It is small wonder that three of Bram's brothers turned to the medical profession and his sister married another famous Dublin surgeon. It was natural that when Bram quotes a letter from a fictional medical specialist in *Dracula*, p. 143, he makes that doctor an Irishman.

Bram's grandfather seems to have had at least four sons. Abraham, born in 1798, was the eldest. William was born in 1806, Edward Alexander in 1808 and Charles Eyre, with a significant gap, in 1821. The three youngest went to Trinity College but there is no record of Abraham senior attending. However, he became a clerk in the office of the Chief Secretary of Ireland in Dublin Castle, the seat of the English colonial administration since medieval times on Castle Street/Cork Hill. First built in the reign of John, the castle was completed in 1220. The civil service was presided over by a London-appointed Lord Lieutenant and a Chief Secretary. It was not the easiest position to hold in the imperial administration. Indeed, on 6 May 1882, the Chief Secretary, Lord Frederick Cavendish, and his under-secretary, T. H. Burke, were both assassinated by Irish revolutionaries in Dublin's Phoenix Park.

William followed his brother into the civil service as an ordnance clerk.

Abraham Stoker had been a clerk for thirty-seven years in the Chief Secretary's office, dealing specifically with parliamentary business, when he retired on a full salary of £650 per annum in 1869. Such a sum was a very respectable annual pension for 1869, yet Bram's biographers stated that his father was not a rich man and that, in fact, his retirement saw him badly in debt. Wealth is, of course, relative but it should be pointed out that the average senior civil servant received a salary (in 1885) of £250 per annum while the top salary for a schoolmaster in the same period was £75 per annum. Abraham senior's income was certainly not 'the modest salary' envisaged by Ludlam. Of course, we know that Abraham was paying fees for the education of his sons, which would have depleted the salary.

Abraham Stoker had married a lady twenty years younger than himself, Charlotte Matilda Blake Thornley. Her father, Thomas Thornley (1796–1850) of Ballyshannon, Co. Donegal, had been commissioned as an ensign in the 43rd (Monmouthshire) Regiment of Foot on 21 October 1813. Known as the Monmouthshire Light Infantry, the 43rd was an Irish garrison regiment, being stationed in Enniskillen in 1789, then in Kilkenny from 1792 with a battalion at Mullingar. They were still in Ireland in 1872, being stationed in Cork.

Thomas Thornley was promoted to lieutenant on 28 September 1815. He apparently saw action in the American war of 1812 (1812–1815) where his regiment of light infantry suffered in the disastrous defeat of Sir Edward Pakenham's army before New Orleans during 23 December/8 January 1815/1816. Returning to Ireland, Lieutenant Thornley was placed on half-pay on 3 April 1817, and he remained as a half-pay lieutenant until his death in 1850. Professor Belford claims that he joined the Royal Irish Constabulary in 1817 but the Royal Irish Constabulary did not come into existence until 1867 and its predecessor, the Irish Constabulary, was not formed until 1836. Lieutenant Thornley married Matilda Blake, one of the Galway Blakes, in 1817 and settled in Sligo. This branch of the Blakes was not that of the Norman Caddell family, nicknamed 'Le Blaca' (the Black), which had settled in Galway, but a family of native Irish origin whose name was originally Ó Blathmhaic. Charlotte had been born in 1818, the eldest child, and spent most of her childhood at the family home in Sligo, which was the second biggest town in the north-west, after Derry. It suffered terribly during the 'famine', losing a third of its population. Charlotte still had relatives in Sligo during this grim period and had many tales to pass on to Bram.

Most importantly, Charlotte instilled in Bram an interest in Irish folk traditions. Christopher Lee, one of the great screen Draculas, recognised Charlotte's importance when he wrote in *The Dracula Book* by Donald F. Glut that 'Stoker was brought up by his mother on a rich diet of Celtic folklore and legend . . .' Charlotte swore that she had heard a banshee wail before her own mother died. The banshee (*bean sidhe*, woman of the fairies) was supposed to wail as a forewarning of a death in a family.

According to Enid Stoker, the wife of Bram's brother Tom, her mother-in-law told gruesome tales of the 1832 outbreak of cholera in Ireland when thousands of victims perished; so fearful did people become that often the living were buried with the dead because no one would go close enough to confirm whether they were alive or not. In burying corpses, sometimes the bones of contorted limbs would have to be broken. In one case, Charlotte told her children, a man believed to be dead, lying with his legs drawn up, was thought to need the bones of his leg broken. A hammer was brought and smashed against the knee. The 'corpse' jerked up with a scream.

In another tale, the family barricaded themselves in their house in Sligo to avoid contamination. Because many wealthy families had fled the area, looting was prevalent. There was a noise: the twenty-four-year-old Charlotte saw a looter was trying to break in, saw his hand creeping through a window to unlatch it. She took an axe and cut the hand off. There is little doubt that Charlotte Stoker was a formidable lady.

Bram listened carefully to her tales. He was to use them to good effect in one of his short stories in the collection *Under the Sunset* (1882). The work is full of Irish folk themes; even the title, which refers to 'the land under the sunset' (i.e. the west), was a euphemism for 'Tir na nÓg' – the land of youth, or the Otherworld. In one tale, 'The Castle of the King', a young man sets out to find his love but she has apparently died in a strange castle – a vast, deathly place shrouded in mist where various horrors await him. Another tale, 'The Invisible Giant', was clearly based on Charlotte Stoker's story about life in Sligo in the cholera epidemic. The young heroine sees the figure of a man in the sky: 'It was shrouded in a great misty robe that covered it, fading into air so that she could only see the face and the grim spectral hands ... the face was that of a strong man, pitiless, yet without malice; and ... the eyes were blind.' One is reminded of Bram's later description of Dracula's face.

It was not until 1889 that Bram was to write his first novel which, again, was significantly set in the west of Ireland, in Conamara, where his hero encounters the legend of the Snake's Pass, an opening leading down to the sea in the mountain of Knockcalltecrore, where French soldiers, landing to help the insurgents of 1798, had lost a fabulous treasure in the mountain's shifting bog. It is the area of which Yeats wrote: 'Come where hill lies heaped upon hill'. The novel appeared as a serial in *The People* and in several English provincial newspapers in 1889 before being issued in book form by Sampson Low dated 1891, although it was officially published in November 18, 1890, at 6s.

Whether Charlotte was also responsible for the basis of this story is uncertain. Charlotte could well have picked up stories of the 1798 uprising in Sligo for, during that year, a French army under General Joseph Amable Humbert had landed in Killala, Co. Mayo, not far from Sligo, in an effort to help the Irish insurgents establish their republic. Charlotte identified the 1798 insurgent, George Blake, one of those who joined

Humbert, as her mother's brother. George was captured on 8 September 1798, after the battle at Ballinamuck, Co. Longford (wrongly given by Professor Belford as 'Ballenamunch'), and immediately hanged. As a concession to his rank he was allowed to soap the rope to ensure a quick death.

In her early forties Charlotte became a determined social reformer: as a Dublin workhouse visitor, she had been appalled by the state of institutions such as the Dublin Union, where young women had little hope but to fall into vice and wretchedness. Indeed, Dublin, under the colonial administration at this time, had a higher death rate than Calcutta or the slums of Moscow. In Dublin 41.9 per cent of all deaths occurred in pauper workhouses. The infant mortality rate was 168 per 1000, double that of the nation-wide average. Some 87,000 out of its 300,000 population lived in dilapidated slum housing, 20,000 families lived in only one room; 5000 more families existed in two rooms. Of the 5000 registered tenement buildings at least 1500 were actually condemned and it was not uncommon for such slum tenements to fall down of their own accord and kill or injure their occupants. Dublin had the biggest 'red light' district of any western city, where women flocked nightly to better their standards of living. Social standards were not to improve until Ireland was able to take control of its own political, social and economic life. At the time Charlotte Stoker was a strident voice calling for equality of the sexes and the provision of dignified work for women. 'A self-supporting woman is alike respected and respectable,' she declared in a pamphlet *On Female Emigration from Workhouses*, published by Alex Thom, Dublin, in 1864.

She had begun her campaigning during the previous year, speaking at a meeting of the Statistical and Social Inquiry Society of Ireland, in Dublin. One of those attending was Dr William Wilde, of whom we shall hear more presently. Charlotte chose to campaign for schools for the deaf and dumb, which she pointed out were available in many countries but not under the colonial administration of England. Her speech *On the Necessity of a State Provision for the Education of the Deaf and Dumb of Ireland* was published by Alex Thom, Dublin, in 1863.

By coincidence, in view of Charlotte's interest in poverty and workhouse problems relating to women, a few months before her death, a widow also named Charlotte Stoker died at the North Dublin Infirmary on 18 December 1900. This Charlotte Stoker had been admitted the previous day from her tenement room at 29 Dunculey Place. She was sixty-seven years old and of the 'labouring class'. She had been taken to the paupers' section of the North Dublin Infirmary and was attended by Dr J. Donohoe of the North Dublin 4 Workhouse who certified her death from 'apoplexy'. The name Stoker was not so common in Dublin. Could she have been a relative, or could the husband of the hapless widow Stoker have been descended from the Cromwellian settlers? There would surely be a touch of irony from an Irish perspective if the latter were the case.

Bram was one of the seven children born to Abraham Stoker senior and Charlotte – five boys and two girls. The eldest was William Thornley, born on 6 Mary 1845. Matilda came next, being a year older than Bram, born in 1846. Bram followed in 1847, with Thomas on 20 August 1849, and Richard Nugent on 31 October 1851. The second Stoker daughter, Margaret Dalrymple, was born in 1853, and lastly came George, on 22 July 1855.

Abraham Stoker and his family lived at No. 15 Marino Crescent, Clontarf, for some years. It was handy for Stoker senior to take the train from the local station, then at the back of Marino Crescent, and travel the three miles to his place of work in central Dublin. The houses in Marino Crescent were Georgian terraced but expensive and the rateable value of No. 15 at the time of Bram's birth was £35 per year.

Sometime before November 1849, however, Abraham decided to move his growing family out of Clontarf, selling the house to a Mr J. Keane. It seems that the move was essential to find more living space for the family.

They moved into the more grandiose structure of Artane Lodge in the village of Artane, on the road to Malahide, just at the back of Clontarf. The population was only 367. It was here that Bram spent his early childhood until the age of ten or eleven. In 1858 the Stokers moved once again, to No. 17 Upper Buckingham Street in the Mountjoy district of Dublin city. This move placed Abraham senior near the home of his brother Edward Alexander, a graduate of Trinity who had become a surgeon and one of the chief examiners at the Royal College of Surgeons, Ireland. Edward Stoker lived at 49 Rutland Square. Rutland Square (now Parnell Square) was soon to feature in Bram's educational life.

In spite of his size, young Bram, who had made it to 6 feet 2 inches in height, weighing 12 stone, by the time he was seventeen, had been a sickly child. He claimed to have been near death at times, but the symptoms or causes of his illness have never been clearly defined. It may well be that he was prone to childhood asthma. His brother William, who would later prefer to use Thornley as a first name, went to Wymondham Grammar School. There is no record of a Wymondham school in Ireland but such a school existed in England. We must presume that William was sent there. Bram's education, however, was supervised at home by his mother with the part-time assistance of William (presumably during school vacations) and Matilda. According to Harry Ludlam (*A Biography of Dracula: The Life Story of Bram Stoker*), Daniel Farson (*The Man Who Wrote Dracula*) and Barbara Belford, when he was fit enough, about the age of twelve years, Bram was sent to a day school whose principal was the Revd William Woods. However, no such school then existed.

William Woods, though he had graduated from Trinity in 1860, does not appear among Dublin's clergy until 1862. He was then a curate of St Mary's, but, significantly, with an address at 14 Granby Row on Rutland Square. Also situated in Rutland Square, at No. 15, was Bective House College, whose proprietor was Dr John Lardner Burke, a former Trinity College man, who had established Bective as a school for 'younger gentlemen'. It was not until 1870 that the Revd William Woods became proprietor of Bective College.

Now while this is too late for Bram to have been a pupil of Woods when he was proprietor of Bective, it is possible that Woods was employed as a master at the school, fitting in with his curacy at St Mary's. This would have made Bram fifteen years of age when he went to have some schooling at Bective in the class of the Revd Woods.

Significantly, Woods was also appointed about this time as chaplain of the Magdalen Lunatic Asylum in Leeson Street, only one house away from where some years later Bram took rooms. One wonders if any of the scenes in Dr Seward's lunatic asylum were born during this time? The Revd Woods, coincidentally, eventually bought No. 20 Marino Crescent, Clontarf.

Of Bram's boyhood, little is now known. Introspective in childhood, Bram had a reputation as something of a 'scribbler' by his early teens. The only childhood friend that we are certain of is Valentine Blake Dillon (1847–1904), who became the lawyer for the Land League and defended Charles Stewart Parnell, the leader of the Irish Party and Land League, when he was arrested in 1880. Bram's friendship with Val Dillon is intriguing and presents a number of questions. The son of a Sligo solicitor, Val Dillon came from a Catholic nationalist background as opposed to Bram's Anglican Unionist one. Also, while Val Dillon was born in the same year as Bram, he was born in Sligo. Nor did he go to Trinity but to the Catholic university, graduating the same year as Bram. He became a solicitor in Dublin.

He was, as his middle name indicates, related to the Blakes of Sligo. And Bram's grandmother was a Sligo Blake. In this might be their boyhood connection for we might assume that Val Dillon and Bram were distantly related. When Val Dillon died on 31 March 1904, it was Bram's brother, William Thornley Stoker, who was leading the medical team in attendance on him in a private hospital in Baggot Street, Dublin.

The question that arises is that if Val Dillon was Bram's boyhood friend, as Bram states, but was born and educated in Sligo until moving to Dublin to enter the Catholic university, then did Bram's mother, a Sligo woman, take Bram to Sligo either on regular visits, or to live for a longer period, during his childhood? Or did Val visit the Stokers in Dublin?

Val was a nephew of the 1848 Irish revolutionary leader, lawyer John Blake Dillon (1816–1866) who became MP for Tipperary when an amnesty allowed him to return from exile in France and settle in Dublin. Val's cousin John (1851–1927) was also elected to his father's seat and was imprisoned with Parnell. When the party split, John became leader of the anti-Parnellites but Val remained a supporter of Parnell and stood for the North Sligo parliamentary seat in 1891. John became leader of the Irish Party in 1918 when it was annihilated at the polls by Sinn Féin and he lost his seat to Eamonn de Valéra. Val became Lord Mayor of Dublin in 1894 and again in 1895. He resigned as Alderman of Dublin in 1896. On a visit to Dublin in 1894, Bram renewed his friendship with Val Dillon during a civic reception for his friend and employer Henry Irving.

Val had married a Margaret Phelan in 1872. Mrs Dillon died in 1903.

Valentine Dillon became 'immortalised' in James Joyce's *Ulysses*. The character Lenehan is describing an annual dinner party presided over by Dillon to the character M'Coy.

– There was a big spread out at Glencree reformatory, Lenehan said eagerly. The annual dinner you know. Boiled shirt affair. The lord mayor was there, Val Dillon it was, and Sir Charles Cameron and Dan Dawson spoke and there was music. Bartell D'Arcy sang and Benjamin Dollard . . .

– I know, M'Coy broke in. My missus sang there once.

Bram described Dillon as 'a man with broad views of life and of the dignity of the position he held for, I think, the third time.' In this Bram was mistaken. Val Dillon held office only twice as Lord Mayor of Dublin. He died at the age of fifty-seven.

By all accounts, Bram was attracted to the weird and supernatural from an early age. In Dublin, in the mist-shrouded twilight, one walked hand in hand with the supernatural along every street. Stories of wailing banshees were not confined to rural areas. Ghostly carriages clattered along in the gloom with headless coachmen cracking their whips; there were mysterious knocks at doors with no one there when answered; and poltergeists were to be found even in the centre of imperial rule at Dublin Castle itself. There were also stories of werewolves haunting the banks of the Grand Canal between the Rialto and Inchicore Bridges. Other tales mention a carriage, drawn by six headless black horses, which would sweep out of Oldbawn House, in the Dublin suburb of Tallaght, and go careening down the road. Tallaght's ghostly visitors did not arrive there coincidentally; the place was the site of plague burials and the very name, Anglicised from Tamhlacht, means a burial ground.

Near to where Bram was born in Clontarf stands Ballybough Bridge across the Tolka River. Nearby was the site of an unconsecrated graveyard where suicides were buried; a local belief at this time was that if a wooden stake was driven through the heart of a suicide it prevented their spirit from returning to haunt the family. It was here at the bridge that a public gallows stood until the early nineteenth century on which miscreants were left hanging as an object lesson to the citizenry.

Citizens would pass down Bridgefoot Street, the site of the old Marshalsea Barracks, with a shudder. Originally a debtors' prison, it was taken over by the military in 1798; here insurgent Irish prisoners were confined, tortured and executed. One prisoner from Limerick, Pádraic Ó Dubhghaill, tried to escape and was killed dropping from the thirty-foot walls. His ghost was popularly said to haunt the street.

While Bram was living in St Stephen's Green, he doubtless became aware of the story of the 'Walking Gallows'. One of the most terrifying ghosts of the area was said to be that of an English soldier, Lieutenant Edward Hempenstall of the 88th Regiment. He was 7 feet tall. During the uprising of 1798 he appointed himself judge and executioner of suspected Irish insurgents. He would use his own silk cravat, placing it around the victim's neck and hoisting them over his shoulders. He would then trot around St Stephen's Green with the struggling victim until they were dead. In 1804 Lieutenant Hempenstall was eventually assassinated but his ghost is said to haunt the Green still looking for victims.

Another story Bram would have become acquainted with in St Stephen's Green was that of the murdered servant. Every Thursday before Good

Friday, people would gather in St Stephen's Green to gaze up at the windows of Iveagh House, the home of Lord Iveagh. It was said that in Cromwellian days a Catholic servant girl had been killed there without being allowed priest or rosary. People swore that a vision of a shining cross appeared on the anniversary of that night at the window of the room where the deed was done. Large crowds would attend to witness the spectacle.

Ardee House, once the town house of Lord Meath, in Ardee Street, was also a famous haunted location. The Dublin writer, Annie Smithson (1873–1948), recounted staying there and experiencing several supernatural phenomena which made her conclude that the place was permeated with evil. She was not a lady to be easily swayed being a nurse, founder of the Irish Nurses' Organisation, who had fought on the republican side during both the War of Independence and the Civil War. In the latter conflict she had been in the dramatic siege of Moran's Hotel where the republican garrison held out for some time despite being faced with machine-guns, an armoured car and an 18-pounder field-gun.

A malevolent spirit was reported to haunt the theatre in Fishamble Street which had formerly been Neale's Music Hall, founded in 1741, where Handel performed his *Messiah* in April 1742. And other ghosts were said to haunt the famous Marsh Library, the first public library in Ireland, built in 1701 and given to the nation by Archbishop Narcissus Marsh (1638–1713). Inside are tiny reading cubicles and dark carved bookshelves with chains that once protected the books from theft. The Library houses some 25,000 volumes from the sixteenth to the eighteenth century. Here Bram, and many another student from Trinity College, studied, and many strange apparitions have been reported by students and professors alike.

Another macabre story was that of 'Billy the Bowl' in nearby Stoneybatter and Grangegorman, north of the river. Billy Davis was born without legs but would sit in an iron bowl and push himself about the streets of Dublin using his powerful arms. He was the terror of the neighbourhood for, despite his disability, he could use his powerful arms to drag his victims to the ground and rob them. He strangled one of his victims and was eventually caught.

From the medical side of his family Bram would have heard about the Dublin body-snatchers. The Royal College of Surgeons, as the main centre for anatomical studies in Ireland, had a great need for bodies for anatomical demonstrations for its students. Stories of 'resurrectionists' were legion in the hall of the college which was said to pay £7 10s. per body, in 'fresh' condition. One of the places renowned for being visited by body-snatchers was the church graveyard of St Kevin's in Kevin Street, a short walk from one of the Stoker houses in Harcourt Street. It is now a park.

In fact, Bram was a teenager when the infamous William Hare died in London. William Burke and William Hare were from the north of Ireland. They had gone to Scotland to work on the Union Canal but became aware of the demand for human bodies for anatomical demonstrations at the city's medical schools. Burke and Hare were never grave robbers, being superstitious. But they had no compunction about murder, suffocating their victims and selling them to a Dr Knox. They murdered sixteen people before they were arrested. As no evidence could be produced, the Lord Advocate Sir William Rae offered an amnesty if one would turn informer. Hare informed on his friend Burke, who went to the gallows on 28 January 1829. Charges against Burke's mistress were found 'not proven'. Hare and his wife fled to London.

The young Bram, with his keen eye for the weird, could not have remained unaffected by the ghoulish atmosphere around him.

One thing Abraham Stoker senior instilled in his son was a love of theatre. He had been a theatre-goer all his life and had regaled Bram with his memories of the great Irish actor Edmund Kean (d. 1833); Bram was old enough to see some of the performances of Edmund's equally famous actor son Charles Kean (1811–1868). One wonders whether old Abraham Stoker was in the audiences which applauded Edmund Kean in the title role of Charles Maturin's play *Bertram* in 1816. *Bertram* won praise from Lord Byron and earned Maturin over £1000. Kean also played in Maturin's second play *Manuel*. Bram and his father went to plays together and once saw Barry Sullivan play the avaricious Sir Giles Overreach in Philip Massinger's famous comedy *A New Way to Pay Old Debts* (*c.* 1625).

Just before Bram was seventeen years old, Abraham decided to move his family once again. This time they moved into south Dublin to No. 5 Orwell Park, Rathgar, next to Rathmines. The Stoker family lived here for the next five years: years which were to see significant developments in Bram's social connections, his political leanings and, especially, his literary pursuits . . .

CHAPTER FOUR

The Curious Class of '65

A<small>T SEVENTEEN YEARS OF AGE</small>, Bram entered Trinity College, Dublin, to study science, specifically pure mathematics. Trinity had been established in 1591 as an institution for Protestant education. In Bram's day it was looked upon as the bastion of the Ascendancy, the Anglo-Irish Protestant and colonial administration. Often, however, the leaders of Ireland's various national movements and of its many republican uprisings were alumni of Trinity. Wolfe Tone (1763–1798), the 'Father of Irish Republicanism' and leader of the 1798 uprising, was one noted graduate. Thomas Osborne Davis (1814–1845), the revolutionary leader of the Young Ireland movement, was yet another who quit the Irish Bar for the political field. Later, Douglas Hyde (1860–1949), the first President of Ireland in 1937, would also be a distinguished alumnus. Just months before Bram entered, yet another famous Trinity man, James Bronterre O'Brien of Longford, the famous revolutionary Chartist leader, had died in London. O'Brien and another Trinity graduate, Feargus O'Connor, a former Repeal of the Union Member of Parliament, had founded the 'People's Charter' of the Working Men's Association in 1838. So, at the same time as being a bastion of the Ascendancy classes in Ireland, Trinity was also a training ground for revolutionary politics. At its foundation, Trinity offered free education to Catholics who were prepared to change their religion. Nowadays, of course, it is non-sectarian and seventy per cent of its student population is Catholic.

When Bram entered Trinity, his elder brother, William Thornley, had graduated from Queen's College, Galway and was already passing through the Royal College of Surgeons, a short walk away in St Stephen's Green, of which institution he was later to become President as well as President of the Royal Academy of Medicine in Ireland.

As we mentioned earlier, Bram soon began to excel in university activities, throwing himself into physical endeavours and winning cups for weight lifting and walking races and a cap for football, and becoming athletics champion of the university. His recovery from being a sickly child was complete. The minute book of the University Foot Races from 1865 to 1873 (presented to the college library in November 1945) shows that Bram frequently chaired the meetings of this athletic group.

Through these committee meetings Bram encountered Isaac Butt, who was often in the chair during the mid-1860s. It would have been surprising if Bram had not also socialised with Isaac Butt elsewhere within the college precincts. Butt was another luminary of Trinity College, born in 1813. He had been a founder of the *Dublin University Magazine* in 1833 and its editor from 1834–1838. He first encouraged his contemporary, Joseph Sheridan Le Fanu, to write for it. The *Dublin University Magazine* has been compared to the *Edinburgh Review* in the way it gathered a group of literati around it. Butt was a lawyer by profession and defended the leaders of the abortive 1848 uprising. He went on to form and lead the Irish National Party seeking 'Home Rule'.

In fact, one of Bram's contemporaries at Trinity, John Gordon Smith MacNeill, from Castlebar, Co. Mayo, was said to have attempted to involve Bram in the Irish Party. MacNeill, on graduation, studied for the Irish Bar and then became an Irish Party Member of Parliament for South Donegal. He remained in Parliament until 1918 when he lost his seat to P. J. Ward of Sinn Féin. MacNeill became a professor of law at University College, Dublin.

Among Bram's contemporaries and friends at Trinity was a grandson of Charles Maturin. William Basil Maturin (1847–1915) was the son of Maturin's eldest son, William. William Basil graduated with Bram and took Anglican holy orders but converted to Catholicism and wrote several theological works. He was drowned when the *Lusitania* was sunk, having been torpedoed by a German submarine off the Old Head of Kinsale, south-west Ireland, on 7 May 1915. Maturin was returning from a lecture tour of America. Some 1201 passengers and crew lost their lives in the disaster.

Alfred Perceval Graves (1846–1931) was another contemporary, and also destined for the civil service but gave it up for a career in journalism, becoming assistant editor of *Punch* in London. He achieved fame with his poetry, translations from Irish and tales of Irish folklore. Bram's uncle Edward Alexander Stoker, the examiner of the Royal College of Surgeons, had married into the Graves family. Edward Stoker's son bore the august name Graves Stoker (1864–1938) and continued the Stoker family's medical tradition, becoming a Fellow of the Royal Irish Academy of Medicine and Licentiate of the Royal College of Surgeons in Ireland. It is of interest that Graves Stoker was educated at Bective College when William Woods was principal.

The Graves family of Dublin combined the professions of medicine, the Church and art. Robert James Graves (1796–1853), the discoverer of 'Graves disease' (toxic goitre), was one-time President of the Royal College of Physicians in Ireland. His nephew Charles Graves (1812–1899) had become Professor of Mathematics at Trinity College, before taking holy orders in the Anglican Church to become dean of Dublin Castle chapel and then Bishop of Limerick, Ardfert and Aghadoe in 1866. He was an expert on the ancient Irish writing known as Ogham and an amateur antiquarian. He became President of the Royal Irish Academy and was responsible for the establishment of a royal commission to edit and translate the ancient Irish law manuscripts, popularly known as the Brehon Laws. Charles' brother, Robert Perceval Graves, was a biographer and his sister Clara was a poet. His two sons were the poet Arnold and, more famously, Alfred Perceval Graves (1846–1931), who was Bram's companion at Trinity. Alfred, in turn, was the father of the poet and novelist Robert Graves (1895–1985) who has achieved even greater literary fame.

Another important contemporary was Standish James O'Grady (1846–1928) from Castletownbere in Co. Cork. He is hailed as 'Father of the Irish Literary Revival'. The son of Viscount Guaillamore, O'Grady is one of the most important yet least known of influential figures in modern Irish literature. W. B. Yeats was to write: 'I think it was his *History of Ireland, Heroic Period* that started us all.' O'Grady was a contributor to the university magazine *Kottabos*.

Kottabos had been launched in 1869 by a newly elected fellow, Robert Yelverton Tyrrell (1844–1914) of Ballingarry, Co. Tipperary, who went on to be Professor of Greek and also of Latin. He was the private tutor and friend of Alfred Graves at Trinity and was recognised as one of the greatest Classical scholars of his day. *Kottabos*, a variant form of *cottabus*, was named after the game played by young men in ancient Greece, much in vogue at drinking parties, which consisted of throwing a portion of wine into a vessel so as to strike it in a particular manner. Aristophanes mentions it. A book, *The Game of Kottabos* by A. G. Brown, was published in 1908, by F. H. Ayres of London. Tyrrell's idea was to use the magazine for Greek and Latin translations and for original pieces of English verse and prose. He edited thirty-six editions between 1868 and 1881 and another fourteen editions were published between 1891 and 1895 by other editors. Tyrrell and Sir Edward Sullivan published a collection of writings from *Kottabos* entitled *Echoes from Kottabos*. Among the distinguished contributors were Oscar Wilde and his elder brother Willie, T. W. H. Rolleston, John Todhunter, Freeman Wills, W. G. Wills, Brabazon Casement (a relative of Roger Casement) and Standish O'Grady.

O'Grady was not just a contemporary of Bram's at Trinity but much involved with him in the athletics life of the university. After he left Trinity, O'Grady was called to the Bar but took up journalism, becoming a leader writer for the *Dublin Daily Express*. O'Grady, however, began to work in the field of Irish manuscripts, the corpus of mythological texts and Céitinn's famous *History of Ireland*. His work was seen as the beginning of the Irish Renaissance. Perhaps O'Grady's description of what he found at Trinity with regard to Irish culture might well have applied to Bram:

> At school and in Trinity College I was an industrious lad and worked through the curriculum with abundant energy and some success; yet in the curriculum never read one work about Irish history and legend, never even heard one word about these things from my pastors and masters. When I was about twenty-three years of age, had anyone told me – as later on a professor of Dublin University actually did – that Brían Bóroimhe was a mythological character, I would have believed him. I knew absolutely nothing about our past, not through my own fault, for I was willing enough to learn anything set before me, but owing to the stupid education system of the country.

O'Grady, it is claimed, later recommended that Bram send the manuscript of his first collection of Irish-based short stories to the publishers Sampson Low, Marston, Searle and Rivington of London. Sampson Low had published the first half-dozen of O'Grady's books and were to publish Bram's *Under the Sunset* (1882) and *The Snake's Pass* (1891) before Bram went on to Constable.

It is hard to tell what influence, if any, O'Grady later had on his classmate after he had discovered the numerous manuscript texts of Irish mythology and folklore. Certainly many others, whom Bram knew, were to acknowledge O'Grady's influence such as Katharine Tynan, John Todhunter, T. W. Rolleston and Aubrey de Vere. The famous 'AE' (George Russell) once declared that 'whatever is Irish in me he kindled to life'. W. B. Yeats also came under O'Grady's spell.

Yet another contemporary of Bram's who became fascinated by Irish folklore was William Larminie from Co. Mayo, who, after graduating from Trinity, spent years collecting folk-tales; *West Irish Folk-Tales and Romances* is his best-known collection. Larminie also achieved a reputation as a poet with such poems as 'The Nameless Fort' in which he speaks of Ireland as a

> – nation slain so utterly
> That even their ghosts are dead, and on their grave
> Springeth no bloom of legend in its wildness;

Bram was not simply a 'physical' student; he plunged into literary studies and appeared in amateur dramatic productions, including those of the Dublin University Dramatic Society and the University Boat Club Dramatic Society. He was once praised for his performance of David in *The Rivals* by the critic of the *Dublin Evening Standard*. Although he would achieve honours in his chosen course of science, he would also win silver medals for essays in history and English composition. He became Auditor of the Historical Society. The Historical Society was a famous debating and literary club founded by Edmund Burke (1729–1797) shortly after his own entry into Trinity in 1744. Among its distinguished members had been the revolutionary Wolf Tone who won two society medals for his oratory. The position of Auditor was the equivalent to President of the Oxford Union in English terms. Bram also went on to be President of the Philosophical Society where his first address was fascinatingly entitled 'Sensationalism in Fiction and Society'. *A History of Trinity College, Dublin 1892–1945*, by Kenneth C. Bailey, points out that Bram's chief distinction at Trinity was that he was one of the few men who became both Auditor of the college Historical Society and President of the university Philosophical Society. To have been elected to these positions certainly meant that Bram was a popular and influential student. We can only lament the lack of letters and papers which might have explored the ideals and hopes of Bram and his fellow students.

One of Bram's addresses to the college Historical Society, on 13 November 1872, was published by the society. The theme was *The Necessity for Political Honesty* in which he seems to be arguing for a

'United Nations'. Later Bram (in his *Reminiscences of Henry Irving*, Vol. II
p. 31) recalled: 'In my University days I had been something of a law
maker in a small way, as I had revised and carried out the revision of the
laws of order of the College Historical Society, Dublin University – our
great debating society founded by Edmund Burke.'

Bram was, as we have said earlier, much influenced at university by
Edward Dowden (1843–1913), a Cork man, who had reached the position
of Professor of English Literature at Trinity by the astonishing age of
twenty-four. His works on Shakespeare, such as *Shakespeare, His Mind
and Art* (1875), became widely read. Among other important studies were
Studies in Literature (1878), *Essays, Modern and Elizabethan* (1910) and
biographies of Southey, Browning, Montaigne and Shelley, not forgetting
his championing of Walt Whitman.

An assistant of Dowden's, another talented young man, was Robert
Henry Martley. He had graduated from Trinity College in 1863, only a
year before Bram entered. While studying for his master's degree, Martley
taught English literature and delivered a series of 'Afternoon Lectures on
English Literature' which were later published in volume form. It was the
only book Martley published, but he published verse here and there and
contributed to Tyrrell's *Kottabos*. In looking for influences on Bram
Stoker, one cannot ignore a poem by Martley in *Kottabos* (Trinity term,
1875) entitled 'The Vampire'. The nine verses begin:

> It is true! It is true! It is true!
> I have seen the terrible thing;
> Its lips are red, and its eyes are bled
> And oh how its fingers cling!

The poem goes on:

> For here the stories have err'd
> It has not the wings of a bat
> It has not the beak nor the claws of a bird;
> It's a hundred times worse than that.

> Its skin was smooth and fair
> And its lips, though steeped in gore,
> Were like some lips I know, and I swear
> I have seen those eyes before.

But whatever the creature be
The fearfulest, cruelest part
Is this, that it fixes its eyes on me,
And smiles as it drains my heart.

One wonders what Bram's attitude to the turbulent politics of his country was during his university life. His Unionist Tory background must have had some effect on his early opinions. But it is hard to imagine that he was oblivious and impervious to the activities of the Irish Republican Brotherhood – known as the Fenians, from the mythological warriors who protected the High Kings of Ireland. In 1865 two former Trinity College men, Thomas Clarke Luby (1821–1901) and John O'Leary (1830–1907), were sentenced to twenty years' penal servitude for their roles in the leadership of the Fenian movement. As with the Irish republican insurrectionist movements of 1798, 1803 and 1848, the Fenians of 1867 were mainly led by some distinguished graduates of Trinity College, men of Bram's own social and educational background.

The year Bram arrived at Trinity the students had turned out to guard the funeral cortège of William Smith O'Brien (1803–1864), the former Ennis Member of Parliament, who led the 1848 Young Ireland uprising. His death sentence was commuted to transportation for life but he was unconditionally pardoned in 1856. When he died, his body was taken to Dublin for transfer to a train to take it to Limerick for burial. Bram's contemporary, Alfred Graves, describes what happened:

For some reason or another it was feared that there would be an unpleasant scene at Kingsbridge Railway Station [now Heuston Station], when the remains of the famous Irish rebel Smith O'Brien were passing through Dublin. This, though in no sense in sympathy with the Rebellion of '48, we undergraduates were extremely anxious to prevent, having had a high respect for the character of O'Brien. So we marched out in large numbers through Nassau Street to the station and occupied it in reverent silence while O'Brien's coffin was being transferred from the hearse to the railway carriage which was to take it for burial to Limerick.

The year after Bram arrived at Trinity, the English administration had moved to suppress the republican movement with arrests and proscriptions of publications. Habeas Corpus was suspended on 17 February 1866. The

Fenian uprising took place in 1867 in Dublin, Cork, Limerick, Tipperary and Clare. Surely young Bram was not unaware of these events? Maybe it is significant that, hard up though the family reportedly were, Bram's father financed a holiday for Bram in England during that crucial, troubled period.

Bram's father remained a Tory Unionist all his life. When Bram told his father that he had applied for a job as Dublin City treasurer, his father retorted that he would not get it as only a Catholic or 'an advanced Liberal' (a supporter of 'Home Rule') would get the post. However, by the 1880s Bram was confessing to being a 'philosophical Home Ruler', supporting Prime Minister Gladstone's attempt to set up federal parliaments for Ireland, Scotland, Wales and England. In fact, in London, Bram, in rebellion against his father's political attitudes, became 'an advanced Liberal' and a member of the National Liberal Club.

We may assume that Dowden, the main literary influence on Bram at Trinity, was also a political influence while Bram was a student. Dowden was not only anti-republican but even anti-'Home Rule'. While he claimed a knowledge of Irish mythology and the ancient texts, he was vocal in condemnation of 'the aboriginal crudity, if not outright obscenity of the Irish sagas'. In this bizarre attitude, Dowden was supported by another Fellow of Trinity College, John Pentland Mahaffy, who became Professor of Ancient History in 1869. Mahaffy had also co-chaired the Foot Races Committee with Bram and may well have been influential on his early ideas. It was Mahaffy, when Provost of Trinity, who organised Trinity's Officer Cadet Corps to defend the grounds against the Irish insurgents of 1916.

It has been argued that Bram only supported 'Home Rule' for Ireland after he became friendly with Gladstone, who was a frequent attender at the Lyceum Theatre. 'I was pleased to think – and need I say proud also – that Mr Gladstone seemed to like to talk politics with me,' Bram wrote (*Reminiscences of Henry Irving*, Vol. II p. 31). But Bram was well acquainted with many leading 'Home Rulers' and nationalists and is said to have attended a number of social functions given by Isaac Butt, the leader of the 'Home Rule' movement in the 1870s, whom he had known since his early days at Trinity.

Butt became President of the Amnesty Association for Irish political prisoners in 1869 and in 1870 founded the Home Rule movement, becoming its first Member of Parliament in 1871. By 1874 his party, the Irish National Party, had won half the Irish seats at Westminster and soon were to hold four-fifths of all the Irish seats. The party held this position until 1918 but were thwarted in their attempts to achieve democratic self-government. Irish representation at Westminster had been designed to be controlled by the majority English vote. This failure led to the Sinn Féin victory in the 1918 General Election in which they took 73 seats out of 105, with the Irish Party reduced to only six seats. The 1918 results gave Sinn Féin the mandate to attempt a unilateral declaration of independence.

Bram graduated from Trinity College in 1870 with honours in science. He then went on to obtain his master's degree in 1875. There is some confusion as to whether he was called to the Irish Bar. In fact, it was not until 30 April 1890, while in England and pursuing his writing and theatrical careers, that he continued his studies on a part-time basis and was called to the Bar of the Inner Temple, in London, to became a qualified barrister-at-law. 'I only took the exams to escape jury service,' he once joked drily.

Although his interests were varied, he had little option in 1870 but to become a minor clerk in the legal department of the civil service at Dublin Castle. According to Thom's Directory, Bram went to work in the Fines and Penalties Department. In 1876 he transferred to the Registry of the Petty Sessions Clerks' Department of the Chief Secretary. The year Bram joined the civil service there was an attempt to reorganise the structure of the offices over which the Chief Secretary attempted to govern. But it was a hodge-podge of bureaucracy. As Elizabeth A. Muenger, in *The British Military Dilemma in Ireland* (University of Kansas, 1991) points out: 'A continuing battle was fought against the deadwood of bureaucracy through-out the nineteenth century ... Those with superior ability became embittered while waiting out their years as clerks, and those of clerkish ability eventually found themselves in offices which demanded talents they did not possess.'

At least Bram, from the outset, was not prepared to wait out his years. He saw his job as a clerk only as a financial basis for the pursuit of other interests. Doubtless, like others with ambitions and of the Trinity fraternity, he made a point of being seen in Bewley's coffee house, in Grafton Street, founded in the 1740s. Here students, intellectuals and artists, as well as businessmen and aspiring politicians, were wont to gather. Bram was determined to use his writing talent and not remain just a clerk.

Bram's father had now retired from Dublin Castle. The family had moved once more before Bram's graduation. By 1870 they were at No. 43

Harcourt Street, Dublin, a splendid Georgian terraced house, where William Thornley Stoker was listed as head of the household. His father, Abraham senior, and Bram are also listed as residents. In fact, the entire Stoker family was living there. Harcourt Street was a very fashionable residential area. At No. 40 a young W. B. Yeats was attending school; at No. 4 lived the Carson family, one of whose sons, Edward, born in 1854, was to be the instrument which destroyed Oscar Wilde. He also organised the Orange Order to resist self-government for Ireland. In spite of forming Unionist paramilitaries to fight the UK government, lunching with the German Kaiser in August 1914, and agreeing a deal under which, had Ireland been given self-government, Unionists would have supported the Kaiser in making an attempt to annex Ireland to the German empire, he was appointed UK Attorney General, helped secure Partition in Ireland and became Lord Duncairn. Harcourt Street is still one of Dublin's best preserved Georgian streets. It is probably indicative of William Thornley's rising position in the Dublin medical world that he was able to afford a home for the entire family in this exclusive area.

But, after two years, Abraham senior decided to move to France, where living was somewhat less expensive. His wife and his two daughters accompanied him when he left Dublin in the summer of 1872. By the next year the family were living in Caen, Normandy.

William Thornley had now joined the City of Dublin Hospital as a surgeon. Bram was starting his career in the civil service. Tom was waiting to graduate from Trinity and planned to join the Indian civil service. He graduated in 1872. With his friend and fellow graduate Vincent Arthur Smith (1848–1920) he went to India. Smith went on to become a historian of India, publishing many studies including the *Oxford History of India* (1918). Tom became a colonial administrator. He eventually retired as Chief Secretary to Government, North Western Provinces and Oudh, having been decorated for services in the 1897 famine there. He also published several studies about India. On retirement, he and his wife and only daughter went to live in London, where he died on 14 June 1925.

Bram's two younger brothers, Richard and George, were still studying medicine at the Royal College of Surgeons. Richard was the first of the two younger Stoker brothers to qualify. He became a Licentiate of the Royal College of Surgeons, Ireland, in 1873; a Licentiate of the Royal College of Physicians, Ireland, as well as a Licentiate of the King's and Queen's College of Physicians, Ireland, in 1874. Why Richard is never mentioned by Bram after that date may be due to the fact that he joined the Indian Army as a surgeon. We find him commissioned on 30 September 1874 and serving in the 1st Gurkha (Rifle) Regiment's second battalion. He was appointed surgeon-major on 6 March 1886. On 30 September 1894, he was promoted surgeon lieutenant-colonel. He was awarded campaign medals for Afghanistan, 1879, and the North-East Frontier, Sikkim, 1888; he also received a medal for the forcing of the Jelapla Pass. Richard retired from the Indian Army in 1897, although the Indian Medical Service records date his retirement as 2 April 1900. He and his wife are reported by Daniel Farson to have moved to British Columbia in Canada where he later died as a recluse.

We will deal with George's career and influence on Bram shortly. Of all his siblings, Bram continued to have a close relationship with his eldest brother, William Thornley, and his youngest brother, George. Bram was to dedicate his novel *The Shoulder of Shasta* (1895) to William Thornley, the only sibling who was so honoured by a dedication; as if to underscore his attachment to his elder brother, Bram named his only son Irving Noel Thornley Stoker.

According to family tradition, Bram was closest to his father and was entrusted with forwarding his father's pension, adding to it whenever he could spare extra cash. Ludlam gives this story, doubtless from Bram's son.

According to Ludlam, as soon as his father left Ireland, Bram moved out of his brother William Thornley's house at 43 Harcourt Street. Ludlam says he took lodgings at 30 Kildare Street, in central Dublin, a fashionable thoroughfare close to Trinity's precincts. No. 30 was Cunningham's Lodging House; the directories of the time do not list the lodgers. Kildare Street was, interestingly, the centre of masculine Ascendancy life in Dublin at that time. Here were to be found the town houses of such Ascendancy peers as the Duke of Leinster, and on the corner was the Victorian Gothic pile which housed the Kildare Street Club, whose membership was a roll call of the Ascendancy grandees. The club restaurant had the reputation of keeping the best table in Dublin. Oysters were brought daily from the club's own oyster beds in Galway, during the season, and muffins were sent in from London. The club had its own Masonic Lodge drawn from its members, and reserved two private pews in the nearby St Anne's Anglican church, where Bram was later to be married. Membership was £10 a year and a bed for the night cost 3s. 6d. The reigning Viceroy of Ireland, the English royal family and their ADCs or equerries did not have to pay any subscription.

'Home Rulers' were excluded from the club and only a few wealthy Catholics of rank, such as The O'Connor Donn, the head of the senior surviving line of the last High King of Ireland, as well as the Earls of Westmeath, Granard and Kenmare, Viscount Gormanston, and Count de la Poer, were admitted.

It was no wonder that the republican leader, James Stephens, after his escape from Richmond Gaol, chose Kildare Street, just opposite the club, as his hideout before going on to Clontarf to make his escape by ship to France. It was the last place that the authorities would ever think of looking for him.

Bram moved several times during his years in Dublin. By 1872 he had rooms at 11 Lower Leeson Street, sharing the house with an artist named William V. D. Delaney and a Herbert Wilson.

Some old friends of the Stoker family decided to keep a paternal eye on the Stoker boys in the absence of their parents. They were Sir William and Lady Wilde who lived in Merrion Square, a minute or two's walk from most of the Stokers. They are better known today as the parents of Oscar than for their own, not inconsiderable, literary endeavours. Oscar, in *De Profundis*, wrote of his parents: 'She [his mother] and my father had bequeathed me a name they had made noble and honoured, not merely in literature, art, archaeology, and science, but in the public history of my own country, in its evolution as a nation.' Some of that heritage they also passed to Bram Stoker and to understand their influence on Bram, we must know something about them.

Sir William Robert Wills Wilde, born in Castlerea, Co. Roscommon, in 1815, was Dublin's leading eye and ear specialist, a graduate from the medical colleges of Dublin, London, Berlin and Vienna. He was the inventor of the ophthalmoscope and created the now general operation for mastoiditis. He had been knighted for his services to medicine in 1864. Among other medical works, he had written on *The Epidemics of Ireland*, 1851. He was part of the Dublin medical fraternity in which members of the Stoker family proliferated and doubtless through this connection he and Lady Wilde had become friends with the parents of Bram and, of course, with Bram and his brother William. Dublin society, anyway, was a close-knit one with most professional families having connections.

Sir William had numerous other interests, particularly Irish folklore, archaeology and history, and he wrote many works covering those fields including *Irish Popular Superstitions*. He also wrote a *Biographical Memoir of Robert James Graves* (1796–1853) (McGlashen and Gill, Dublin, 1864), whom we have already mentioned as the discoverer of 'Graves disease' – toxic goitre. Sir William was a man of great generosity; he gave freely to the poor and founded St Mark's Ophthalmic Hospital in Dublin. In contrast to this, he was something of a womaniser and had three illegitimate children before his marriage.

Lady Jane Francesca Wilde, the daughter of a Wexford cleric named Elgee, was born in 1826. She became involved in the Young Ireland movement, converted by the work of Thomas Davies. Firstly under the pseudonym of 'James Fanshawe Ellis' and then under that of 'Speranza', she wrote fiery republican material for the patriot newspaper *The Nation*. Her verses and articles became widely read in the period leading up to the Young Ireland republican uprising of 1848. One of her pieces, '*Jacta Alea Est*' (the die is cast), was used against the editor, barrister Charles Gavan Duffy (1816–1903), on a charge of sedition. She had written:

We must be free! In the name of your trampled, insulted, degraded country ... lift up your right hand to heaven and swear by your undying soul, by your hopes of immortality, never to lay down your arms, never to cease hostilities, till you regenerate and save this fallen land.

Jane Elgee acknowledged that she was 'Speranza', the authoress of the 'seditious material'. But because of her well-connected family – she was granddaughter of Archdeacon John Elgee of Wexford – the colonial authorities made no move to arrest her. She was a firm supporter of the lawyer John Mitchel (1815–1875), the Derry-born son of a Presbyterian minister, educated at Trinity College, who was arrested in 1848 for high treason and sentenced to transportation, but who escaped from Tasmania to the USA in 1853. 'Speranza' was bitterly disappointed by the failure of the 1848 uprising.

It is an interesting aside to note that Duffy went on to be elected Member of Parliament for New Ross, was forced to emigrate to Australia, where he become Prime Minister of Victoria in 1871 and, ironically, received a knighthood for his services, and then devoted himself to literary work. His son George was one of the five signatories on the treaty which brought the Irish War of Independence of 1919–21 to an end.

As 'Speranza,' Lady Wilde's best-known poems were 'The Year of Revolution', 'The Voice of the Poor' and 'The Famine Year' (1848) – her most stirring poem – which begins:

Weary men, what reap ye? – 'Golden corn for the stranger.'
What sow ye? – 'Human corpses that wait for the avenger.'
Fainting forms, hunger-stricken, what see ye in the offing?
'Stately ships to bear our goods away amid the stranger's scoffing.'
There's a proud array of soldiers – what do they round your door?
'They guard our master's granary from the thin hands of the poor.'
Pale mothers, wherefore weeping? 'Would to God that we were dead –
'Our children swoon before us, and we cannot give them bread!'

She wrote numerous books, even translating from the German Gothic
tales, such as W. Meinhold's *Sidonia the Sorceress*, for the Popular Library
in 1849, and collected Irish folk-tales which she eventually published in
volume form in 1888 as *Ancient Legends of Ireland*.

Isaac Butt had been a close friend of Lady Wilde. Butt's relationship
with her was soured when he took over the legal representation in 1864 of
Mary Josephine Travers who sued Lady Wilde for something she had said
in a letter. In the course of the trial, Miss Travers claimed Sir William
Wilde had raped her, a charge immediately dismissed by the judge. While
the court awarded one farthing damages to Sir William the case damaged
his reputation.

The Wildes had married in 1851. Their first child, born in 1852, was
named William Charles Kingsbury Wilde – but called Willie to differentiate him from his father. He went to Trinity and graduated in 1873,
taking his master's degree in 1876. Willie studied law but turned to
journalism for a livelihood. He had been a contributor to *Kottabos*;
incidentally, in view of his younger brother's more famous work, it is
interesting that one of his poems was entitled *Salomé*. Willie Wilde wrote
stories for the *The World* and then, having moved to London, he wrote for
Vanity Fair before launching a satirical journal called *Pan* which seemed
to survive for only one issue, dated 25 September 1880. He then wrote for
the *Daily Telegraph*, mainly as a leader writer, and became an active
member of the Irish Literary Society. He had an unhappy marriage to an
American widow and newspaper owner before marrying an Irish girl
named Sophie Lees by whom he had a daughter, Dorothy Wilde. Willie
was to die at his Chelsea home, No. 9 Cheltenham Terrace, on 13 March
1899.

In 1856 the Wildes' second child was born. Lady Jane patriotically
named him Oscar Fingal O'Flahertie Wills Wilde. Oscar was the name of
the son of the mythical Oisín and grandson of Fionn Mac Cumhail; Fingal

was the derivative of Fionn; O'Flahertie was said to have been after the Galway antiquarian and writer (1629–1718) whose work was the first published history of Ireland, written by an Irishman from an Irish point of view, to reach the English public. The Wildes also had a daughter, Isola Francesca, born two years after Oscar, but she died at the age of ten years.

Oscar was only sixteen years old when Bram left Trinity and would enter Trinity himself a year later, in 1871. In fact, Bram stood as sponsor for Oscar to join the college Philosophical Society. Trinity College was but a short walk from Merrion Square, home of the Wildes, and it is obvious that Oscar and his elder brother Willie would have been present at their parents' dining-table when Bram was a guest. As Oscar Wilde's biographer, Richard Ellmann, points out, Stoker 'had often come to 1 Merrion Square'.

The paths of Bram, Oscar and Willie would, in fact, continue to cross and recross for the rest of their lives.

CHAPTER FIVE

The Drak'ola of Irish Folklore

DURING THE YEARS between 1870 and 1876 the Wildes acted *in loco parentis* to Bram and undoubtedly had an influence imparting information on Irish folklore to him, laying the seeds of many stories in his fertile imagination. As well as Lady Wilde's fascination with Irish folklore and tales, Sir William had written *Irish Popular Superstitions* (1852), *Ireland, Past and Present; the Land and the People* (1864) and *On the Ancient Races of Ireland* (1874). Both he and Lady Wilde were particularly fascinated by tales of the macabre.

There can be little doubt that Sir William's interest and explorations in Egypt, plus his papers on Egyptian archaeology, provided the background for Bram's famous weird novel of a pharaoh's curse, a long-dead Egyptian queen who returns to life and some extraordinary reanimated mummies. *The Jewel of Seven Stars* (1903), one might justly claim, started the 'mummy cult' in both literature and films. Stoker's novel was given a boost in the 1920s following the widespread stories of the curse of Tutankhamen. In 1932, Boris Karloff starred in Karl Freund's film *The Mummy* as a 3000-year-old on the track of his lost love. The only film, however, to acknowledge its origin in Stoker's novel was *Blood from the Mummy's Tomb* (1971) directed by Seth Holt, who died just before shooting was completed, and starring Andrew Keir and Valerie Leon. When it was refilmed as *The Awakening* (1980), with Charlton Heston and Susannah York, its origin was not acknowledged and, ironically, author Ronald Chetwynd-Hayes wrote a novelisation of the screenplay. So one had a novel of a screenplay of a novel! Later credits did point out that the film was originally based on the Stoker novel.

The fact that Sir William and Lady Wilde were experts on Irish folklore and mythology was, we believe, an essential ingredient in the creation of Bram's major weird novel – *Dracula*.

It has been accepted without question that Bram Stoker took all his ideas for his vampire novel from the traditions of the Carpathian region of Eastern Europe. Indeed, when the Irish actor, Ivan Stokes Dixon, once argued that *Dracula* owed more in essence to Ireland than to Rumania, he was not regarded with any degree of seriousness.

Dracula was born in the mind of an Irishman [Dixon wrote] – therefore he is Irish. The Rumanians get a lot of money out of tourists, but the truth is that Bram Stoker never visited their country. He got his information from guide books. I want the Irish Tourist Board to set up a Bram Stoker Museum so that we can have some of the credit for this remarkable work.

The first question to consider, therefore, is: Was there a vampire tradition in Ireland? The short answer is that there are such traditions in most ancient cultures and Ireland is no exception. And, in fact, it can be argued that Bram Stoker, though a city man from Dublin, was well placed to hear stories of the *deamhan-fhola* or blood-sucking demons which peopled the shadowy places of the rural Ireland. Whatever he may initially have picked up from his mother, there is surely no doubt that over convivial dinners with the Wildes on dark winter evenings, Sir William and Lady Wilde recounted to Bram tales of the *neamh-mhairbh* or the Un-Dead that permeate Irish legends and folklore.

There are two folk-tales in particular, collected and published by Lady Wilde, which we suggest were told to young Bram and which influenced his own work.

The first concerns a farmer named Connor who, in search of some lost cows, comes to a lonely house on a bleak and desolate heath. Connor knocks at the door. 'It was opened at once by a tall, thin, grey-haired old man, with keen dark eyes. "Come in. You are welcome. We have been waiting for you."' By the fire is the man's wife: 'an old, thin grey woman, with long sharp teeth and terrible, glittering eyes'.

As Connor sits there, growing more afraid by the minute, there are three separate knocks on the door, and each time the tall man opens the door. Each time he admits a wolf. The three wolves sit in a row watching him. They then transform into three young men who are the sons of the house. The story ends well because Connor has performed a good deed and saved the life of one of the wolves. He is allowed to go away unharmed.

The second story features a tall, dark horseman, who waylays a farmer named Jemmy Nowlan near Slane. He orders Jemmy to mount behind him on his night-black horse and takes him off to a grim, shadowy castle. Inside, beautiful young women present Jemmy with garlands of flowers and fight over who should dance with him. They each insist on dancing in turn until, near dawn, Jemmy is exhausted and desires nothing but sleep. The tall, dark horseman demands he tell a story. Jemmy can tell none and so is thrown out of the castle into the inhospitable first glimmers of dawn. Three men, carrying a coffin, come by and insist that he help them carry the coffin to a desolate spot where they then demand that he dig a grave. When he sees that the coffin is empty and asks who they are going to bury, they tell him that it is himself. Jemmy, desperate to escape, remembers that the hazel has magic properties, seizes a hazel wand from a nearby tree and is thus able to get away by fending off the three men. As he runs off, Jemmy staggers and falls, and finds himself back on the castle steps. He is so exhausted that he passes out. But, thankfully, he is still clutching the hazel stick, so is able to fend off the attentions of the tall, dark horseman. Finally, on waking, Jemmy finds himself safe in his own hay-rig.

There are themes enough here which find echoes in *Dracula*.

Indeed, it is reasonable to suppose that young Bram's friendship with the Wildes, particularly Lady Wilde, also drew him towards the wealth of German Gothic vampire literature. Lady Wilde was at this time making translations from German Gothic tales.

It has been suggested by the prolific Irish author and novelist Cathal Ó Sándair (1922–1996), in 'Dracula Domharfa' (Dracula the Immortal), *Irish Times*, 18 May 1993, that while at Trinity College, Bram undoubtedly came across and read Seathrún Céitinn's *Foras Feasa ar Éireann*, the History of Ireland, written between 1629 and 1631. Dr Céitinn dwelt on the subject of the *neamh-mhairbh* (the Un-Dead) in Volume I, Chapter 10. Trinity College library, in fact, possessed two manuscript copies of the work. It was translated from Irish into Latin and published in St Malo, Brittany, in 1660. While there is no known evidence that Bram had a knowledge of the Irish language, even though he does use a verse in Scottish Gaelic in Irish script together with a translation in *The Mystery of the Sea*, there is no reason why he could not have read Céitinn's work in translation. In 1723 Dermod O'Connor published his translation of Céitinn's work under the title *The General History of Ireland*. Patrick Weston Joyce also made a translation and printed it side by side with the Irish text, which was published by M. H. Gill, Dublin, in 1880.

Joyce had received his master's degree from Trinity in the same year that Bram entered the college and was awarded his doctorate in the same year that Bram graduated. Joyce had been brought up bilingually in Irish and English in Co. Limerick and wrote numerous studies on Irish history and culture. Elected to the Royal Irish Academy in 1863, Joyce – whose brother Dr Robert Dwyer Joyce was a committed IRB man – attended many of Trinity's Historical Society meetings and doubtless met Bram as the society's Auditor. Joyce had collected several Irish werewolf and vampire legends.

It was Ó Sándair, writing to the authors in April 1995, who also made the observation that Bram might have been guided to use the name of the historical Wallachian hero – Dracula – because it sounded the same as the Irish *droch-fhola* (pronounced drok'ola), bad blood; he might even have connected the name with a Kerry folk-tale about 'Dún Dreach-Fhola' (pronounced drak'ola), the castle of blood visage. The castle was said to be high up in a lonely pass among the Macgillycuddy's Reeks, a range in Co. Kerry which contains Ireland's highest mountain. Ó Sándair may well be right: Seán Ó Súilleabháin, the Kerry-born one-time registrar and archivist of the Irish Folklore Commission, mentioned this same oral folk-tale in a lecture at UCD in 1961, prior to the publication of his book on Irish death customs, *Caitheamh Aimsire ar Thórraimh*, translated into English six years later as *Irish Wake Amusements*. He said it was told to him in the Macgillycuddy's Reeks. The story concerns an 'evil fairy fortress' – Dún Dreach-Fhola – inhabited by *neamh-mhairbh* (Un-Dead) who sustained themselves on the blood of wayfarers. Unfortunately there is no reference to the story in *Caithreamh Aimsire ar Thórraimh*.

What is fascinating, given the location of the story, is that Bram's younger brother George married Agnes, a daughter of Richard McGillycuddy, The McGillycuddy of the Reeks of Beaufort, Co. Kerry, in 1884. Bram attended this wedding. George had become a friend of Agnes' brother John ('Jackgillycuddy') McGillycuddy (b. 20 March 1855) while he was studying at Trinity College. Once again George might well have passed on this folk-tale of the area from which his wife's father took his title and estate. And did the name Dreach-Fhola (drak'ola) remind George of the legends of the Wallachian ruler, Dracula, which he must have come across while serving in the Turkish army in the Balkans? It is a possibility.

The Dreach-Fhola goes back to stories of vampires and werewolves which proliferated in Ireland as early as the sixth century AD. One early tale maintains that a St Nath-í (sometimes Anglicised as St Natalis) cursed a family so that every member, both male and female, had to assume the shape of a wolf once every seven years and live on the blood of their kin. St Nath-í had his foundation at Achadh Chonaire (Achonry, Co. Sligo), perhaps significantly in the same county where Bram's mother spent her childhood.

This is doubly interesting as Achadh Chonaire means 'Conaire's field' and the name Conaire means 'hound' or 'wolf'. The popular eighteenth-century Irish name for a werewolf was *conríocht*. The name occurs in the saga of 'Da Dearga's Hostel' for, in the hostel, the legendary king Conaire Mór is killed and decapitated. Dr Dáithí Ó hÓgáin, in his *Encyclopedia of the Irish Folk Tradition*, points out: 'It is striking that the name of his host Da Dearga, also called simply Dearg, signifies redness; and the original story must have had the character in the role of foe rather than of friend. Dearg, indeed, was a common personification of death in early Irish literature.'

Writing on the subject of metempsychosis, P. W. Joyce, in his still seminal *A Social History of Ancient Ireland*, confirms that in the Irish 'Nennius' it is stated that the people of the petty kingdom of Osraige (Ossory), lying on the eastern border of Munster, could turn themselves into wolves and ravaged and devoured cattle and people. Giraldus Cambrensis, in his twelfth-century *Topographia Hibernica*, also mentions werewolves in this area. 'Certain men of the Celtic race have a marvellous power which comes to them from their forebears for by an evil craft they can at will change themselves into the shape of a wolf and have sharp long teeth.'

We find another version of the story of Nath-í in the AD1250 Norse saga *Kongs Skuggsjo*, or *Speculum Regale*, which says that St Patrick found a race of werewolves in Ireland with which he had to fight. Even the sober William Camden (1551–1623), in his study on the British Isles, *Britannia*, mentions werewolves in Tipperary. The werewolf tradition certainly continued as oral folklore well into nineteenth-century Ireland for the wolf population of the country was not eradicated until the start of that century. Several spots recall the wolves in Ireland, such as Feltrim in Co. Down, which is Fealdruim, or wolf-ridge; Ballinabrackey in Meath is Buaile na

Bréamhaí, the milking place of the wolf-plain; Breaghwy in Sligo and also in Mayo comes from Bréachmhaigh, wolf-plain.

In their studies of vampirism, both William Woods and Anthony Masters refer to the fact that Irish vampires were known as *dearg-dul* and *dearg-due*. Dr Clive Leatherdale, in *Dracula: The Novel and the Legend*, says: 'Similarly, the Leanhaun Shee (the fairy mistress) was supposedly an eye-catching fair maiden whose charms were irresistible to men. Energy would be drawn from the ensnared male until he eventually wasted away, or else procured an alternative victim to take his place.' Dr Leatherdale is only partially right. The *leannán sí* is a phantom-lover but not really a blood-sucking vampire. Though it is true that many Otherworld creatures were thought to be bloodless and abducted humans merely to consume their blood.

In the eighteenth century, stories of a vampire called the *dearg-dul* were recorded. William Woods suggests that the approved method of disposing of the vampire was to pile stones on its grave. Anthony Masters speaks of these vampires as *dearg-due*, which he says means 'red blood sucker'. *Dearg* does mean 'red', while the word for 'one who sucks' is *diúlaí*. Among the various stories of the *dearg-diúlaí* was that of a beautiful young woman in Waterford who lured strong men to their doom by flaunting her sexuality and then sucking their life's blood from them. A similar tale of a beautiful female vampire is found in Antrim where the female corpse is said never to achieve peace until she can be replaced by another beautiful girl whom she makes into a vampire. From the Dingle peninsula in Co. Kerry comes the story of a *dearg-diúlaí* said to have haunted the road between Dún Chaoin (Dunquin) and Baile Feirtéaraigh (Ballyferriter) near a stretch known as Casadh na Gráise, where two streams twine. A man going along the road, a little the worse for drink, encountered the female Un-Dead but, instead of running away, blessed and prayed for her and thus released her from her purgatory. Such stories are to be found in places whose names warn the traveller – Glennascaul in Galway is Gleann an Scáil, the valley of the phantom of evil supernatural being; Drumarraght in Fermanagh is Droim Arracht, the ridge of the apparition; Anascaul, Co. Kerry, is Abhainn an Scáil, the river of the phantom; Glengesh in Donegal is Gleann Geis, the taboo valley, one among several places where the warning word '*geis*', taboo, tells strangers to shun the place.

One of the most fascinating stories of a *dearg-diúlaí* or Un-Dead comes from Co. Derry. Near Garvagh stands a place called Slaughtaverty. The name is from the Irish Leacht Abhartach. Legend goes that a local

chieftain named Abhartach was a cruel and evil man; an awesome tyrant
who inflicted pain and suffering on the people whom he ruled. Some
accounts have Abhartach grossly misshapen. The people turned for help
to a neighbouring ruler named Cáthan. This Cáthan fought and slew
Abhartach. In Celtic tradition, they buried the chieftain standing in his
grave. But the next day Abhartach appeared and sought the blood of the
living to sustain his vile corpse. He was as cruel and as evil as ever. Cáthan
came on him again and slew him a second time; he was buried a second
time but, as before, the next day Abhartach appeared once more and
spread terror throughout the land. Cáthan then sought the advice of a
Druid. Accordingly, Cáthan met Abhartach a third time and this time slew
him using a sword of yew wood. The corpse was buried in the same place
but this time it was placed head downwards. Mountain ash twigs were
placed on top of the grave and then a great stone. Thus the corpse's evil
powers were subdued and it was never seen on earth again. A *leacht* or
sepulchral monument was raised, called the Leacht of Abhartach, which is
why the place is still called Slaughtaverty. This tale was recorded by
several enthusiasts in the nineteenth century including P. W. Joyce.

The yew and mountain ash, which feature in the story of Abhartach, are
also mentioned in *Dracula*, and these references have much in common
with Irish folklore. On p. 30 Jonathan Harker is given a crucifix made of
mountain ash to protect him because it is May 'St George's' Eve, when
evil things are about. The mountain ash, which is, of course, the rowan, or
luis in Irish (this is also the name of the letter 'l' of the Ogham alphabet)
goes back to Druidic times in England. Another early name for the rowan
in Irish is *caorthann*, a word found in many Irish place-name compounds
such as Ballykeeran, Co. Westmeath, which is Bealach Caorthainn, pass of
the rowan tree. In ancient Ireland, and, indeed, in rural Ireland in the last
century, an effective means of warding off evil was to place branches of
rowan over the doors of houses to keep all evil spirits at bay, especially on
May Eve. A wand of rowan was placed in a milk pail and around the churn
to prevent evil spirits contaminating the milk; another wand was kept in
the house to prevent the same evil from setting fire to it.

Bram refers several times in *Dracula* to a yew tree, *idad* in Irish and the
letter 'i' of the Ogham alphabet. Twice his characters use yew trees to hide
behind and Lucy Westenra, in her graveyard scene, moves down an avenue
of yews. The yew, in Ireland, has a significant role as symbolising a place
of religious importance. The Yew Tree of Mughain, near Ballaghmoon in

Co. Kildare, was a major religious focal point. Places named after the sacred yew tree proliferate in Ireland.

There is even a potential model for Castle Dracula in Ireland, although Bram used a Scottish castle as his model as we will discuss later. Two miles west of Macroom, Co. Cork, on the Killarney road stand the ruins of a fifteenth-century Mac Carthy stronghold, still rising to four storeys in height. It is significantly called Carrigaphouca Castle, the castle of the 'rock of the *púca*'. The *púca* is an evil spirit. Even today locals will genuflect as they pass the castle, some refusing to pass it at night. Mrs Mai O'Higgins (writing as recently as October 1993, in *Ireland's Eye*) says:

> The castle acquired an evil reputation as a place of weird happenings and ghoulish sights. A place of ghosts and fairies. The country folk around would report that the strange cries and noises came from the depths of the castle. People returning from fairs and markets would hasten their steps when passing the place before the strange lights at midnight would appear.

It was reported that screaming could be heard in the castle at night and the next morning the brooding entrance would be splattered with blood. According to an article in *The Irish Monthly* (1874), which Bram might well have seen, Carrigaphouca Castle was inhabited by a '*derrick-dally*' obviously an Anglicisation of *dearg-diúlaí*, a vampire. Who this would be is uncertain. The castle was the scene of many sieges and battles between the Irish and English. In 1601 the castle was held by Cormac Tadhg Mac Carthy who is regarded as an Irish traitor, having betrayed his countrymen and joined the English, accepting a knighthood and becoming Sheriff of Cork. Cormac captured James Fitzgerald and, together with Sir Walter Raleigh and Sir Warham St Leger, supervised while James Fitzgerald was 'cut into little pieces while alive'. The descendants of Cormac held on to the castle until 1690 when it was confiscated during the Williamite Conquest; it finally fell into disuse. Some local people say that it is the unquiet spirit of the traitor Cormac who haunts the place, still sustaining himself on the blood of the innocent.

The numbers three and seven, much favoured in Irish story-telling, also appear in *Dracula*. Once Bram actually changes the number in a well-known Biblical story from ten to make it fit the Irish seven. This is the reference to the seven young women with lamps, on p. 62. The New

Testament specifically refers to ten women, 'five of them wise, and five were foolish' (Matthew 25:1–10). Incidentally, while seven is considered lucky in Ireland – such as the seventh son of a seventh son – in the Balkans it is a sign of evil and bad luck. The number three is also significant, and we have the example of the three young vampire women, on p. 39. Deities in Irish myth, both good and evil, appear in threes; the deity is usually a triune figure. The goddess of death and battles, the Mórrígán, appears as three personalities.

According to Dr Leatherdale the fact that Dracula was killed on 6 November is 'one specific instance of Irish lore discernible in *Dracula*'. His argument is that according to Seán O Súilleabháin it was the custom in Ireland for blood to be shed either on St Martin's Eve 11 November or earlier to propitiate the saint. Hardly a Christian concept. If St Martin fails to receive his blood sacrifice in the year ahead then ill luck befalls. Dracula, therefore, has to be destroyed on this day. We find this rather unconvincing. If the symbolism is so explicit, then why did Stoker not use the actual date of 11 November rather than 6 November to make clear his point?

Such symbolism would admittedly have come easily to Bram from his cultural background. He did not, as many claim, have to research all his vampire law and symbolism in the British Museum.

Bram, if he did not read Céitinn's work, could equally have read, or been told about, the work of Dubhaltach Mac Firbisigh (1585–1670), one of the most industrious Irish academics of his time. He taught in Galway, and not only wrote his own works but copied and preserved older books to prevent their destruction. He, too, was aware of the Irish tradition of vampirism. In *Genealogies, Tribes and Customs of Hy-Fiachrach*, Mac Firbisigh asks an interesting question while discussing folklore: '*ni dogabh bás gan marbhadh agus arambí drochghnuis mairbh?*' Who achieves death without killing and on whom is an ill-countenance of death? He is talking about a *mairtchenn* whose description certainly resembles the vampire's victim, who dies but is not dead, and who has to pass on the Un-Dead state to another victim, thus achieving death without killing.

There is another possible Irish connection in *Dracula*. Bram says, on p. 32, '. . . as the Turks say, "water sleeps, and enemy is sleepless".' In *The Annotated Dracula* Professor Leonard Wolf comments: 'So far, I have not been able to identify this proverb . . . It may be that Stoker had in mind the French proverb "*L'enemi ne s'endort pas*" – one's enemy does not sleep.' Professor Wolf, however, was specifically looking for the proverb in Turkish or Balkan culture. Wolf himself was born in Transylvania. Again, the obvious is overlooked – that fact that Stoker was Irish. The Celtic scholar Whitley Stokes (1830–1909) picked up a *seanfhocal* or old saying written in a medieval Irish tract which he recorded as: '*uisce codladh, an namhaid neamchodladh*' – literally, water sleeps, the enemy is without sleep or sleepless. Stokes believed that it derived from a saying connecting water and the downfall of an enemy, which Niall Ó Dónaill records in his *Foclóir Gaeilge-Béarla* (Irish–English Dictionary, 1977): '*uisce faoi thalamh a dhéanamh i gcoinne duine*', literally, to put water under the ground of someone, meaning to attempt their downfall or to intrigue against them. Incidentally, Stokes was another Trinity College graduate. After years in India he went to London in 1882 and, also like Bram, was called to the Bar of the Inner Temple. He settled in Kensington and his path may well have crossed Bram's at the Inner Temple. Stokes became a leading authority on Celtic philology and published a number of tracts on Sanskrit as well as on Hindu law.

Stokes also knew about werewolves and found, in an old glossary, the word *conoel* meaning a female werewolf. In the eighth-century story *Fled Bricrend* (Bricriu's Feast) there appears a character named Uath Mac Immomium (horror, son of terror) who turned himself into both wolf and bat and was called a *sirité*, which nineteenth-century philologists have interpreted as 'elf-man'. However, modern consensus is that it meant something more in the way of a supernatural being and might be derived from *síraide*, meaning everlasting, an eternally living entity. Werewolves are also mentioned in the *Leabhar na hUidri*, a book compiled in 1100 by Mael Muire Mac Ceileachair (d. 1106). Known sometimes as 'The Book of the Dun Cow' and 'The Book of Clonmacnoise' (where it was compiled), it contains the 'Red Branch Cycle' of Irish myths, an incomplete version of the 'Táin Bó Cuailgne' and the *Leabhar Gabhála* (Book of Invasions, origin legends of the Irish) amongst other items.

Cormac Mac Art is said to have been High King of Ireland in the third century AD. He is the most celebrated of the semi-mythical kings and the subject of many legends. In one version of Cormac's birth, it is said that his father Art the Solitary was slain at the battle of Magh Mucramha. His pregnant wife, Éachtach, fled in a chariot, with her handmaiden, to find sanctuary with her brother-in-law, Luighne. Passing through a forest at nightfall, Éachtach felt the birth pangs approaching. She halted the chariot and told her handmaiden to prepare a bed of dried leaves by the forest path. She gave birth and her son was called Corbb-Mhac (chariot-son), i.e. Cormac.

While she and the new baby slept, the handmaiden was supposed to watch over them. However, she was exhausted and also fell asleep. While they slumbered, a large wolf-bitch came along, seized the child and took it away to her den. In one early text the word *conoel* describes the wolf-bitch; this, according to Stokes, actually meant a 'female werewolf'. The next morning the distressed mother and her handmaiden reached the sanctuary of Luighne's fortress. Luighne offered a reward for the recovery of the child.

Meanwhile, the wolf-bitch reared Cormac among her own cubs and taught him many things. Finally, a trapper, Lugnae Fer Tri, found the boy and he was returned to his mother. She then took the boy north to Fiachrae Cassán of the Airgialla, who was to foster him. Their path lay across some mountains and once again they found themselves alone at night. The baying of wolves closed in on them. Blazing red eyes of predators shone in the darkness, surrounding them. The young boy, Cormac, told his mother not to fear; he walked out to the encircling wolves and spoke to them, and they ceased their attack and slunk away. There seems no further development, at least none that survives, to the idea that Cormac was raised by a female werewolf until he was taken to be fostered. This, incidentally, would mean that he lived with the wolves until he was seven, the age of fosterage in ancient Ireland.

In this tale we have one of the earliest versions of a story motif that has been popular throughout European cultures and even in many other parts of the world – the story of the boy reared with wolf-cubs. It is a story made popular in twentieth-century literature by Rudyard Kipling's tales of Mowgli, the boy raised by wolves, in *The Jungle Book* (1894) and *The Second Junge Book* (1895). It is an easy step from the story of Cormac to more full-blooded tales of werewolves.

According to Dr Joyce, there are numerous stories of werewolves and blood-sucking demons scattered through Irish folklore, but he felt that 'these stories are scattered and have no thread of connection; they do not coalesce into a system; they are told of individuals, in palpable exception to the general run of people, and many of them are stated to be the result of magical skill.'

Dracula apart, one can also argue that Irish folklore themes form part of Bram's other weird fiction. In his last novel, for example, *The Lair of the*

White Worm (1911), filmed by Ken Russell in 1988 and starring Hugh Grant, we have an ancient and monstrous white worm, secreted for thousands of years in a bottomless well in ancient Mercia, which is able to metamorphose into a woman and demands blood to sustain itself. It has been debated whether the basis for this story lies in the tale of the Oilliepheist, the great white worm which appears to threaten Patrick; the same theme crops up in tales of the Ó Ruairc family of Breifne.

The evidence is thus surely overwhelming that Bram Stoker regularly dipped into his own memories and the rich storehouse of Irish tradition when he put pen to paper in order to create macabre stories.

CHAPTER SIX

The Vampire Lovers

IT DOES NOT HAVE TO BE ARGUED, perhaps, that Bram Stoker, with his taste for the weird in literature, was well acquainted with the works of his fellow Irishmen in the field, from Maturin to O'Brien, and from Mangan to Le Fanu. One writer whose work he would have certainly come across was William Carleton (1794–1869) from Clogher, Co. Tyrone, who arrived in Dublin with less than three shillings in his pocket and launched a career as a writer with his *Traits and Stories of the Irish Peasantry* (1830). One of these stories, 'Wildgoose Lodge', often appears in weird tale collections such as *Irish Tales of Terror*, edited by Jim McGarry, Fontana Books, 1971. Carleton's stories of rural Ireland, such as *Fardorougha the Miser* (1839) and *The Black Prophet* (1847), a story of the 'Great Hunger', are full of brooding despair. Patrick Kavanagh once claimed in a BBC talk that Carleton was one of the two great native writers of Ireland – the other being James Joyce. Carleton's strength was in his knowledge of the rural and peasant Ireland, an Ireland which existed beyond the safety of the houses of the rich Anglo-Irish.

In 1872 there appeared a story which was to have, perhaps, the greatest influence on Bram. It was the vampire tale 'Carmilla', written by Joseph Sheridan Le Fanu. Sheridan Le Fanu was born on 28 August 1814, at the Royal Hibernian School in Phoenix Park, Dublin. His father, Joseph, was chaplain there as well as Dean of Emly. The Le Fanus were intertwined with the Sheridan family whose most famous literary scion was the Dublin-born playwright Richard Brinsley Sheridan (1751–1816), to whom Le Fanu was a great-nephew. Sheridan's father, Thomas (1719–1788), also achieved distinction as Jonathan Swift's godson and biographer. He compiled a *General Dictionary of the English Language* in 1780, becoming a close friend of Samuel Johnson.

Sheridan Le Fanu went to Trinity and graduated with honours in Classics, becoming Auditor of the Historical Society, as Bram later became. From 1837 poems, short stories and novels, proceeded from his pen. He has been acclaimed by many as the greatest writer of the supernatural who ever lived. Certainly he is rightly hailed as Ireland's equivalent to Edgar Allan Poe. His ability to build up suspense by an implied horror and maintain it at a frightening level was an inspiration to many writers, and he was seen as the link between the Gothic horror school and the writers of modern psychological fear tales. When he died on 7 February 1873, he had produced fifteen novels and some forty-three short stories.

His 'A Chapter in the History of a Tyrone Family', published in the October 1839 issue of the *Dublin University Magazine*, has been seen as a source for *Jane Eyre* by Charlotte Brontë. It is true that the Brontë family subscribed to the *Dublin University Magazine* and, indeed, Charlotte is reported to have written Le Fanu a letter of appreciation about his work. When *Jane Eyre* appeared eight years later, the critic William Makepeace Thackeray (1811–1863) wrote to Charlotte to point out that the plot of her book was familiar. She replied that she was sure it was original, but Edna Kenton, in *A Forgotten Creator of Ghosts: J. S. Le Fanu, Possible Inspirer of the Brontës*, argues that echoes of his work also appear in *Wuthering Heights*.

One writer who clearly acknowledged Le Fanu's inspiration in his work was M. R. James (1862–1936), who edited a memorable collection of Le Fanu stories in *Madame Crowl's Ghost* (1923) as a tribute.

By the time Bram came to write *Dracula*, he had already been inspired by Le Fanu's short story 'Mr Justice Harbottle' (1872). Its influences on his short story 'The Judge's House' (1891) are obvious. In Le Fanu's story two young university students rent rooms in an old Dublin mansion. They see a vision of an old man in a crimson, flowered silk dressing-gown. They also hear ponderous footsteps. 'Horror of horrors! within a stair or two of the plot where I stood the unearthly tread smote the floor. My eye caught something in motion; it was about the size of Golian's foot – it was grey, heavy and flopped with a dead weight from one step to another. As I am alive, it was the most monstrous grey rat I ever beheld or saw.' In the malignant expression of the rat the student beholds the evil visage of the judge.

In Stoker's story a student rents an old mansion house. He, too, is bedevilled by noises and apparitions, particularly the appearance of a rat. 'There on the great high-backed carved oak chair by the right side of the fire-place sat an enormous rat, steadily glaring at him with baleful eyes.' The features of the rat eventually turn into the vindictive face of the judge and back again. 'There, in the judge's arm-chair, with the rope hanging behind, sat the rat with the judge's baleful eyes, now intensified with a fiendish leer.'

However, there is another episode behind Bram's short story that it would be wrong to ignore. Bram himself had lived in the house of a notorious 'hanging judge'. Towards the end of 1874 Bram's brother, William Thornley, moved from No. 43 Harcourt Street to No. 16 Harcourt Street. No. 16, together with No. 17, had comprised 'Clonmell [sic] House', built in 1784 for John Scott, Earl of Clonmell (1739–1798). Lord Clonmell, a Trinity man, became Chief Justice of Ireland and was called 'Copper-faced Jack'. He has been described as 'unscrupulous, passionate and greedy'. In 1792 he hanged a father and son for a minor theft. The son had actually committed the theft but 'Copper-faced Jack' held the father responsible as well. He was the judge, according to Eamonn Mac Thomais, in *Me Jewel and Darlin' Dublin*, at the trial in 1795 of the Anglican minnister, Revd William Jackson, a prominent figure in the republican United Irish movement. When Jackson collapsed, dying, in the dock, Clonmell insisted that he be held up so that sentence could be passed. Perhaps Thornley told Bram the stories about the notorious previous occupant of No. 16; this might explain why, in Bram's short story, a character named Dr Thornhill is the one who recounts the tales about the 'hanging judge'. Clonmell House had been divided into two parts in 1830. Prior to this, Clonmell House, which had wings on each side, was surrounded by a large-sized garden while fields stretched in front to the south side of St Stephen's Green to Clonmell Street, which was renamed Earlsfort Terrace in 1839. A subterranean passage stretched from the house under Harcourt Street to the Green but it is uncertain whether this secret passage still existed when Bram lived there.

Curiously enough, the year after Bram's story 'The Judge's House' appeared, Thornley moved into No. 8 Ely Place, next to No. 6 where another famous 'hanging judge' had been resident. This was the infamous 'Black Jack' John Fitzgibbon, Earl of Clare (1749–1802) formerly attorney general and then Lord Chancellor, who took a leading role in securing the Union of the Irish parliament with that of Great Britain. He once boasted his intention to make the Irish a nation of tame cats. Enraged crowds attacked his house several times and when he died, dead cats were thrown at his funeral cortege which was followed by jeering crowds.

Le Fanu's story 'Carmilla' was the quintessence of vampire lore. It is set in a lonely castle in Styria, and is narrated by Laura, a trusting and innocent girl. The languorous and beautiful stranger Carmilla arrives and becomes Laura's friend. There is a dextrous working of a lesbian relationship between the two girls, the mortal and the vampire. Laura suffers terrifying nightmares and displays curious symptoms of lethargy and pallidness. Eventually her father and his friends realise that a vampire is at work – none other than Countess Mircalla of Karnstein who had been buried 150 years before! She and Carmilla are one and the same. The monster is tracked to its blood-filled coffin where a stake is driven through its heart, the head cut off, the body burnt and its ashes dispersed in the river.

'Carmilla' was a powerful story and its effect on Stoker was, we believe, to lead directly to his own classic. The story so impressed Bram that when he came to write *Dracula* his first chapter, as we have seen, carried such clear echoes of 'Carmilla' that Otto Kyllmann had it deleted. That chapter is now an independent story entitled 'Dracula's Guest'.

It is inconceivable that Bram Stoker did not meet Sheridan Le Fanu at some point. Professor Belford's claim that he was Bram's 'employer' at the *Dublin Evening Mail* is unlikely: Le Fanu had sold his interest to Maunsell before Bram began to write his unpaid theatre criticisms for the newspaper. However, not only were both men, at various times, Auditors of the Historical Society at Trinity, but Le Fanu continued to attend Trinity College in his later years. The year after Bram arrived at Trinity, Le Fanu created a controversy by publishing, as a joke, a pamphlet entitled *The Prelude, Being a Contribution towards a History of the Election for the University* under the pseudonym of 'John Figwood Esq' in which he castigated the principal university candidates for office; this was a talking point among all the students.

Le Fanu certainly encouraged Trinity students with a 'literary bent'. Bram's fellow student at Trinity, Alfred Graves, won the Shakespeare Prize Ode and Le Fanu published it in the *Dublin University Magazine*. Graves (in his autobiography *To Return to All That*) comments: 'Thus were laid the foundations of a friendship of many years' standing, and I was often invited to spend the evening with Le Fanu at Merrion Square.'

The paths of Bram and Le Fanu could well have crossed at Merrion

Square: when Le Fanu was living at No. 18 (now No. 70), Bram was a
regular visitor to the home of Sir William and Lady Wilde at No. 1. In
fact, M. Pozzuoli, in his biography, claims that Bram and Le Fanu did
meet in the home of the Wildes in 1871, but does not state his source. It
is, of course, possible and likely. Merrion Square, Dublin, was one of the
most splendid residential squares in Europe, with tall, Georgian houses
conveying an impression of nobility and grandeur. We do know that Bram
knew George Brinsley Le Fanu (1854–1929), Sheridan Le Fanu's younger
son, and that both were members of the Irish Literary Society. Odds are
that Bram also knew his contemporary Thomas Philip Le Fanu, Sheridan
Le Fanu's elder son, who apparently drank himself to death on 20
December 1878

After graduating from Trinity, Le Fanu was called to the Irish Bar but,
instead of practising, he became involved in journalism and was encouraged
by Isaac Butt, then editor of the *Dublin University Magazine*, to write
stories for it. He became editor and proprietor of several Dublin newspapers, including *The Warder*, which Bram wrote for, and the *Dublin Mail*.
In 1861 Le Fanu also became editor and proprietor of the *Dublin University
Magazine*, following in Butt's footsteps. The magazine achieved a reputation as a leading literary journal. Le Fanu gave up his active role in
journalism sometime between 1869 and 1872, the exact date being
uncertain.

In his later years, Le Fanu was a widower, for his wife Susan Bennett,
whom he had married in 1844, died on 28 August 1858. Gradually, as his
sons and daughters grew up, Le Fanu became more and more reclusive.
As Graves recalled: 'Le Fanu led a strange life in those days. He had lost
his wife, beautiful and accomplished Miss Bennett, the daughter of an
Irish QC, and had become a recluse. He spent his time between his office
at the Dublin *Evening Mail* and his home in Merrion Square, never getting
to bed till two or three in the morning or being up till midday.' He was
only fifty-eight when he died on 7 February 1873. Yet his reclusiveness, as
Graves testifies, did not prevent Le Fanu entertaining some Trinity men
with literary ambitions. According to Graves, Le Fanu loved to tell his
student guests strange tales.

He told me once how a big Dublin business man had been on the
point of making a large venture. One night he dreamt that when he
went into his office he found a crow on his desk, resisting all attempts
of his clerks to 'shoo' it away. The crow warned him to desist from

his speculation and flew off. Next morning he went to his office, and as he entered the room found his clerks, with great amusement, trying to chivvy away a crow that had flown in at the open window and perched upon his desk. The crow looked at him, very knowingly, turned round, and flew out of the window. So much impressed was the merchant by this realisation of his dream that, fortunately for him, he abandoned his speculation.

This story contains much Irish mythological symbolism, the crow being the symbol of the Celtic goddess of death and battles, who often appears to warn of ill fortune.

Another Dublin story for the truth of which he vouched was this. A jeweller was about to set a very valuable diamond, which he was holding with a pair of pincers, when, owing to a mishandling of it, the pincers slipped and the diamond was shot through the open window into the court below. Search was at once made for it, and carried on continuously, but to no avail. The owner of the diamond was naturally not only highly incensed but highly suspicious of the truth of the jeweller's story. Years went by; the jeweller, in consequence of this incident, which was a good deal talked about, lost custom, and died in poverty. But long afterwards the diamond was discovered deeply embedded in the whitewash of the wall opposite his shop.

Sheridan Le Fanu was not the first Irishman to write a vampire story. The prolific Dublin playwright Dion Boucicault (1820–1890), who wrote more than 140 plays, and whose successes included *The Corsican Brothers*, *The Colleen Bawn* and *The Shaughran*, wrote a played called *The Vampire*. The three-act play opened on 19 June 1852, at London's Princess' Theatre. In the play Alan Raby is the vampire who 'dies' in the period of Charles II but cannot be destroyed until Dr Rees, a student of the supernatural, shoots him with a charmed bullet.

The play was apparently based on a story called *The Vampire*, published as 'A Tale By Lord Byron' in the 1 April 1819 issue of *The New Monthly Magazine*. In fact, the story was written by Dr John Polidori as a result of his 1816 sojourn at Byron's summer house in Geneva, the Villa Diodati, when a storm caused Byron to suggest that the assembled guests write a weird supernatural tale to help pass the time. Mary Godwin (the future wife of Shelley) began to create her novel *Frankenstein* as a result. Bryon had outlined the story which Polidori then worked into a novel. The vampire (Lord Ruthven) is obviously modelled on Byron himself: the handsome Ruthven has the physical deformity of a club foot and 'dead grey eyes'. When Byron broke with Polidori the true authorship of the work became known because Byron disowned it.

The Vampire, issued in volume form, was immediately translated into many languages. Cyprien Bérard wrote a sequel, *Lord Ruthven ou les Vampires*, in 1820. A stage adaptation of the story, entitled *The Vampire, or The Bride of the Isles*, opened on 9 August 1820 at the Lyceum Theatre. The play was written by James Robinson Planché; he later produced a new version, *Der Vampyr*, which also played at the Lyceum in 1829.

In the year that Stoker was born E. Lloyd of London published a lengthy part-work novel which can hardly be classed as simply a 'penny-dreadful'; at 868 pages *Varney the Vampire, or The Feast of Blood* remains the longest vampire epic ever written. The story was published anonymously although a clue was given in that it was said to be 'by the author of *Grace Rivers*'. Even so, its authorship has long been in contention. Montague Summers claimed it was written by Thomas Preskett Prest, a prolific writer of popular novels of mystery and horror, such as *Sweeney Todd, the Demon Barber of Fleet Street, The Skeleton Clutch, or The Goblet of Gore* and the like. But the authorship can in fact be attributed to James Malcolm Rymer (1814–1881), another popular writer of the day. Rymer used the pseudonym of Malcolm J. Errym, also called Merry, and was an exceedingly prolific author of adventure tales and mysteries. In 1972 an expert of genre, Everett F. Bleiler, in a Dover (New York) edition of *Varney*, concluded from a study of the cultural milieu and stylometric analysis of the work that the author was, indeed, Rymer.

Sir Francis Varney is condemned to exist as a vampire having committed suicide in the seventeenth century. He haunts Ratford Abbey, unable to curb his thirst for the blood of young maidens. He is killed by a stake in the heart, by magical bullets and by hangings, but the rays of the moon always revive him. He finally finds a way to end his life by throwing himself into the active crater of Mount Vesuvius.

Another vampire tale appeared in a volume called *Odds and Ends* about 1860. It was a translation from German concerning a vampire called Azzo. This is set in the Carpathian mountains at Castle Klatka. A young woman named Franziska is lured to the castle and finds the man Azzo. He is thin and pale but as she begins to develop symptoms of anaemia he grows younger. There are wounds on her neck. A young man named Woislaw learns the secret of Azzo and takes Franziska to the ancient coffin of Ezzelinus de Klatka where she drives three iron nails through the coffin lid into the vampire's body.

Bram had certainly discovered supernatural and 'vampiric' literature during his student days and had already developed a talent for writing when a sickly child. We saw in Chapter Four that when he entered the Irish civil service in 1870 he did not see his entire life being spent in it as his father's had been. Like Le Fanu before him, the profession for which Trinity had qualified him was not to have his full attention. He was soon to follow in Le Fanu's footsteps and start a career in journalism. In 1871 he approached Henry Maunsell who had taken over from Le Fanu as editor and owner of the *Dublin Mail*. Stoker, aged twenty-four, bearded Maunsell in his office and complained that the *Mail* did not carry any theatrical criticism. Maunsell admitted this was so. Stoker volunteered his services to write such pieces and in November that year he began his new career as the *Mail*'s part-time, unpaid theatrical critic.

Before long Bram was also contributing to another weekly journal once owned by Le Fanu, *The Warder*. Business contacts soon brought a new offer to the energetic civil servant. A new evening newspaper was planned for Dublin, to be called the *Irish Echo*. Would he be editor? It would be part-time, after the hours of his regular job at Dublin Castle. The paper first appeared on 6 November 1873, but two days later – on Bram's twenty-sixth birthday – had to retitle itself *The Halfpenny Press* as another *Irish Echo* had just been launched. It was too much work and after four months Bram reluctantly resigned.

He still threw himself into his theatrical reviews, and even took a part in some amateur performances himself. Bram was able to predict the success of several budding actresses like Geneviève Ward whom he first saw at Dublin's Royal Theatre in 1873. She had married the Count Constantine de Guerbel of Nicolaeiff at the age of eighteen in 1856, but had left him on the steps of the church. She never divorced him but went on to have a career as 'Madame Ginevra Guerrabella' the acclaimed opera singer, before losing her voice and turning to drama. Bram recalled that he predicted she would be a great success in his diary at the time and he later dedicated his weird novel *The Lady of the Shroud* (1909) to her. She became a lifelong friend and was one of the few who attended his funeral.

In addition to all this critical activity, Bram found time to write fiction. In September 1872, he had a fantasy story published in *London Society* called 'The Crystal Cup', featuring an evil king 'pallid with the hue of Death'. Most intriguing is the fact that *London Society*, in the January – June issue of that year, had been serialising Sheridan Le Fanu's 'The Room in the Dragon Volant'. One wonders whether Le Fanu suggested Bram submit his story there or even recommended it to the editor? Bram did not apparently have any further success in his writing career until 1875. In the Irish magazine *The Shamrock*, a ten-chapter mystery serial appeared from 6 February to 6 March entitled 'The Primrose Path'. This was successful enough to be followed by another serial, 'Buried Treasures', on 13 and 20 March. In May came a further serial, 'The Chain of Destiny'. This four-part weird fantasy had such ingredients as an evil curse, a nightmare villain, and a romance.

In May 1874, Bram had set off to Switzerland, to visit his parents and sisters who were now staying there. But he stopped off in Paris where, according to Ludlam, presumably quoting Bram's son Noel, he met an actress called 'Miss Henry'. He alarmed his father by saying that he was going to throw up his clerk's job and become a writer. It was clear that Bram had become infatuated with 'Miss Henry'. In 'The Burial of the Rats', much has been read into the paragraph: 'In this year I was very much in love with a young lady who, though she returned my passion, so far yielded to the wishes of her parents that she promised not to see me or correspond with me for a year.'

His father begged him to continue in the civil service for he would soon be made a senior clerk with job security. 'You know that there are few men of your standing now in the Castle who have a larger income,' Abraham Stoker wrote on 19 September 1874, 'and you can also guess how many competitors there would be if a vacancy took place tomorrow in your office.' The infatuation ended and Bram 'hung on', obeying his father's advice.

It might well be that his father's concern for Bram's lifestyle was communicated to his elder brother William Thornley for Bram was persuaded, for a time, to move back into his house. By the end of 1874, Bram had returned as a resident to his brother's new house at No. 16 Harcourt Street. This was also the address given by his younger brothers, Richard and George, at this time. By mid-1875 Bram had moved out again.

Perhaps the reason for his departure, along with Richard and George, was that William Thornley had decided to marry. In 1875 he married Emily Stewart, a daughter of Captain William Stewart of Sallymount, Ranelagh. Stewart had been commissioned into the Royal Regiment of

Artillery on 16 December 1816. He had retired as a half-pay captain in May 1840. Towards the end of her life Emily Stoker, who died in 1910, developed what seems to have been a form of Alzheimer's disease.

In 1892 William Thornley was to move from 16 Harcourt Street to Ely House, 8 Ely Place. He was to be knighted for his services to medicine in 1895. Living in Ely Place about 1907–1910 was the young Oliver St John Gogarty (1878–1957). Gogarty was the model for James Joyce's character, 'stately plump Buck Mulligan' in *Ulysses*. He had graduated in medicine in 1907 and became a surgeon. Later he would secure his reputation as a writer. He published a book of reminiscences in 1937, *As I Was Going Down Sackville Street*, which became the centre of a famous libel action. In this book, Gogarty devotes several pages to Sir Thornley Stoker (as William Thornley now liked to call himself).

Sir Thornley's house was No. 8 while Gogarty lived at No. 15. Another well-known Irish author, George Moore, lived at No. 4. According to Gogarty:

> Sir Thornley Stoker, the famous surgeon lives in Ely Place, and in the Eighteenth Century, which he never really leaves; hence the house is filled with period furniture, of which he is a collector and connoisseur. Chippendale Adams and old silver candelabra, match the silver jambs of the doors, and are contemporary with the silver linings of the great fire places, under their mantels of Sienna and statuary marble.

According to Gogarty, Sir Thornley had arranged a dinner party one evening. The Rt. Hon. Augustine Birrell, Chief Secretary to the Lord Lieutenant, had been invited, and so had George Moore, whom Farson refers to erroneously as 'Henry Moore'. George Moore's reputation had been consolidated with his novel *Esther Waters* (1894). He was later to help W. B. Yeats and Lady Gregory establish the Abbey Theatre as the national theatre of Ireland. They all sat down to dine.

> . . . Then Birrell says, 'How is your brother Bram, Sir Thornley?'
> 'Haven't seen him for some time.'
> 'Is he living in Herbert Street, or is he in London at all these days?'
> 'He is engaged on scientific research somewhere,' said Sir Thornley.

'Not on the habits of Dracula?' said Birrell, with a laugh.

At this stage the mahogany door bursts open, and a nude and elderly lady came in with a cry, 'I like a little intelligent conversation!' She ran round the table. We all stood up. She was followed by two female attendants, who seized whatever napery was available, and sheltering her with this and their own bodies, led her forth, screaming, from the room.

Our consternation held us in the positions we had suddenly taken. Birrell looked like a popular figure in Madame Tussaud's, Sir Thornley, with his knuckles on the table, inclined his head as if saying a silent grace. At last he broke silence with: 'Gentlemen, pray sit down.'

Nobody liked to begin a conversation, because the farther it was off the subject, the more purposefully self-conscious it would seem. Sir Thornley recovered himself and spoke:

'Gentlemen, under my mahogany, I hope you will keep this incident, mortifying as it is to me, from any rumour of scandal in this most gossipy town. And now, Moore, I conjure you most particularly, as you are the only one who causes me grave misgivings.'

'But it was charming, Sir Thornley. I demand an encore.'

Sir Thornley rose, went over to Moore's chair, and pointing his beard into Moore's ear, hissed something. Then, taking the novelist by the shoulder, he pushed him to the door and into the hall, and out into the street. We heard the door banging and the yapping of her Ladyship's Pomeranian dog.

Sir Thornley insisted on his guests drinking more wine. The dinner dragged on, Sir Thornley asking questions without waiting for answers, from each of us in turn. I was counting the minutes towards the end of this melancholy feast. After some minutes the butler leant over and said something to Sir Thornley.

'Did you admit that scoundrel?' said Sir Thornley harshly.

'He says, sir, it's a matter of life and death.'

'Will you, pray, excuse me, gentlemen? I have to leave the room for a moment.'

We could hear the inarticulate sound of voices, and suddenly two loud screams. It transpired that George, on his way home, had been bitten by a mad dog and was in danger of hydrophobia. Sir Thornley had enlarged the two slight scratches on Moore's right calf and was screwing caustic into the wound. The yells increased, and through the door, which Sir Thornley had forgotten to close, we could hear him saying, 'I don't care whether you're in a dinner-jacket or not. You'll have to send to your house for my honorarium, which is five guineas, before you leave this hall.' Moore produced a wallet of flexible green and handed Sir Thornley a five pound note with 'I'll send the silver in the morning by my cook'. The butler opened the door, to let out George Moore, and to let in a little Pomeranian dog . . .

After Lady Stoker had died in 1910, Sir Thornley sold up his home at Ely House and in November moved into a house at 21 Lower Hatch Street, Dublin, where he remained until his death in 1912. Bram himself was ill by 1910 and forbidden to travel to Ireland to attend Lady Stoker's funeral.

It seems that Bram and his brothers had moved out of Harcourt Street in order to give the newly wed William Thornley and his bride more 'space'. In mid-1875 Bram moved into rooms at No. 116 Lower Baggot Street, still only a walk away from Merrion Square. The significance of this was that No. 119 was the home of a close friend of Bram's brother William, John Todhunter (1839–1916). Todhunter was a literary confidant for Bram at this time. He was another Trinity College graduate who had practised medicine in Dublin from 1870–1874. Tiring of medicine he devoted himself to literature. Todhunter wrote several plays with suggestive supernatural backgrounds such as *The Banshee* and *The Black Cat*. Like Willie Wilde, Oscar's brother, he had also been a contributor to *Kottabos*. Bram mentions him and his wife as attending first nights at the Lyceum Theatre. Todhunter was to be a founder of the Irish Literary Society in London of which Bram became a member.

In 1876 Bram was promoted to Inspector of the Petty Sessions. Travelling around the Irish law courts, he realised that the system was in a mess. Clerks of the courts of the Petty Sessions had no idea of their duties and so he set to work on researching and compiling a book which, after publication, was the standard work for many years – *The Duties of Clerks of Petty Sessions in Ireland*, published by the authority of the civil service by John Falconer, of Upper Sackville Street, Dublin, in 1879.

Bram also continued to work on his fiction with a series of eight tales, mystical, supernatural allegories which were later to be collected in *Under the Sunset*. Bram dedicated this to his son Irving Noel Thornley Stoker. A friend of Bram's had agreed to illustrate the stories. This was William

Fitzgerald who, after graduating from Trinity in 1873, had become a lawyer. Ludlam is totally in error when he identifies William Fitzgerald as 'a parish priest in Killaloe, Co. Clare'. Bram's other biographers have followed his lead. The *Thom's Law Directory* of 1879 certainly lists a William Fitzgerald at Clarisford House, Killaloe, but as a lawyer. Clarisford House was, in fact, the home of William's father and perhaps confusion occurred because William's father was the Right Revd William Fitzgerald, Anglican Lord Bishop of Killaloe, Kilfernora, Clonfert and Kilmacduagh. Bishop Fitzgerald (1814–1883) had been one of the professors at Trinity College, and was a prolific author on ecclesiastical history and theology, many of whose works caused controversy. His entry in the *Dictionary of National Biography* is impressive. Bram's friend, and illustrator, William Fitzgerald practised as a lawyer until 1882. Bram appears to have visited him at Clarisford House, Killaloe, several times, ostensibly to discuss the illustrations but also to take a holiday.

Killaloe is a beautiful spot at the foot of Lough Dearg where the Shannon winds between Slieve Bernagh and the Arra mountains, a town of narrow streets and steep hills where St Lua founded his community in the sixth century. It was also the ancestral seat of the Dalcassian princes of whom Brían Bóromha became the most famous High King of Ireland, defeating the Danes at Bram's birthplace of Clontarf.

The ancient cathedral, built by Donal Mór Ó Brían in the twelfth century, had been taken over by the Anglican Church after the Reformation and it was now the centre of the Anglican diocese. Doubtless Bishop Fitzgerald, as a former professor of history, took the opportunity to show his son's guests the ancient crosses and Ogham inscriptions and an intriguing monument to one Thorgrimr, a Viking who apparently converted to Christianity. With its old Celtic oratory and hill-forts and other ancient sites, Killaloe was a place of fascination for Bram. It put him in physical touch with the folklore that he had imbibed in Dublin.

The year after his illustrations appeared in *Under the Sunset* William Fitzgerald turned from law and studied for ordination in the Anglican Church, becoming a curate in Cork.

The break-up of the Wilde family during this period had a profound affect on Bram.

Sir William Wilde died on 19 April 1876. The May issue of the *Dublin University Magazine* ran an unsigned obituary which may well have been written by Bram. Oscar had already left Trinity, having won a demyship to Magdalen College, Oxford in 1874. This scholarship was so called because it was half a Fellowship. Oscar was beginning to make a name for himself with contributions to the *Dublin University Magazine, Kottabos* and the *Month and Catholic Review*. It was in *Kottabos* that his haunting 'Requiescat' was first published. It begins:

> Tread lightly, she is near
> Under the snow,
> Speak gently, she can hear
> The daisies grow.

His elder brother, Willie Wilde, had already left for London to pursue his journalistic career and so, at the end of that year, Lady Wilde decided to follow her sons to England and set up home in much-reduced circumstances in Oakley Street, Chelsea. When Bram himself followed to England, he found houses in Cheyne Walk and in St Leonard's Terrace, both only a short distance away from Lady Wilde, and he continued his friendship with her until her death in 1896.

In October 1876 word came from Naples, where Bram's parents and sisters had moved. They were living in the Pensione Suisse in the Cava di Tirreni district. Bram's father had died on 12 October, aged seventy-eight. Bram left for Naples immediately to arrange affairs for his mother. In a letter to a friend, James McHenry (9 April 1885), Bram says that when he reached Cava di Tirreni he was allowed to see his father's body before burial. 'I pressed [kissed] my dear father's forehead in the vault of the church at La Cava.' It was Bram who formally registered his father's death on 4 November before the acting consul, P. G. Barff. He gave his father's profession, and his own, as 'gentleman'. To Bram's surprise he found that his mother and sister Matilda wished to remain living in Naples. Presumably, Matilda, as eldest daughter, remained as companion to Charlotte Stoker. Having made the necessary financial arrangements, Bram returned to Dublin with his sister Margaret.

Margaret went to live with her brother William Thornley and his wife at 16 Harcourt Street. A colleague of William Thornley's, William Thomson, a Fellow of the Royal College of Surgeons, Ireland, had just moved into 31 Harcourt Street. It was no coincidence that Thomson had, in the early 1870s, lived a couple of houses away from John Todhunter's house where Bram rented rooms. Thomson was now a surgeon at the Dublin hospitals of Richmond, Whitworth and Hardwick. Romance immediately blossomed between Thomson and Margaret. On 27 June

1878, Margaret and William Thomson were married at St Peter's Anglican church in Dublin. Bram gave his sister away and was one of the witnesses together with a friend, Kate Harden.

Like Bram's brother, William Thornley, William Thomson was to be knighted (1897) for his work for medicine in Ireland. Bram notes that Thomson used to visit London and attend the Lyceum Theatre when he was manager there.

William Thomson's career was interesting. He had been born in Downpatrick, Co. Down, but his father, a government clerk, died when he was young. His mother married the proprietor of the *Galway Express* and, at first, Thomson seemed destined for a career in journalism. Indeed, after graduating from Queen's College, Galway, William went to work on the Dublin *Daily Express*. But while working as a reporter he also studied medicine and took his medical degree from the Carmichael School of Medicine in 1872. In 1874 William Thomson became a Fellow of the Royal College of Surgeons. He began to publish several medical works and was considered 'a surgeon of considerable ability'. In 1896 he became President of the Royal College of Surgeons succeeding Sir William Thornley Stoker in the position. He was editor of the *Transactions of the Royal Academy of Medicine, Ireland.*

During the South African war Thomson joined Bram's younger brother, George, in organising field hospitals and was mentioned in despatches. He also received the Queen's Medal with three clasps. While in South Africa he was appointed surgeon in ordinary to Queen Victoria in Ireland and in 1901 became honorary surgeon to King Edward VII. From 1905 until his death on 13 November 1910, he was Inspector of Anatomy for Ireland. He and Margaret had a son and a daughter.

Perhaps some of his brother-in-law's medical writings might have appealed to Bram – those on the workings of the arteries and blood supply! Among other works, Thomson edited the third edition of *Power's Surgical Anatomy of the Arteries* (1881).

While some critics have been disparaging about Bram's medical knowledge, as demonstrated in *Dracula*, Bram certainly had no lack of contacts to help him out within his immediate family circle. In fact, from the notes and original manuscript in the Rosenbach Foundation Library, it appears that Bram did consult members of his family for 'a surgeon's' notes and suggestions appear in the margins of three pages concerning blood transfusions and autopsies. Bram adjusted his text accordingly. Just who this surgeon was is almost impossible to establish. The most likely authority would be Bram's brother William Thornley, being the most accessible of his medical siblings.

Bram's mother and sister Matilda finally returned to live in Dublin in the early 1880s and took a house at 72 Rathgar Road, Rathfarnham. Matilda seems to have devoted most of her youth to being a companion to her mother. She was, however, an accomplished illustrator and a literary critic. She wrote several articles for the *English Illustrated Magazine* to which she also sold illustrations and 'illustrative headings' for articles. Oscar Wilde commented favourably on her article on 'Sheridan and Miss Linley' (*English Illustrated Magazine*, April 1887).

She finally married late in life. It seems that while in France she had met a personable Frenchman. She married at the Rathfarnham parish church on 5 March 1889. Her husband was Charles Auguste Petitjeán of 18 Rue Morboeuf, Paris, whose profession is given on the certificate as an '*administrateur délégué des Ardoisiers de la Corrèze*', which would be a French government official (administrator) of slate workings at Corrèze. His father, Denis Eustace Petitjeán, was a Chevalier de la Légion d'Honneur. This ceremony was, curiously enough, conducted, according to the registrar, 'by consent of bridegroom's father – all formalities complied with a previous contract executed before the Church Council in Dublin'. Matilda's brother-in-law, Dr William Thomson, was a witness together with William Thornley Stoker and André Petitjeán.

Matilda was the last of the Stoker children to marry and leave their mother's house in Rathfarnham – Bram, as we shall see in the next chapter, having married in 1878.

In 1895, Bram dedicated his novel *The Watter's Mou'* (Constable, 1895) 'To My Dear Mother in her loneliness'. Mrs Charlotte Stoker was still living at 72 Rathgar Road, where she remained until her death. Just before she died in 1901 (not 1902, as recorded by Professor Belford), Charlotte Stoker wrote to Bram:

I have not been well at all lately, time tells very severely on me and even the drops in my eyes begin to lose their effect. I only hope God will be good enough to take me home before I get quite blind. Situated as I am it is a terrible look forward to me but I can't complain. I have had a happy and healthy life and must take the bad as well as the good. If I had lost my sight in the early part of my life, when it needed me to be useful, how much worse it would have been . . .

Charlotte Stoker died on 15 March 1901, at her home in Rathfarnham. She had been suffering with influenza for six days which led to cardiac arrest. The information was given to the registrar by her illiterate maid, Eliza Kavanagh, who had to sign with an 'X'. She was the only person who had been present at the death. Charlotte was eighty-one years old.

When Bram had returned from Naples at the end of November 1876, he had once more moved back to his brother's house at No. 16 Harcourt Street. His career began to change that December when, after he had written a piece of theatre criticism about a performance at Dublin's Theatre Royal, in which Henry Irving was playing, the actor asked the manager of the theatre to introduce him to the critic. Irving was, by then, famous and Bram was already one of his more fervent admirers. He had first seen Irving on the actor's second visit to Ireland when he was performing a repertoire of plays by some of the leading Irish playwrights, such as Sheridan and Goldsmith, at the Theatre Royal, Dublin, in August 1867.

Bram had been an undergraduate at the time of Irving's first Dublin performance as Captain Absolute in Sheridan's *The Rivals* and he had been greatly impressed. Coincidentally, the same repertoire of 1867 included a play by Mary Elizabeth Braddon (1835–1915) which she had adapted herself from her best-selling novel *Lady Audley's Secret* (1862). Mary Braddon went on to write nearly seventy popular novels during her career and became a close friend of Bram and his wife. In *The Strand Magazine* of February 1896, she published a vampire story 'Good Lady Decayne' concerning a seductive female vampire. The story may well have been lingering in Bram's mind in the summer of that year as he was working on *Dracula*. He certainly used one of Mary Braddon's ideas, that of blood transfusion, in Chapter Ten of his novel. When *Dracula* appeared, Mary Braddon wrote him a letter of congratulations dated 23 June 1897: 'We will talk of it more anon! when I have soberly read and meditated thereupon. I have done my humdrum little story of transfusion in the Good Lady Ducayne – but your "bloofer lady" . . .'

Irving had returned to Dublin in 1871 and 1872, confirming Bram's estimation of him as the world's greatest actor. Irving had been born John Henry Brodribb, in Somerset, England, on 6 February 1838. His mother was a Cornishwoman, Mary Behenna (it is suggested that the name comes from the Cornish word *byghenna*, smaller). Irving was three years old when he was sent to live with his aunt Sarah and her husband Isaac Penberthy,

15 The Crescent, Clontarf, the house where Bram Stoker was born.

The famous mummies in the vaults of St. Michan's Church, Dublin, where the Stoke family had a crypt.

Bram's first bachelor apartment was at 30 Kildare Street, Dublin.

The Merrion Square home of Sir William and Lady Wilde and their sons Oscar and Willie.

Bram Stoker, taken in 1884, the year he met Walt Whitman.

Florence Stoker,
a drawing by Oscar Wilde.

Florence Stoker,
a drawing by Sir Edward Burne-Jones.

Henry Irving and Bram Stoker (hand in pocket) leaving the Lyceum to
board a hansom cab. *The Tatler*, October 9, 1901.

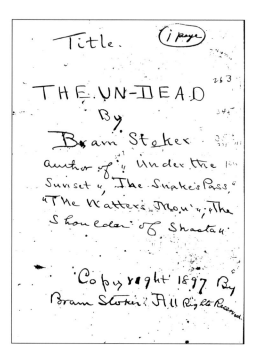

Title page of the original manuscript of 'The Un-Dead'.

A corrected and re-pasted page of the original manuscript.

DRACULA

6d.

BY

BRAM STOKER

6d.

WESTMINSTER

Archibald Constable & Co Ltd

2 WHITEHALL GARDENS

The jacket cover of the rare, abridged 1901
Constable sixpenny paperback edition of *Dracula*.

Arminius Vambéry who is claimed by many as a source of material for the novel.

One of the early fifteenth century, German propaganda pamphlets depicting Vlad Dracula (the Impaler).

VAMPIRES IN NEW ENGLAND.

Dead Bodies Dug Up and Their Hearts Burned to Prevent Disease.

STRANGE SUPERSTITION OF LONG AGO.

The Old Belief Was that Ghostly Monsters Sucked the Blood of Their Living Relatives.

ECENT ethnological research has disclosed something very extraordinary in Rhode Island. It appears that the ancient vampire superstition still survives in that State, and within the last few years many people have been digging up the dead bodies of relatives for the purpose of burning their hearts.

Near Newport scores of such exhumations have been made, the purpose being to prevent the dead from preying upon the living. The belief entertained is that a person who has died of consumption is likely to rise from the grave at night and suck the blood of surviving members of his or her family, thus dooming them to a similar fate.

The discovery . . . . . rival in highly . . . . ted Ne . . . . . a superst . . .

was driven through the chest, and the heart being taken out was either burned or chopped into small pieces. For in this way only could a vampire be deprived of power to do mischief. In one case a man who was buried eat up in his coffin, with fresh blood on his lips. The official in charge of the ceremonies held a crucifix before his face and, saying, "Do you recognize your Saviour?" chopped the unfortunate's head off. This person presumably had been buried alive in a cataleptic trance.

WERE THEY BURIED ALIVE?

How is the phenomenon to be accounted for? Nobody can say with certainty, but it may be that the fright into which people were thrown by the epidemic had the effect of predisposing nervous persons to catalepsy. In a word, people were buried alive in a condition where, the vital functions being suspended, they remained as it were dead for a while. It is a common thing for a cataleptic to bleed at the mouth just before returning to consciousness. According to the popular superstition, the vampire left his or her body in the grave while engaged in nocturnal prowls.

The epidemic prevailed all over southeastern Europe, being at its worst in Hungary and Servia. It is supposed to have originated in Greece, where a belief was entertained to the effect that Latin Christians buried in that country could not decay in their graves, being under the ban of the Greek Church. The cheerful notion was that they got out of their graves at night and pursued the occupation of ghouls. The superstition as to ghouls is very ancient and undoubtedly of Oriental origin. Generally speaking, however, a ghoul is just the opposite of a vampire, being a living person who preys on dead bodies, while a vampire is a dead person that feeds on the blood of the living. If you had your choice, which would you rather be, a vampire or a ghoul?

One of the most familiar of the stories of the Arabian Nights tells of a woman who annoyed her husband very much by refusing food. Nothing more than a few grains of rice would she eat at meals. He discovered that she was in the habit of stealing away from his side in the night, and, following her on one such occasion, he found her engaged in digging up and devouring a corpse.

Among the numerous folk tales about vampires is one relating to a fiend named Dakanavar, who dwelt in a cave in Armenia. He would not permit anybody to penetrate into the mountains of Ulmish Altotem or to count their valleys. Every one who attempted this had in the night the blood sucked by the monster from the soles of his feet until he died.

At last, however, he was outwitted . . . . cunning fellows. They began to . . . he w . . . and when night cam . . .

Two views of Whitby as Stoker knew it. (*Above*) Whitby Harbour, with the famous abbey in the background. (*Below*) The 199 steps which Mina runs up when she discovers Dracula has enticed her friend Lucy away, known as the Church Steps.

Slains Castle, the inspiration for Dracula's castle.

The model of Dracula's Castle built for the 1979 version of *Dracula* bears more than a striking resemblance to Slains Castle.

a Cornish miner, living near St Ives, Cornwall. When he was twelve years old he went to live in London with his mother. So Irving had a sympathy and understanding for the Celtic background. In 1876 Bram and Irving struck up a close friendship.

It was Irving who introduced Bram to Celtic Cornwall and sent him down to visit his aunt, then in her eightieth year. Bram visited Cornwall several times and his favourite spot became the coastal village of Boscastle where Thomas Hardy (1840–1928), who began his career as an architect and restored St Juliot's church nearby, wrote *Under the Greenwood Tree* (1872). In Stoker's work Boscastle became Pencastle and featured in his short story 'The Coming of Abel Behenna' (using Irving's mother's maiden name). Two fisherman are in love with the same girl, Sarah Trefusis. One of them wins her by guile and on the day of the wedding the body of the other is washed ashore in a wild storm.

Irving was back in Dublin with a play in June 1877. Bram spent his summer holiday in London that year and took the opportunity to meet James Knowles, who was just about to launch a new publication, *Nineteenth Century*. (Coincidentally, Constable were to buy this magazine in 1921 and continued its publication until 1950. Otto Kyllmann helped Helen Waddell in its editing. Later, the man who bought *Dracula* became chairman of Constable, retiring in 1954. Kyllmann died in his ninetieth year on 14 May 1959.)

Bram confessed to Knowles that he wanted to emigrate to England to pursue a career as a writer. Knowles was himself a Scot and knew the pitfalls of such a move. 'Why do you think it better to be in London?' he enquired. 'Could you not write to me, for instance, in Dublin?' Bram argued that he believed being in London would give him better access to editors. 'I could write well enough,' he replied, 'but I have known that game for some time. I know the joy of the waste-paper basket and the manuscript returned unread.' This implies that Bram, as well as writing for Irish newspapers and magazines, had been unsuccessfully sending material to English publications. Indeed, after his first success with *London Society*, Bram had submitted many more stories in the 1873–75 period and to other London magazines like *Temple Bar*, but they were all rejected. Bram's desire to go to London to be a writer significantly started at the time the Wildes left Dublin in the autumn of 1876 and after Bram had become friendly with the London-based Irving. Did either of these events influence him? After all, he had been having an extremely good period in

Dublin literary circles. Surely, on the face of it, it was better to consolidate his growing reputation in Ireland? But it seems other factors were guiding his decision to emigrate.

By coincidence, 1876 was the year when another Dublin clerk, aged only twenty, left his employment to seek fame and fortune as a writer in London. George Bernard Shaw was later to observe: 'Every Irishman who felt that his business in life was on the higher planes of the cultural professions felt that he must have a metropolitan domicile and an international culture: that is, he felt that his first business was to get out of Ireland.'

At this time there was no Irish Literary Revival taking place, and no native Irish theatrical tradition of worth. Although Dublin had a permanent theatre as early as 1637, it was essentially an Anglo-Irish cultural establishment and so generations of writers such as Congreve, Farquhar, Goldsmith and Sheridan felt obliged to leave for London to establish themselves as 'English' writers. However, Shaw was, perhaps, being a little harsh in his judgement as a means of self-justification, for writers like Maturin, Le Fanu and many others had established international reputations without the necessity of leaving their native country.

When Irving brought *Hamlet* to Dublin in November 1877, he and Bram discussed the possibility of Bram joining him as his manager. Bram had already made up his mind. In his diary for 22 November 1877, he wrote: 'London in view!' It was now a matter of time and opportunity. In the meantime, Bram once more moved out of William Thornley's house and took rooms at 7 Stephen's Green North. This was the main business premises of Robert Smyth, a grocer and wine merchant. There were fifteen other business offices in the house, mainly offices of barristers and solicitors. At the top of the house Bram and two others had rooms. This was to be Bram's last home before leaving Dublin.

About this time it appears that Bram met Julian Hawthorne, the son of the famous American writer Nathaniel Hawthorne, when the young man was on a tour of Ireland. Nathaniel (1804–1864) had been American consul in Liverpool for three years; Julian (1846–1934) followed in his footsteps as a writer and editor with a penchant for the weird. In his 1888 collection *David Poindexter's Disappearance*, the younger Hawthorne included a short story he had written, using the background of his Irish visit, called 'Ken's Mystery'. It is one of the few vampire stories actually set in Ireland. Julian continued his friendship with Bram and was a frequent visitor to the Lyceum. Did Bram receive any sort of inspiration from Julian's Irish vampire tale published nine years before *Dracula*, or could it be that Hawthorne was himself inspired by Bram's own tales of Irish folklore? It is one more intriguing possibility in the legend of this great novel.

On 7 June 1878, Bram went to Paris for a holiday and passed through London, taking the opportunity to visit his friend Irving once again. He found Irving in a troubled state for the next day he was to put on a new play at the Lyceum entitled *Vanderdecken*, an eerie Gothic drama based on the legend of the Flying Dutchman. The play had been especially written for Irving by William Gorman Wills, the Irish playwright from Kilkenny.

Wills was a cousin of Violet Martin and Edith Somerville – the writers Somerville and Ross whose *Some Experiences of an Irish RM*, 1908, has become a classic of humorist writing. He was the son of Dr James Wills of Roscommon (1790–1868), another writer and poet, who had been a close friend of Charles Maturin and saved him from financial disaster by allowing him to publish a poem 'The Universe' under his name. Indeed, the Wills family were also related to the Wildes. William Gorman Wills (1928–1891) had been a painter before becoming a novelist, poet and playwright. His best known plays were *Charles I* (1872), *Jane Shore* (1876) and *Olivia*, based on fellow Irishman Oliver Goldsmith's *The Vicar of Wakefield* (1885). Irving acted in *Charles I* and *Olivia*. Wills was also to write a stage version of *Faust* in 1886. His son Freeman Croft Wills wrote a biography of his father published by Longman of London in 1898. Both William Gorman Wills and Freeman Croft Wills had contributed to *Kottabos*.

But the new eerie mystery of *Vanderdecken* would not work. Indeed, Bram attended the first night on 8 June and saw it flop. It was too poetic, with none of the macabre feeling necessary for such a drama. Bram joined Irving the next day, being Sunday, and then spent all day and most of the night, in his rooms in Grafton Street, redrafting the script. On Monday they went exhausted to the Lyceum and the cast were summoned to rehearsal. The second performance was infinitely better and Bram and Irving celebrated with a meal in the Devonshire Club before returning to Irving's rooms and talking about the macabre in literature until 5 a.m.

When Bram continued his trip to Paris a few hours later, the die for his future career was already cast.

CHAPTER SEVEN

The Colonel's Daughter

WHILE THE PART-TIME DUBLIN THEATRE critic was developing his friendship with Henry Irving, another significant friendship was also blooming. Bram had met Florence Balcombe, an eighteen-year-old girl of extraordinary beauty. She was, he was told, the daughter of a colonel who lived in Clontarf. Further, she was 'walking out', as the phrase had it, with young Oscar Wilde. Within a short time she had rejected Oscar and agreed to marry Bram.

In 1876 the Balcombe family had taken up residence in Clontarf, close by where the Stoker family had once lived, at No. 1 Marino Crescent. All Bram's biographers are confused, appearing to think that the Stokers and Balcombes had lived as neighbours in Marino Crescent. In fact, the Stokers had moved out in 1849 while the Balcombes did not move in until 1876. In that year also, twenty-six-year-old James William ('Willie') Balcombe became secretary to the Commissioners of Clontarf Township (the local town council).

There might have been some nepotism here for it seems there was a connection between the Balcombe family and the Lemon family. The family tradition is that Lemon was the name of Florence's great-grandfather. Graham Lemon of Clontarf, a leading Dublin businessman, originally from Armagh, was one of the twelve-man Clontarf Commissioners and a Justice of the Peace. It seems likely that this connection was the cause of young 'Willie' settling in Clontarf.

The Lemons had come to Ulster in the early nineteenth century and were in trade. By the 1860s they had moved their business premises to

Sackville Street (O'Connell Street), Dublin, where they were first described as 'Confectioners to HM The Queen'. Then from 1878 they bore the title 'Lozenge and Confit Manufacturers to HM The Queen'. As well as his home in Yew Park, Clontarf, Graham Lemon, the head of the family, had a second home at Ross Castle (now Derriwillingham House), Armagh.

Within weeks of 'Willie' arriving in Clontarf, his retired father, Lieutenant-Colonel James Balcombe, together with his wife Phillippa (this eccentric spelling of the name appears in official documents thus differentiating the mother from a daughter named Philippa) and his second son and six daughters, came to share No. 1 Marino Crescent. Both Ludlam and Farson believed that there were only five daughters. One of those daughters was Florence Ann Lemon Balcombe, whom Bram was destined to marry.

Lieutenant-Colonel James Balcombe was an extraordinary character. The son of an army corporal, with no formal education, who had joined the army himself at the age of fourteen, Balcombe had managed to transcend early nineteenth-century class prejudice and had risen from the ranks to become an 'officer and a gentleman'. We make no apology for a digression into his story for, while it has been ignored by Bram's biographers, it is nevertheless a worthy one.

Bram's future father-in-law was born on 15 May 1820 at Kilkenny. His father was Bernard Balcomb (the 'e' was added later), a corporal in the 57th Regiment of Foot (later the West Middlesex Regiment of Foot), one of the Irish garrison regiments. Corporal Bernard Balcomb's wife was named Mary. James' sister, Hester, was born on 6 May 1822, when Bernard Balcomb, now a sergeant, was stationed at Shandon, Cork. The regiment was sent to India soon after. Sergeant Bernard Balcomb took his family with him. In India, a second sister was born, named Catharine. By now the 'e' had materialised on the end of their name.

Sergeant Bernard Balcombe died in Poona in April 1837. He had been ill for some time and perhaps it was to help family finances and security that young James Balcombe, aged only fourteen years, joined his father's regiment as a 'boy soldier' on 20 April 1835. He joined the regiment at its base in what was then called Tellicherry (Telli) in Madras province, now the Tamil Nadu state.

Young James Balcombe was obviously intelligent and resourceful and willing to study hard to make himself literate in adverse circumstances. From merely a 'boy soldier' on enlistment, a few weeks later, on 15 May he was made 'private' and two years later, at seventeen years of age, he became a corporal while technically regarded by the army as 'under age'. This was the year when his father died in Poona. He now became head of the family with his mother and two sisters to support.

On 8 October 1839, he was promoted acting sergeant, then colour sergeant on 2 November 1842, quartermaster sergeant on 1 February 1846, and senior quartermaster sergeant on 7 November 1851.

The responsibility of providing for his family was somewhat alleviated when, on 10 February 1845, his youngest sister Catharine married the 57th Regiment's sergeant-major, Thomas Edward Jones, at Fort St George, Madras. Catharine was only fourteen years old while Jones was thirty-six. Jones was from Bow in London and had initially served in the St Helena Regiment. He had served in New South Wales before joining the 57th in India. Two years after his marriage to Catharine he was invalided out of the army because of 'physical deterioration due to overseas service'. It has been impossible to trace what then became of James' two sisters.

James Balcombe was in England in April 1847. He was married on 20 April at Hougham parish church, near Dover, Kent, to Phillippa Anne Marshall, born in 1824. Phillippa was the daughter of a barracks sergeant, William Marshall, stationed at Shorncliffe.

The 57th Regiment returned to garrison duties in Ireland. James and Phillippa were to have eight children, six daughters and two sons: Philippa Anne (26 March 1848, Enniskillen), James William (13 January 1850, Enniskillen), Mary Rachel Juliana (11 October 1851, Kilkenny), William Francis (22 January 1853, Cork), Catharine Mary (14 January 1855, Corfu – Florence Stoker always spelt her sister's name with a 'K'), Florence Mary Lemon (17 July 1858, Falmouth), with Bertha Maude and Alice Grace being the youngest children.

Life for Quartermaster Sergeant James Balcombe was to change dramatically when the 57th Regiment's quartermaster officer, a lieutenant, died in October 1851. The regiment was then at Kilkenny. The officer commanding, Lieutenant-Colonel Thomas Goldie, took an unusual step – highly unusual in those days. He promised to raise James Balcombe from the ranks to be 'an officer and a gentleman' as replacement. Goldie wrote from Kilkenny to Viscount Hardinge, the Colonel of the Regiment, and to Lieutenant-General Lord Fitzroy Somerset, commander-in-chief, on 28 October seeking permission. It was granted. Quartermaster Sergeant James Balcombe was commissioned on 7 November 1851 in the 57th as its quartermaster officer with the rank of lieutenant.

It is difficult to imagine from the modern social perspective just what adjustment had to be made in the move from one social class to another. The class system in the mid-nineteenth century was extremely rigid, especially within the British Army. The fact that Balcombe continued in the same regiment would have undoubtedly caused resentment among his late comrades of the sergeants' mess and friction with his new fellow officers. One also wonders how Phillippa Balcombe, daughter of a barrack sergeant, adjusted to being the wife of an officer. Such things mattered in those days.

After a further two years in garrison duties in Ireland, the 57th were ordered to the Ionian islands off Greece, which were then a British Protectorate. From 22 March 1853 to 22 September 1854, Lieutenant James Balcombe and his family lived on Corfu where his daughter Catharine was born. Then came the Crimean War and from 23 September 1854 to 6 August 1856 he saw service there, receiving the Crimean Medal with clasps for participation in the battles of Balaclava and Inkerman and the siege of Sebastopol, as well as the Turkish Crimean Medal.

From 12 January 1857 to 7 June 1858, Balcombe and his family were stationed in Malta. He had been promoted captain quartermaster on 1 April 1857. On 8 June 1858 he was ordered to India. This time he went without his family. His wife, Phillippa, with her then five children, all under ten years old, and also eight months pregnant with Florrie, took the family to England where she was assigned quarters in the garrison port of Falmouth, at that time not only a major military base but a commercial port. Professor Belford imaginatively assigns her 'a house on the Falmouth moor': in fact she was allocated lodgings in the centre of Falmouth, in Killigrew Street. Sir Peter Killigrew (d. 1704) began the foundation of the town in the seventeenth century. Bram would have loved the nice theatrical connection in that Sir Peter's brother Thomas Killigrew, a former page of Charles I, formed the King's Company of theatrical players and built the first playhouse in Drury Lane, reviving some of the forgotten plays of Shakespeare. Samuel Pepys, in 1660, saw Killigrew's production of *Othello* 'which was well done'. There is a Killigrew Road which leads into a square named The Moor, which has obviously confused Professor Belford. It had been a marshland before the seventeenth-century harbour was constructed. This connects with the quayside High Street and Market Street. The town was a staging post not only for the Royal Navy but for troops going on overseas service which is undoubtedly why the Balcombes were assigned accommodation there.

The reason why Captain Balcombe had to leave his family behind was that the Indian National Uprising (known in British history as the Indian Mutiny) had begun. The British Army needed soldiers with service experience in India. But the last major battle of this campaign took place at Gwalior just a week after Balcombe arrived at his Indian posting. On 25 September 1859 the 57th Regiment dispensed with Balcombe's services and he returned to England, with his family, to be placed on the half-pay list. So far as the regular army lists are concerned, he remained as a half-pay quartermaster captain until he formally retired from the army on 1 July 1881, and was then allowed the 'honorary rank' of major.

How, then, does he appear in Bram's world as *Lieutenant-Colonel* James Balcombe?

Balcombe, since his birth, had known no other life but the army; no permanent home, only army camps and barracks and postings. He and his family had been living in Enniskillen, the 57th regimental headquarters, when he was discharged from the regular army in 1859. He now had to provide a home for his large family. Knowing no other profession he joined the Militia in Ireland, a forerunner of the Territorial (part-time) Army, as a means of boosting his half-pay as a quartermaster captain. The militias in Ireland were especially in need of recruits at this time as the authorities had become aware that a new revolutionary movement (the Irish Republican Brotherhood, founded in 1858) was planning an uprising. After the experience of the Indian National Uprising, the authorities began to suspect that the Irish regiments, like their Indian counterparts, were planning to mutiny and, as time went on, they began to transfer the 'suspect' regiments out of Ireland. Later figures revealed that 15,000 serving soldiers in the Irish garrison regiments had joined the republican movement together with 5000 serving in Britain; 80,000 others had taken the Fenian oath. Reports showed that the Fenians could rely on 100,000 rifles stored in British Army depots in Ireland. Irish soldiers, former officers of the United States Federal and Confederate armies, now discharged, were returning home to prepare for the rising. When it did take place, in March 1867, the Irish uprising was confined to Dublin, Cork, Limerick, Tipperary and Clare. From the colonial administration's viewpoint, local militias needed all the 'tried and trusted' officers they could get.

On 4 February 1860, James Balcombe was appointed captain and adjutant of the Royal South Down (Light Infantry) Militia, whose headquarters were in Downpatrick, Co. Down. He was appointed major on 31 December 1875. The Annual Army List and Militia List for 1879 acknowledges that James Balcombe was able to use the honorary militia rank of 'lieutenant-colonel' as from 6 December 1876, when he retired from the Militia. Bram's great-grandchildren still have the pair of silver candlesticks presented by the South Down Militia to James Balcombe on his retirement.

As we have seen, young James William ('Willie') Balcombe left his family in Ulster and moved into Clontarf in 1876. For many years he held numerous positions under the Commissioners for Clontarf Township, including secretary, executive sanitary officer and apparently running the Clontarf Baths and Assembly Rooms. He was to marry in June 1880.

His sister, Florence, had become an exceedingly beautiful young woman, though she was surely not the exception among the Colonel's six daughters. Farson claims that she was named after the Italian city and not after Florence Nightingale in contradiction to Rupert Hart-Davis, in his *Letters of Oscar Wilde*, who says of Balcombe: 'he had fought in the Crimea and it seems likely that Florence was named after Miss Nightingale.' George du Maurier, the artist and author of the classic novel *Trilby*, which introduced the mesmeric Svengali to the world of popular villains, considered her one of the three most beautiful women he had ever seen. Edward Burne-Jones painted her portrait while Oscar Wilde himself tried to capture her likeness in an excellent sketch.

Bram in 1895 decided to commission the famous Irish artist Walter Frederick Osborne (1859–1903) of Rathmines, Dublin, to paint Florrie's portrait. Osborne, whom Ludlam dismisses as just 'a young Irish artist', actually had quite a reputation at this time and was a member of both the Royal Hibernian Academy and the Royal Academy, and a highly sought after portrait painter. Today the National Gallery of Ireland holds some fine examples of his work. Osborne's portrait of Florence was exhibited in the Royal Academy and drew much attention. Bram had paid him £75 for the commission. Osborne also painted portraits of Bram's mother, Charlotte, and his father, Abraham, the latter from a photograph, both of which were hung in the Royal Hibernian Academy.

At the age of seventeen, Florence met the then twenty-one-year-old Oscar Wilde. Richard Ellman, in his biography *Oscar Wilde*, is clear: 'They met at her house at 1 Marion Terrace [*sic*], Clontarf.' This is confirmed by Oscar in a letter to Florence where he recalls the meeting in her mother's house in Clontarf. Ludlam's claim that Bram probably introduced Oscar to Florence is based on the misinformation about the Clontarf Stoker/

Balcombe connection. It seems more likely that Bram eventually met Florence at the Wildes' house or was introduced to her by Oscar.

It is clear that Oscar Wilde had, for some reason, been invited to No. 1 Marino Cresent and there met the seventeen-year-old Florrie, as she was called. He had obviously become a family friend. In one letter to Florence, Oscar Wilde sends his regards to her brother 'Willie' and her sister 'Gracie'. Alice Grace, in fact, married the Irish writer Francis Frankfort Moore (1855–1931). Moore was born in Limerick and educated in Belfast. He started his career as a journalist and became a prolific author, writing poetry, some successful plays, biographies and romantic adventures; *The Jessamy Bride* (1897) became the bestseller of the year in which Bram's *Dracula* appeared. Bram's sister-in-law Grace and her husband were, Bram noted, among the regular attenders at the Lyceum Theatre when they were in London. Grace Balcombe was to die in 1901 and Moore eventually remarried Dorothea Hatton. He died in 1931.

Bertha Maude, the other young sister we know so little about, was married in November 1886, to District Inspector Pierre Bavillier Pattison of the Royal Irish Constabulary at Clontarf.

During the summer of 1876 Oscar returned to Dublin to spend some time with his mother. He wrote to his friend Reginald Harding from Merrion Square, (Sunday, 6 August 1876): 'I am just going out to bring an exquisitely pretty girl to afternoon service in the Cathedral. She is just seventeen with the most perfectly beautiful face I ever saw and not a sixpence of money. I will show you her photograph when I see you next.' Oscar was still courting her the next spring, in May 1877, when he wrote again to Reginald Harding: 'Florrie [is] more lovely than ever.'

In April 1878, Oscar was writing to Florence from Bournemouth, and showing himself as a friend of the Balcombe family. 'I hope you are all well especially Gracie: Willie's success in the North is most encouraging.'

But a few months later, in the summer of 1878, Florence Balcombe was not only 'walking out' with Bram – they had already fixed the date of their wedding.

According to both Ludlam and Farson, the Balcombes had moved into a house next door to William Thornley Stoker's house in Harcourt Street. This is incorrect. Lieutenant-Colonel Balcombe and his family were still living at No. 1 Marino Crescent, Clontarf. Florence had, sometime in the period prior to her wedding in December 1878, gone to stay with William Thornley Stoker and his wife at No. 16 Harcourt Street. This is rather unusual for those days of adherence to etiquette. It was William Thornley's address that was given on Florence's letters at the time and on her marriage certificate. This seems to have misled both Ludlam and Farson.

Why had Florence given up Oscar Wilde for Bram Stoker? According to Ludlam and Farson, Florence Balcombe was a 'no nonsense' character and she preferred a more practical man, someone who did not have the outrageous lifestyle of the young poet. That is contradicted by Oscar's biographer, Richard Ellmann, who believed the break was due to Oscar: 'Wilde could not marry while still a student.' Ellmann also says that Oscar was suffering from syphilis at this time. He is, however, also a little disparaging of Florence.

Stoker was better than Wilde for Florence Balcombe, who had aspirations to become an actress. In any case, Wilde, though he now almost had his degree evidently did not feel he was in a position to marry. His obligatory two years' wait after syphilis had been diagnosed was not over. He wrote to her a proud and eternal farewell.

The letters, however, do seem to contradict the idea that it was Oscar who broke up the relationship. In fact, Oscar seems petulant. He wrote to Florrie from his mother's house in Merrion Square:

Though you have not thought it worth while to let me know of your marriage, still I cannot leave Ireland without sending you my wishes that you may be happy; I, at least, cannot be indifferent to your welfare; the currents of our lives flowed too long beside one another for that.

Oscar, in the same letter, demanded the return of a small golden cross that he had given her one Christmas with his name engraved on it.

I need hardly say that I would not ask it from you if it was anything you valued, but worthless though the trinket be, it serves as a memory of two sweet years – the sweetest of all the years of my youth – and I should like to have it always with me.

Oscar suggests that Florence use her sister, Philippa, as an intermediary as he was meeting her that Wednesday afternoon. He ended emotionally:

We stand apart now, but the little cross will serve to remind me of the bygone days, and though we shall never meet again, after I leave Ireland, still I shall always remember you at prayer. Adieu and God bless you. Oscar.

Florence, by return, wrote to suggest that Oscar come to 16 Harcourt Street, the Stoker household, to retrieve his present, but Oscar replied, now dropping the endearment 'Florrie' for 'Dear Florence':

I could not come to Harcourt Street: it would be painful for both of us: but if you would care to see me for the last time I will go out to the Crescent on Friday at two o'clock. Perhaps it would be better for us both if we saw one another once more.

He also promised to send back her letters when he returned to Oxford and enclosed a 'scrap I used to carry with me: it was written eighteen months ago: how strange and out of tune it all reads now'. Presumably this was a poem dedicated to Florence.

Whatever Florence replied, Oscar wrote again on Thursday:

Dear Florence, As you expressed a wish to see me I thought that your mother's house would be the only suitable place, and that we should part where we first met. As for my calling at Harcourt Street, you know, my dear Florence, that such a thing is quite out of the question: it would have been unfair to you, and me, and to the man you are going to marry, had we met anywhere else but under your mother's roof, and with your mother's sanction. I am sure that you will see this yourself on reflection; as a man of honour I could not have met you except with the full sanction of your parents and in their house.

When Florence finally made her stage debut at The Lyric on 3 January 1881, as a Vestal Virgin in *The Cup* by Alfred, Lord Tennyson, along with a hundred other young women, Oscar anonymously sent her a crown of flowers. He had sent one to Ellen Terry, whom he called 'Nellie', and enclosed the other. In his note he said:

The other – don't think me treacherous, Nellie – but the other please give to Florrie from yourself. I should like to think that she was wearing something of mine the first night she comes on the stage, that anything of mine should touch her. Of course if you think – but you won't think she will suspect? How could she?

She thinks I never loved her, thinks I forget. My God, how could I?

Oscar was eventually to marry another Irish girl, Constance Mary Lloyd, the daughter of a Dublin barrister, then living in London, in 1884.

That Oscar continued to be a friend of Florrie and Bram Stoker is seen in a letter sent on 21 February 1893 from Babbacombe Cliff in which he says:

My dear Florence, Will you accept a copy of *Salomé* – my strange venture in a tongue that is not my own, but that I love as one loves an instrument of music on which one has not played before. You will get it, I hope, tomorrow, and I hope you will like it. With kind regards to Bram, believe me, always your sincerely friend, Oscar Wilde.

Bram certainly accepted Florrie's and Oscar's previous *amour* with equanimity.

Oscar also remained friendly with Florrie's sister Philippa who married a Dr J. Freeman Knott of York Street, Dublin. He was a Fellow of the Royal Academy of Medicine, Ireland, and a Member of the Royal Irish Academy, and had published extensively on medical matters. On a visit to Dublin in January 1885, Oscar writes to 'My dear Phil' that he will visit them. 'Pray remember me to your husband and to all at the Crescent [Clontarf]: I will be delighted to see them and Florrie again.' Philippa's daughter, Dr Eleanor Knott, was to become a leading authority on Middle Irish and Early Modern Irish, publishing many scholarly works and translations of Middle Irish Poetry. Her first publication was *Foclóir d'Eisirt* (1910), a study of the vocabulary of the mythical poet Eisirt. Her most highly regarded works are *An Introduction to Irish Syllabic Poetry of the Period 1200–1600* (Cork University Press, 1928), *Irish Classical Poetry* (Dublin, 1957) and *Early Irish Literature* (with Professor Gerard Murphy, Routledge, 1966).

Lady Wilde, Willie and Oscar continued to socialise with the Stokers in London until the accusations made by the Marquess of Queensberry, the father of Lord Alfred Douglas. Oscar's unsuccessful libel action led to his prosecution for gross indecency and in May 1895 he was sentenced to two years in gaol. No evidence has come to light about Bram's attitude but on 16 July 1895, Willie Wilde wrote to him:

> Bram, my friend, poor Oscar was not as bad as people thought him. He was led astray by his Vanity & conceit, & he was so 'got at' that he was weak enough to be guilty of indiscretion and follies and lies – that is all – I believe this thing will help to purify him body and soul. Am sure you & Florence must have felt the disgrace of one who cares for you both sincerely.

In the light of the emotions Bram had expressed all those years earlier in his 'fan' letter to the American poet Walt Whitman, we are inclined to conclude that he sympathised with Willie's opinion and – in all probability – felt deeply, if secretly, for Oscar in his pain and humiliation.

CHAPTER EIGHT

George Stoker: The Real Progenitor of Dracula?

IN THE EARLY SUMMER OF 1878 Bram's youngest brother George returned to Dublin having spent two years as a surgeon with the Imperial Ottoman Army. Abdul-Hamid II's Turkish forces had smashed a Bulgarian insurrection in 1876 causing Russia to enter the war on behalf of their fellow Slavs. George had just turned twenty-one years in the summer of 1876. He was already a Licentiate of the Royal College of Surgeons, Ireland, and a Licentiate of the King's and Queen's College of Physicians, Ireland. He volunteered to serve as a surgeon in the Turkish army and arrived in Constantinople (Istanbul) on 27 August 1876.

George Stoker was not the first Irishman to serve in the Turkish army and to traverse the very ground where the historical Dracula fought against the Turks.

Indeed, both the Stoker and the Blake families had married into the Browne family of Galway, Mayo and Limerick, and herein lines a fascinating connection with Transylvania, the land Bram was to make synonymous with Dracula. It was a Browne from Moyne (Castle Mahan), Co. Limerick, who became Governor of Transylvania, on behalf of the Austrian empire, during the Russian-Austrian-Turkish War of 1736–39. Another Irishman, Charles O'Donnell, also of the Austrian service, became Governor of Transylvania from 1767 to 1770, as well as President of its government. Austria established its rule in Transylvania in 1711 and, as part of Hungary, it formed a province of the Austro-Hungarian empire from 1867 to 1918 when it was ceded to Romania. The Stoker family's connection with the Browne family, in this respect, is well worth considering.

Certainly, Transylvania and the Balkans generally were not as remote to the Irish as they seemed to be to the Victorian English. Thousands of Irish, banned from the professions of Ireland after the Williamite Conquest of 1691, had sought religious and social freedom in Europe, mainly in France and Spain. Many became soldiers and politicians in the Austrian empire. Christopher Duffy, in *The Wild Goose and the Eagle* (Chatto and Windus, 1964), points out that a small group of Irish exiles 'exercised an influence in Austrian politics out of all proportions to their numbers'. In the very year Bram left Dublin to settle in London an Irishman, Edward Taafe, became President of the Austrian Council of Ministers, the equivalent of Prime Minister. Among the Irish exiles in Austria was Maximilian Ulysses Browne of Moyne, Co. Mayo (1705–1757), who was educated in Co. Limerick. He commanded the O'Neillan (O Nualláin) Regiment of the Austrian army and rose to become Field Marshal and Governor of Prague being ennobled and using the style 'Count von Browne'.

His nephew, Count George Browne de Camas, also from Moyne, Co. Limerick (1698–1792), had served in the Russian army against the Turks. He was a major-general when he was captured by the Turks in a campaign to relieve Crotska and sold as a slave in a public slave market. He was bought by a merchant living in Adrianople (Edirne) where Bram's brother George was based for a while. Browne was made to carry sacks of currants between Adrianople and Constantinople. Browne's plight was noticed by an unnamed Irishman in the Turkish service who enlisted the help of the French ambassador to Constantinople, de Villeneuve, and they helped Browne escape. He was able to make his way back to St Petersburg bearing Turkish state secrets. His adventures did not end there for he became a friend of the Tsarina Catherine the Great.

He rose to become Field Marshal of the Russian army and Governor General of Livonia (modern-day Latvia). Browne is still regarded with honour in Latvia for in 1762 he ordered a thorough investigation into the conditions of the serfs and submitted far-reaching proposals on reforms to the Livonian Diet in 1765. He proposed that serfs be allowed time to cultivate land for themselves, that they should be able to own movable property, and that the barons' rights of punishment for trivial offences should be restricted. He also proposed to set up schools in every village and made literacy an obligation. In short, Browne tried to throw out feudal law but was met with outraged hostility by the barons. Sadly, his reforms were ignored.

There is another speculative link between the Stokers and Transylvania. Bram Stoker's brother Richard was, as we have seen, named Richard Nugent Stoker, from which we might speculate that the Stoker family had some connection with the famous Nugent family of Westmeath. It was Christopher Nugent, 14th Baron Delvin of Westmeath, who had compiled an Irish language primer to help Elizabeth I understand and converse with Gráinne Ní Máille during the Connacht chieftainess's famous visit to Greenwich. The Nugents fled to Europe after the Williamite Conquest; one was killed at the battle of Fontenoy (1745) and another became Governor of Prague. Robert Nugent (1702–1788) saved the family fortunes in Ireland by converting to Protestantism, making friends with the Prince of Wales and receiving the titles Viscount Clare and Earl Nugent. Before he died he converted back to Catholicism.

However, Count James Robert Nugent of Castelnugent was an officer in the Austrian army, fighting in Transylvania during the Turkish War of 1737. He became a Field Marshal in the Austrian service. The tradition of the Nugent exiles was that they returned to Ireland for the birth of their children. James' son Laval, who became an Austrian privy councillor and Field Marlshal, was born at Ballincor, Co. Wicklow in 1777. His son was born in Dublin in 1796. Laval Nugent commanded Austrian troops in Naples in 1816 and was created a prince of the Holy Roman Empire by Pope Pius VII. He was also made a magnate of Hungary, representing Transylvania, with an hereditary seat in the upper house of the Hungarian Diet. He died at Bosiljero, near Karlstadt, on 21 August 1862.

One can speculate whether the stories of these Irish military heroes permeated the household of the Stoker family of Clontarf whose ancestors they seem to have been. Irish exiles had fought in various armies in the Balkans for many centuries. In the eighteenth century the Austrian Emperor's Dalmatian army was commanded by General Thomas, Baron von Brady, from Co. Cavan, fighting against the Tsar's army commanded by Field Marshal Peter Lacy, from Co. Limerick.

During the period 1850 to 1855, by which time the Irish had a strong tradition of supplying military brigades to fight all over the world, plans by two Irishmen, Andrew O'Reilly and R. S. Moore, to form brigades for the Ottoman army were calculated to serve English interests in the Balkans. O'Reilly was the son of Andrew O'Reilly senior (d. 1862). The father was for many years the *Times* correspondent in Paris but was dismissed at the end of 1848 for extravagance. He was replaced by J. B. O'Meagher (author of *Reminiscences of an Emigrant Milesian*, 1853).

A General Colman, who is said to have fled to Turkey after the 1848 uprising in Ireland, became known as Fehti Bey, while a General Richard Guyon, (d.*c*.1856) a native of Cratloe, Co. Clare, also took service with the Turks and was known as Kurschid Pasha. Guyon served in Transylvania and in Wallachia, the home territories of the historical Dracula.

During the mid-1850s many Irishmen arrived in the town of Varna on the Black Sea as part of the British Army *en route* to the Crimea. The army of the Russian Tsar Nicholas I had occupied Dracula's principality of Wallachia, driving out the Turkish soldiers of the Sultan Abdul Medjid I. On 4 October England and France entered the war on the side of the Turks. This was known as the Crimean War, as most of the action was fought there. On 22 July 1854, the 31st Regiment from Fermoy, Co. Cork, arrived at Varna. Letters from Varna survive written by Francis Crotty of Mitchelstown, Co. Cork. The 31st Regiment was not the only Irish unit present. The 5th Dragoon Guards (The Green Horse) and the 7th Dragoon Guards were among several other Irish regiments assembled there.

Until the peace signed on 30 March 1856, Varna was a military encampment where many Irish regiments were stationed. Who knows what local history and legend they transmitted back to Ireland? Even more intriguing is the fact that Bram's father-in-law, then Lieutenant James Balcombe, passed through Varna with the 57th Regiment on his way to the Crimea, and Varna was used as the staging post when Balcombe and his regiment returned at the end of the war. The letters of Francis Crotty, who became an NCO and one of the only nine to be awarded a French War Medal, a Turkish Medal, the Crimean Medal and three clasps and a Good Conduct Medal, is full of fascinating facts about life in Varna. Of the Turkish army he says:

> I do not believe that any European nation had such a lot of ragamuffins. Their infantry wear white trousers; at least they might be once white, and a round jacket the same colour of the Irish Constabulary, a red cap called a fez with a small plate of brass on the centre of the crown, a blue tassel hanging behind the ear. Shoes they have the remains of, and some have pieces of old cloth and bits of hides tied round their feet. They carry a long queer looking flint gun and bayonet.

It was at Varna, on 10 November 1444, that the troops of the Turkish Saltan Murad II defeated his old ally Vlad Dracul II and his combined

army of Rumanians from Transylvania and Wallachia. This defeat paved
the way for Vlad Dracul's son Dracula, who had been a hostage of the
Turkish sultan, to assume the throne of Wallachia in 1448.

Vlad Dracul II had initially been an ally of the Turks when together
they crushed the independence of Serbia and Bulgaria in 1437, but he then
pursued an independent line, turning on his former Turkish allies. The
battle of Varna saw the rise of his son Dracula, the historic character, who
had served in the Turkish army. As soon as he was installed as ruler of
Wallachia, Dracula embarked on a similar policy of fighting the Turks,
becoming their most implacable foe, earning him the title of Vlad the
Impaler.

Vlad's victories over the Turks, such as that in 1461 when, during his
march south of the Danube near Zimnicea, he is said to have put 23,883
Turks to the sword, were still talked about as folklore throughout the area.
In December 1476 Dracula's enemy, the Turkish puppet-ruler, Laiota
Basarab, defeated and killed him with the aid of a Turkish army.

To the Rumanians and Bulgarians Dracula had become a national hero.
There were many poems written in the nineteenth century hailing his
heroic life, such as Dimitrie Bolintineanu's 'Battles of the Romanians'.
Even plays about Dracula, such as G. Mavrodullu's *Vlad Tepes*, a drama
in five acts, performed in Bucharest in 1856, were very popular. Certainly
any visitor to the area could not fail to encounter the legends, either of
Dracula as a hero, or of Dracula as the personification of evil, depending
whether you view him from the Rumanian or Turkish and Saxon
viewpoint.

Dracula's enemies, the Saxon settlers against whom he had conducted
campaigns, had begun to turn out propaganda against him as early as 1462.
Two of the oldest manuscripts about his atrocities were written in Low
German at this time, one of which survives, coincidentally, at the Irish
foundation of St Gallen in Switzerland (Gall was an Irish *religieux* who
established the monastery with a band of followers in 612). The other
manuscript survives in the Lambach monastery in Austria. They were the
start of the first 'Dracula industry'. No fewer than fourteen pamphlet
accounts from the period have been identified including Ambrosius
Huber's 1499 Nuremberg pamphlet entitled 'About the wild bloodthirsty
berserker, Dracula Voevod' and Matthias Hupnuff's pamphlet of the same
title published in Strasbourg in 1500. A 1491 pamphlet about Dracula
published in Bamberg was purchased by the British Museum before the
appearance of Stoker's novel and it has been argued that he consulted this.

When one examines the evidence, Dracula country does not seem so removed and isolated from Ireland after all. So when Bram's youngest brother George, with his new medical qualifications, left Ireland to seek service in the Turkish army, it was neither an unusual nor, perhaps, a surprising event.

Why did George decide to volunteer to serve the Turks? It is clear from his writings that he was very supportive of the Turks and had a dislike for Greeks, Bulgarians, Rumanians and the other small nationalities under Turkish rule. Certainly England's foreign policy at this time, as it had been in the Crimean War, was to support the Turkish empire against what was seen as the potential dangers of the Russian empire. George seemed to share his father's Unionist and High Tory background and this could have made him into a blind supporter of empire. He seems to have believed in the 'civilising vocation' of the Ottoman empire. However, there are records of many Irishmen serving in the Turkish forces at this time and not all were from the Unionist elements. In fact, in 1877 a Colonel O'Reilly (known as Hussein Bey) was to be found serving on the Turkish general staff; he is mentioned in H. M. Hozier's *Russo-Turkish War*. O'Reilly was a nationalist when it came to Ireland but apparently found no conflict in fighting for the Turkish empire.

Incidentally, Achmed Abdullah (1881–1945), the Eton-educated British Army officer who became a prolific writer for the pulp magazines in the realms of fantasy and mysticism and is most famous for his novel *The Thief of Bagdad* (1924), refers to Irishmen still in the service of the Turks during a later war. In his memoirs *The Cat Had Nine Lives*, he mentions the death of O'Gorman Pasha while leading a cavalry charge against Bulgarian guns at Adrianople during the Balkan War of 1912–13.

On the other hand the Irish independence movement knew clearly about the implications of the Russo-Turkish War and the fact that England's interest was to support the Turks against the Russians. The leaders of the Irish Republican Brotherhood's American wing, Clan na Gael, approached the Russian Ambassador to the USA, Nikolai Shishkin, with the proposal that the Russians should aid insurgents in Ireland. Clan na Gael felt that war between England and Russia was again possible in 1876–77 and believed that with Russian help the Irish insurgents could hold down a major part of the English army in Ireland to prevent them reinforcing the Turks as they had done in the Crimean War. Shishkin rejected the idea of entering into negotiations with the Irish Republican Brotherhood in the belief that the claims of a separatist, republican movement in Ireland were grossly inflated, according to John Devoy, in *Recollections of an Irish Rebel* (1929).

George Stoker expresses his reasons for siding with the Turks as simple prejudice.

For George, the Turk was 'educated as a thoroughly honest and trustworthy man' but 'my experience is that lying is more natural to the Greeks than truth, and, to my sorrow, I know that they never failed to swindle me when such a chance presented itself'. In spite of this statement, George's account of his time among the Turks shows that they, also, seized every opportunity to swindle him. Although he records the incidents, he passes over them without any disloyal comment. He had nailed his pro-Turk colours firmly to the mast and adhered to them. While it was the Ottoman suppression of the Christians in Bosnia-Herzegovina that was the immediate triggering point of this war by the nations fighting for independence against the Turkish empire, George blandly states: 'There is no doubt that the oriental Christians, especially, the Bulgarians, have been oppressed for centuries, *but they have prospered and become rich* [our italics].' One has to remind oneself how young George was and allow for some political naïvety on his part.

By contrast, however, Oscar Wilde, a year younger than George, was moved to write a sonnet on the massacre of the Bulgarian Christians by the Turks at this time, in which he despairingly cries:

> Come down, O Son of God! incestuous gloom
> Curtains the land, and through the starless night
> Over thy Cross a Crescent moon I see!
> If thou in very truth didst burst the tomb
> Come down, O Son of Man! and show thy might,
> Lest Mahomet be crowned instead of Thee!

Writing from Merrion Square in April 1877, Oscar sent a copy of this poem to William Ewart Gladstone (1809–98), then leader of the Liberal opposition to Disraeli's Tory government.

An indication of George's attitudes is made in the following passage:

An Italian from Cor-r-r-k [a play on the local pronunication of Cork, Ireland] who afterwards distinguished himself at Plevna, favoured us with 'The Wearing of the Green'; and to counterbalance the rebellious sentiment therein expressed we all sang, or rather howled, 'God Save the Queen'.

As an officer in the Turkish army, George was sent to the Bulgarian town of Tartar Bazardjick, near Philippopolis (Plovdiv). Here a local Jewish landowner had been thrown out of his house by the Turks, who converted it into a military hospital. George had another interesting tale to tell.

One morning, about four o'clock, the governor of the town sent for me, and said there was a countryman of mine who had arrived during the night, and that he had got a room in the *khan* [hotel], that nobody would go near him, and he begged me to find out what he wanted – adding, 'he has a revolver, and you had better approach cautiously.' Accordingly, I stole along the verandah, and peeping in at the window indicated, saw a wild-looking fellow stretched asleep on the bed with a revolver beside him. I retreated at once and got a long pole, and standing well to one side of the window, tapped loudly. The answer came through the window in the shape of three bullets. Then I heard some frightful cursing in broad Irish to the effect that the 'd--d ammunition was out'. So I approached the door and knocked, stating my nationality. This time my advances were better received, and the door was opened. I found my countryman was a doctor going to Nisch. I got him a place in a *britska* with an Armenian also going to the front.

Alas, George does not explain why the Irish doctor should have behaved in such a fashion.

It is significant that George appears to understand Irish, at least enough to know what the doctor was cursing about. By the late nineteenth century, most Anglo-Irish families had ceased to use Irish as the language was severely in decline during this period. There was no longer the need to use the language to 'communicate' with the native Irish. Some, however, did not drop the language. One intriguing personality, almost an exact contemporary of Bram's, and whom Bram met on the Dublin theatre circuit, was 'Barney' Fitzpatrick, Baron Castletown of Upper Ossory (1849–1937). A keen theatre-goer, Lord Castletown owned a 20,000 acre estate at Doneraille, Co. Cork, and a manor at Abbeyleix. He was a former colonel of the Prince of Wales' Leinster Regiment and a founder, with the then Lord Longford, of the Irish Loyal and Patriotic Union. Even so, he annoyed the English peers in the House of Lords by insisting on his right to address them in the Irish language. He would also turn up to Unionist meetings in an Irish saffron kilt and deliver a speech in Irish. Lord Ashbourne, on the other hand, not only wore a saffron kilt but refused to speak English. To those who knew no Irish he would speak only in French as an alternative.

In October 1876, Emily Anne, Viscountess Strangford, arrived in Bulgaria to distribute aid to the Bulgarian victims of atrocities. Lady Strangford was the widow of Viscount Percy, a President of the Royal Asiatic Society, who had thrown herself into charity and medical work in the Middle East, founding a hospital in Damascus and another in Beirut. Her most famous foundation was the Victoria Hospital in Cairo. She died on 24 March 1887, on board the *Lusitania* (this was, of course, an earlier ship than the famous Cunard liner which went down in 1915). Lady Strangford asked George Stoker if he would accompany her as she needed a doctor to look after the distribution of medical aid. George agreed, providing the Turkish army gave him leave. This was arranged by Lady Strangford, who had good connections with the Turkish authorities.

Lady Strangford and George made their way to Panagjuriste, a village in the Planina mountain range just east of Sofia. The Turks had first captured Sofia and the surrounding district in 1382 but in September 1443, the Wallachian ruler, Vlad Dracul, Dracula's father, liberated Sofia from them. The Turks eventually recaptured it with the fall of Dracula and it was not until 1596 that Wallachians drove the Turks out again. Uprisings and wars to throw the Turks out of the Balkans continued from then on. As George Stoker recorded: 'Panagurista [*sic*] was noted as having been the centre of the foolish and futile attempt that was made at insurrection during the early part of 1876.' Here, at least, George was able to talk with some of the people fighting the Turks and perhaps hear some of their side of the story.

> While I was in Panagurista I made the acquaintance of an insurgent who was in hiding there. He was a native of the place, and had been the standard bearer of the insurrection. The Government [Turks] were searching for him everywhere; but although he lived in the village, they never succeeded in catching him. He used to come out during the night for exercise and our house was his favourite resort.

Very often he brought a three stringed banjo with him, and used to entertain us with rebellious songs. He was a very fine fellow, almost the only Bulgarian I ever met who had any courage – tall, well built, with fierce black eyes, and an enormous black moustache – in fact, the very picture of an insurgent. He was noted for his powers of endurance . . .

In this mountain area, George was well placed to hear tales of Vlad Dracul and his son, Vlad Tepes, Vlad the Impaler, otherwise known as Dracula, and the many strange legends which had been built up about him.

On 21 May 1877, Rumania also declared independence from Turkey. Mihail Kogalniceanu, Minister for Foreign Affairs, declared: 'We are not depending on any authority, we are an independent nation . . . we are a free and independent nation.' Rumania then allowed a Russian army under the Grand Duke Nicholas, cousin to the Tsar, to march through its territory to face the Turkish army of Abdul Kerim. The Russians were joined by Rumanians and marched across the Danube.

George now volunteered to accompany a Turkish task force going to Soukoum Kaleh on the Black Sea in eastern Turkey under the command of Feizly Pasha. The plan was an attempt to prevent the Russians driving through Armenia across the eastern border. George was the only European with this Turkish army. He sailed with them on the *Esseri Djid* to Trebzond (Trabzon) and then went on to Kars.

General Count Mikhail Loris-Melikov assaulted Kars and, after a savage encounter, the Turks under Ahmed Mukhtar Pasha fell back to Erzurum having lost 7000 killed and wounded. George accompanied the retreat and then was ordered to return to Constantinople. He was now appointed *Chef de l'Ambulance du Croissant Rouge* (the Red Crescent equivalent of the Red Cross). As Chief of Ambulance he was placed in command of a dozen ambulance wagons and a mobile hospital and sent back to the Bulgarian front. He arrived at Plevna (Pleven) in time for the start of the siege of its Turkish garrison from 19 July to 10 December. Units of Rumania's 4th Division were involved in the first onslaughts. Plevna was under the command of Marshal Osman Nuri Plasha with 30,000 troops. After several attempts to break out, Osman Pasha finally surrendered to a Rumanian Colonel Cerchez, commanding the Reserve Division.

Meanwhile, before the fall of the town, George had been sent to General Suleiman Pasha's army holding the Shipka Pass where General Fedor

Radelski was pressing forward. The Turks held the Russians back from 21 August until 8 January. Then the Russian General Osip Gurko took command of a reinforced Russian army and launched a new offensive which saw 4000 Turks killed and 36,000 wounded at a cost of only 5000 Russians killed and wounded. The end of the war was in sight with Plovdiv (Philippopolis) falling on 17 January and Edirne (Adrianople) shortly afterwards.

For George, this was undoubtedly the worst part of the campaign.

It is a terrible feeling, and one which I hope that few of my readers may ever have to experience, to see hundreds, nay, – as I saw at Schipka [*sic*] – thousands of men lying prostrate without help or hope; to hear the half suppressed groans and sharp, wild cries of pain, to pass amongst acres of dead and dying, feeling bewildered, and not knowing why, where to turn, or where to begin! It is terrible to see strong men, overcome with cold, and pain, and hunger, gradually succumbing, to know all the time that even a little help, opportunity given, would have saved them, and might still save were it to hand. In Plevna the wounded were without help, for the doctors' hands were idle for want of splints. In Schipka, were it not for the prompt concurrence of Suleiman Pasha with my view, in giving me *carte blanche* for the use of the Red Crescent Ambulance, then under my charge, to bring the wounded to Philippopolis that terrible Pass would have been memorable for the death of many hundreds of men more than the number that even now rest on its slopes.

George, with a column of Red Crescent doctors and nurses, was captured by Cossacks on 17 January 1878, near Ashkala. They were taken to the headquarters of General Sistovitch at Illidja who treated them well and telegraphed his high command at Tiflis for instructions. The Red Crescent doctors were then released. They crossed to join the Turkish force of General Ahmed Mukhtar again in Erzurum, on the upper Kara Su (western Euphrates), where they were besieged by Count Mikhail Loris-Melikov's forces. George points out that there were thirty-five European doctors in Erzurum when the siege started, of whom twenty-three died before the town surrendered on 31 March. He does not bother to record the number of Turkish doctors or doctors of non-European nationalities who also died.

When the news came of the surrender of the town, George writes:

... immediately the priests (mullahs) rushed to the minarets of the mosques and called on the faithful to defend themselves against the 'Giaour';. At once the men and boys seized their arms, and the women ran shrieking through the street, calling on their sons and fathers and brothers to defend them.

'Giaour' is a Muslim term of contempt for an unbeliever and is sometimes used in the Balkans as an alternative name for an 'Un-dead'. One is reminded of Lord Byron's poem 'The Giaour' (1813):

> But first on earth, as Vampyre sent,
> Thy corpse shall from its tomb be rent;
> Then ghastly haunt thy native place,
> And suck the blood of all thy race . . .

George managed to leave Erzurum on 31 March, avoiding capture, and fourteen days later he was back in Constantinople. The Russians, with Rumanian, Serbian, Montenegrin, Bulgarian and other allies, had pushed the Turks back to the Chatalja (Catalca) line just outside the Turkish capital. The Turks finally agreed to abide by the Treaty of San Stefano on 3 March 1878, which allowed independence to Serbia, Montenegro, Rumania and Bulgaria, and gave the administration of Cyprus to Great Britain. The war over, George was awarded a Turkish medal for his services – Champcharee, 4th class, Medjiide.

Before leaving the area, George travelled to Bourgas (Burgus) and on to Varna where he found the United Kingdom consul was an Irishman named Brophy; his brother, A. Brophy, showed George the historical sites of the area. If George had not encountered the legends of Vlad Dracula before at Sofia, he surely must have done so in Varna.

We contend that George Stoker, returning to Dublin in 1878 with his tales of the campaigns in the Balkans, was undoubtedly the main and, perhaps, the initial source for his brother's interest in the historical character of Dracula. It is amazing that other researchers, attempting to link Bram with the historical Dracula, have singularly failed to consider the role of Bram's brother George.

George was so full of stories about the campaigns in the Balkans that Bram, it is claimed by the family, encouraged him to sit down and get it all on paper; later that year, in December 1878, his book about the war was published – *With 'The Untouchables', or Two Years campaigning in*

European and Asiatic Turkey. The book appeared just before Bram left Dublin for good. While issued under the imprint of Chapman and Hall of London, it was actually printed and published by John Falconer, of 53 Upper Sackville Street, Dublin. There was good reason for this, for Bram had been in contact with John Falconer throughout the year and doubtless recommended his brother's book to him.

Bram, of course, had been compiling his own book linked to his job as Inspector of the Petty Sessions which Falconer was to publish: *The Duties of Clerks of Petty Sessions in Ireland*. He finished it the very month his brother's book appeared and wrote his introduction on 31 December 1878. The book was published a few months later in 1879 and remained a standard work for many years.

It has been argued that another contemporary of Bram's at Trinity College might well have been a source of information on the Balkans. This was James David Bourchier from Co. Limerick, who had been at Trinity while Bram was there, although slightly younger than Bram. He was appointed the Balkan correspondent for *The Times* in 1888. Bourchier was not content to be an observer of events but acted as an intermediary between the Cretan insurgents against Turkish rule and the Greek government. He also took part in the secret negotiations which resulted in a Balkan alliance against the Ottoman empire. Wandering through Greece and the Balkans, Bourchier finally settled in Sofia, which – since the victory over the Turks in 1878 – was now the capital of an independent Bulgaria. Bourchier wrote an introduction to a volume entitled *The Bulgarian Peace Treaty* (1920). He eventually died in Sofia and was given a state funeral at the Rilo Monastery. Ellinore Grogan became his biographer with *The Life of J. D. Bourchier*.

Some, noticing the connection, have specualted that Bram could have been fed material by Bourchier. This is certainly a possibility, reinforced by the fact that Bourchier's younger brother, Arthur, and his wife were Lyceum actors at the time Bram was manager there. Arthur wrote introductions to both *The Dramatic Author's Companion* (1910) and *The Actor's Companion* (1912) and wrote lengthier studies on the theatre with *Some Reflections on the Drama* (Basil Blackwell, Oxford, 1911) and *Art and Culture in Relation to Socialism* (Independent Labour Party, London, 1926).

In August 1878 Irving had arrived for a short tour. Bram and his brother William Thornley met him at Kingstown (Dún Laoghaire). Bram's brother was now one of the pillars of the medical establishment in Dublin. He had left the City Hospital to become chief surgeon at Swift's Hospital in 1876;

he was a Professor of Anatomy and Fellow of the Royal University, and an Honorary Professor of Anatomy at the Royal Academy; and he was already publishing several academic papers in connection with his profession. Both Ludlam (p. 50) and Farson (p. 37) state that Irving stayed with William Thornley 'at his home in Kingstown'. Of course, William Thornley's house was then at 16 Harcourt Street. There was a 'Mrs Stoker' living in Kingstown, at 28 Clarinda Park in 1875 and later at 1 Royal Terrace East in 1878. This was not Bram's mother, however, nor, of course, William Thornley's wife. We have to assume that Irving must have stayed in Harcourt Street and not in Kingstown. Bram accompanied Irving on trips to Bray, Leixlip and Belfast. He also introduced him to his fiancée, Florence Balcombe. Irving then returned to Ireland in September for another two weeks of performances and further discussed the plan for Bram to become his manager.

In November came a telegraph summons from Irving, then in Glasgow. Bram headed there immediately. Irving had acquired a lease on the Lyceum Theatre in London and planned to open a season there on 31 December. He now asked if Bram would become his manager as they had been planning for so long. His initial salary would be £22 per week. Bram agreed. He would not be the first Irishman and graduate of Trinity College to manage London's Lyceum Theatre. John Brougham (1814–1880), the Dublin actor and dramatist, after graduating from Trinity and abandoning a career in medicine, took to the stage and became manager of the Lyceum in 1840. He wrote over seventy plays and libretti for operas. Bram now headed back to Dublin to make a whirlwind of arrangements: resigning from the civil service and finishing his book for clerks of the Petty Sessions. His final act, before leaving Dublin, was to marry Florence Balcombe.

Florrie and Bram were married at St Anne's church, the famous neo-Romanesque building in Dawson Street, on 4 December 1878. Bram was now thirty-one years old; Florrie was twenty. Bram was still living at No. 7 St Stephen's Green North, while Florrie gave her address, as we have mentioned, as that of Bram's brother at No. 16 Harcourt Street. Bram's best man and witness was Thomas W. Martelli, who had worked with him and was now Registrar of Petty Sessions Clerks Office. This seems to contradict Professor Belford's theory that Bram did not get on with his fellow workers at Dublin Castle and avoided them outside working hours. Philippa Anne Balcombe was the second witness. It would seem that this was Florrie's sister even though the middle name is given as 'Anne' and not 'Annie' for her mother usually gave her name as 'Phillippa Anne'. Five days later Bram and Florrie left for England. They were to join Irving and his company, who were finishing a tour in Birmingham, before setting up home in London.

Bram continued to return to his native country fairly regularly. We know that Florrie also returned and, in 1885, was staying with her parents in Clontarf. A photograph of Florence taken at a Dublin ball appeared in *The Gentlewoman* of 6 February 1897. Bram would visit his mother in Rathgar, his brother William Thornley and sister Margaret and her husband in central Dublin. He would also attend Trinity College functions and was there, significantly, in 1892 when Professor Arminius Vambéry of the University of Buda-Pesth (Budapest, the city founded by the historical Dracula) received an honorary degree. Of Vambéry we will have more to say later. Bram would also return when he accompanied Irving on theatrical business.

Indeed, Bram was not only in Dublin in 1907 but also in Belfast. He utilised this visit to write two articles for the May 'Irish Special' number of *The World's Work*. In an article 'The Great White Fair in Dublin', Bram wrote of his visit to the scene of some boyhood adventures at Donnybrook where a 'New Exhibition' had risen on the site of the old Donnybrook fairground. The fair had officially been sanctioned in 1204 although there are references to fairs held in the area going back to the seventh century. The fair lasted for a week, including 'Walking Sunday'. It was increasingly criticised in the nineteenth century for its drunkenness and lewd standards of behaviour, and by 1855 a body of people containing both Catholic and Protestant clergy, led by such men as George Nugent, the Marquess of Westmeath, had persuaded the Lord Mayor of Dublin, Joseph Boyce, to close it. But the Dillon family, who owned the fairground, fought a running battle with the authorities so that it was not until 1868, when Bram was a twenty-one-year-old Trinity student, that the fair was finally closed. It is obvious that Bram, like most Dubliners of the middle class, would have attended some of the fairs.

His second article described his impressions upon visiting the famous Harland and Wolff shipyard in Belfast. This was where the White Star liner *Titanic* was to be built, only to sink on its maiden voyage a week or so before Bram died.

The regular visits to Ireland apart, from 1879 Bram's home would be in London and his brother George would soon follow him there. In fact, of the five Stoker brothers, only William Thornley was to remain in Dublin all his life.

Some, seeking to justify the 'English' epithet for Bram, have argued that
once he left Ireland, he turned his back on his country of birth. This, as
we have shown, was patently not so. And, indeed, when W. B. Yeats and
some fellow Irish literary exiles in London formed the Irish Literary
Society in 1892, Bram, along with other Irish writers, became a firm
supporter of the society. It has been suggested that he was introduced to
the society by Maurice Comerford, a fellow Dubliner, who was editor of
The Stage, and a confidant of Bram. On the other hand, Bram's old Dublin
friend and former neighbour, John Todhunter, was one of the three
founding members of the society and doubtless it was he who persuaded
Bram to join.

The objects of the society were to afford a centre of social and literary
intercourse for persons of Irish nationality, and to promote the study of
the Irish language, history, literature, music and art. Charles Gavan Duffy,
who was then living mainly in the south of France but also kept a house in
London, became its first president. Lady Wilde was an early member
along with the actress Maud Gonne and the Harmsworth brothers, Alfred
and Harold, from Chapelizod, Co. Dublin. Alfred became Viscount
Northcliffe and Harold became Lord Rothermere, two of the major names
in publishing. It was Alfred who conceived *Tit Bits* and *Answers* and
founded Amalgamated Press, turning it into the largest publishing empire
of its kind in the world, taking control of *The Times* in 1908. (Incidentally,
Chapelizod, now a suburb of Dublin, was a town which featured in many
of Sheridan Le Fanu's weird stories, a place he described as a 'melancholy
and mangled old town . . .' with 'the village church, with its tower dark
and rustling from base to summit, with thick-piled, bowering ivy . . .')

The Irish Literary Society, which continues in existence today, attracted
a wide variety of members, from Sir Robert Stawell Ball (1840–1913),
Astronomer-Royal for Ireland, also a Trinity College graduate, to Michael
Davitt (1846–1906) the former republican revolutionary, sentenced to
fifteen years' penal servitude for being the organising secretary of the Irish
Republican Brotherhood. He became a founder of the Irish National Land
League and Member of Parliament in 1882. Every well-known Irish
literary figure who lived in London, or was passing through the city,
became enrolled in the Irish Literary Society.

The secretary of the society at this time was yet another Trinity College
man, from Co. Offaly, Thomas William Hazen Rolleston (1857–1920), also
a *Kottabos* contributor and one of whose essays had been on Walt
Whitman's *Leaves of Grass*. He was editor of the *Dublin University Review*,

which sought to replace the *Dublin University Magazine*. He had also studied in Germany from 1879 to 1883 and given a series of lectures at Oxford on modern German literature. Among his better known books were *Imagination and Art in Gaelic Literature*, 1900, and *Myths and Legends of the Celtic Race*, 1911, still in print today from Constable. Rolleston could well have reinforced Bram's youthful memories of Irish folklore and mythology and pointed him to the Gothic tradition and Germany's extensive vampire literature.

Stoker was at the annual dinner of the Irish Literary Society in the autumn of 1896 when Arthur Conan Doyle, recent creator of another legendary fictional character, Sherlock Holmes, took the chair. Bram knew Conan Doyle through the Lyceum and the staging by Irving of his first play *Waterloo*, performed in 1894. It was Bram who read the script; when Irving asked him what he thought of it, he replied: 'I think this, that that play is never going to leave the Lyceum. You must own it – at any price. It is made for you.' Doyle's play had originally been called 'A Straggler of '15' but it was Irving who changed the title. Doyle was to send Bram a letter of congratulations on the publication of his novel *The Mystery of the Sea* in 1902. At the 1896 Irish Literary Society dinner the thirty-eight-year-old Doyle was said to have astounded his audience by blandly assuring them that the best in Irish literature was not produced by native Irish writers but 'by those with Saxon blood'.

> The Celt is the most conservative of mankind. His thoughts turn backwards, and his virtues and his vices are alike those of his prehistoric ancestor. His life in Ireland is one of unremitting toil, and with a soul which is full above all others of fire and sympathy and humour, he has spent himself in dreams upon the hillside or stories round the winter fire. Give him culture, give him that Catholic University of which we hear, and Celtic Ireland may send its Renans and its Pierre Lotis to London as Celtic Britanny sends them to Paris.

There must have been a certain irony in Doyle's statement unless the vanity of the man blinded him. One can, to a degree, understand his vehement support of the empire but the arguments in his speech are curious. There was little of 'Saxon blood' in Doyle, who was the grandson of a dispossessed native Irish Catholic family. The name Doyle could not be more Celtic, being the Anglicised form of Ó Dubhghaill (black stranger).

Conan Doyle's grandmother Marianna Conan, who gave him his middle name, also could not have possessed a more Celtic name: it means 'hound' or 'wolf'. His grandfather, John Doyle, had fled to England ironically to escape the English colonial Penal Laws against Catholics and Dissenters which were being enforced in Ireland. His father Charles had been raised a devout Catholic. His mother was Mary Foley, the name being the Anglicised form of Ó Foghladha (plunderer), a Co. Waterford family. Conan Doyle was born and raised in Scotland and given the name of the great Celtic hero, Arthur. And here he was, addressing a society devoted to Irish literature, particularly that in the Irish language. One could, perhaps, forgive Doyle's ignorance of the fact that the Irish language was Europe's third oldest written language (after Greek and Latin) and that its literary wealth was beyond measure, but one would have expected him to be more circumspect in his address. The confusion between the meaningless concept of race (i.e. 'blood') and culture was, alas, all too common. No wonder the Irish Literary Society were somewhat taken aback by his outburst.

Bram was later to interview Conan Doyle at his house at Hindhead, Surrey, for *The World* (New York, 28 July 1907), reflecting on his career, work and marriage. This was later reprinted in an abridged version in the London *Daily Chronicle* of 14 February 1908. It is interesting that Conan Doyle made no reference to his paternal Irish lineage but said:

> But my real love for letters, my instinct for storytelling, springs, I believe, from my mother, who is of Anglo-Celtic stock, with the glamour and romance of the Celt very strongly marked. Her I do resemble physically, and also in character, so that I take my leanings towards romance rather from her side than my father's.

When Ivan Stokes Dixon said, 'The creator of *Dracula* was born, raised, lived and died as an Irishman. To separate him from his culture is impossible,' he was making a very valid point about culture, not 'race'.

A knowledge of Bram Stoker's nationality and background is essential to an understanding of his personality and work. His fascination with the supernatural and weird in literature was, we believe, the result of his cultural background. Irish writers, writing both in their own language as well as in English, often choose subjects where there is a tendency to suspend natural laws. They have the enviable ability to present breaks in natural laws as vivid and realistic. Fantasy, especially the fantasy of the macabre, has been a fascinating tradition in Irish writing, dating from early mythology and folklore to modern times. Had Stoker not come from such a background then *Dracula* might never have become an intricate part of world folklore.

CHAPTER NINE

The Writing of 'The Un-Dead'

WHEN AND WHERE Bram Stoker actually began to work on *Dracula* has been the subject of a great deal of argument and controversy. As with many elements concerning the book's creation, the facts have, with the passage of time, become obscured in rumour, myth and plain nonsense.

The story which Stoker liked to tell – because it was a good story and he was a man of the arts who knew all about the value of publicity – suggested that the idea had come to him in a nightmare. It was a concept that had several notable literary progenitors, in particular Charles Dickens' *A Christmas Carol* (1843), Robert Louis Stevenson's *The Strange Case of Dr Jekyll and Mr Hyde* (1888) and, of course, the other great classic of the horror genre, *Frankenstein*, begun by Mary Shelley after a night of fearful dreams in 1816.

Harry Ludlam gave posthumous credibility to this colourful story in his biography of Stoker, explaining that Bram's restless sleep had followed from 'a too generous helping of dressed crab at supper one night'. Although the picture of Bram tossing and turning in his bed with images of a blood-sucking creature prowling about in his mind is an intriguing one, and certain to appeal to any journalist seeking copy, the account is quite apocryphal. Nor is it possible to give any more credence to a claim made to Ludlam by Stoker's son Noel (who was eighteen when *Dracula* was published) that his father's nightmare had been specifically about 'a vampire King rising from the tomb to go about his ghastly business'.

Another account has suggested that *Dracula* was written as the result of a bet Stoker made with a fellow writer. This tale originated with the writer Louis Jelf-Petit (1844–1913) and was made public in December 1971, by Jelf-Petit's grandson, F. H. Tate, in a letter to *The Times*. Mr Tate claimed that his grandfather had known Stoker 'when they were both young men' and he had told him an account of the writing of *Dracula* that he had never heard elsewhere. 'The story was,' wrote Mr Tate, 'that Bram Stoker and a friend entered into a wager as to which could write a more horrible and frightening story. When the time limit for the wager had expired and the tales were submitted to the adjudicator, it was decided that Bram Stoker had lost his bet. The other story has never been published!'

Again this is a colourful story about an event without a single fact to substantiate it. Exhaustive research that we have conducted among the literary remains of Bram Stoker's friends and acquaintances – both those of his youth and others he knew around the time he was writing the book – has failed to unearth a single candidate for this author whose manuscript, if we are to believe the Jelf-Petit account, was superior to Stoker's masterpiece.

The theme of a book being written for a wager often crops up. *Frankenstein* was also said to be the result of a friendly competition between Byron, Shelley, his wife Mary and Dr Polidori, as to who could create the best tale of terror. Peter Berresford Ellis, in his biography of Henry Rider Haggard – *A Voice from the Infinite* (1978) – reveals that *King Solomon's Mines* (1885) was written after a wager between Haggard and one of his brothers, when Haggard said he could write a book just as good as Robert Louis Stevenson's *Treasure Island* which had just been published.

The brutal murders committed by Jack the Ripper in London in 1888 have also been advanced as the inspiration for the book. It has been suggested that the Ripper's violence and the subsequent public panic so caught Bram's imagination that he planned a book about a man of the night preying on unsuspecting victims, and this eventually developed into *Dracula*. Again this contention, advanced by the historian Professor Grigore Nandris (1895–1968), has absolutely nothing to substantiate it. Nor is there any evidence to support an equally imaginative theory advanced in America some years ago that *Dracula* is actually a cryptic novelisation of the Jack the Ripper case based on certain secrets known only to Bram and a close circle of friends.

A fourth source, which has been even more widely circulated, claims that Stoker was inspired as a result of a meeting in the spring of 1890 with a Hungarian-born expert on the supernatural, Professor Arminius Vambéry (1832–1913). This vain, rather pompous man, with his thick, black beard, heavily lidded eyes and domed forehead, was certainly amongst those who enjoyed the after-performance hospitality of Sir Henry Irving in his Beefsteak Room above the auditorium of the Lyceum, and in all probability did delight his fellow diners, amongst them Stoker, with his talk of adventures and travels. But there is not a scrap of evidence that he subsequently entered into a correspondence with Bram about the vampire lore of Transylvania and by so doing gave the book its authentic flavour as Ludlam, especially, has claimed.

Vambéry was certainly an extraordinary figure, as his biography *Arminius Vambéry: His Life and Adventures*, published in 1883, makes very evident. Born in Budapest, he had a gift for languages, being able to speak sixteen, and spent many years travelling in central Asia, disguising himself as a dervish in order to discover the origins of the Magyar language, as well as tracking the footsteps of Marco Polo. Eventually he took the less rigorous job of Professor of Oriental Languages at the University of Budapest where he lorded it over staff and students alike. He produced a number of books about his expeditions including *Travels in Central Asia* (1864) and *The Story of My Struggles* (1886). A great Anglophile, Vambéry also wrote a number of letters and essays for English publications and visited the country on several occasions where his obvious interest in fostering British interests in Asia gained him access to the highest political circles. His honours included the Grand Cordon of Medjide and the Japanese Order of the Holy Treasure, and in 1889, he was made a Commander of the Royal Victorian Order and lionised by fashionable society.

The professor attended the Lyceum on 30 April 1890 to see a performance of Irving in *The Dead Heart* and afterwards dined in the Beefsteak Room. Stoker saw Vambéry once more in Ireland in 1892 when the professor was receiving an honorary degree from Trinity College. But it was at the meeting in the Beefsteak Room that Stoker later recalled asking the Hungarian if he had ever been afraid of death during his travels and being somewhat taken aback when Vambéry tapped his jacket and said that he always protected himself against the danger of capture and torture by carrying a vial of poison hidden behind the lapel. According to Ludlam's biography, the professor also 'spoke of places where mystery and intense superstition still reigned: places like Transylvania. It was then that Count Dracula began to stir in his tomb.' Bram's subsequent biographer, his great-nephew Daniel Farson, went even further: 'There is good reason to assume that it was the Hungarian professor who told Bram, for the first time, of the name of Dracula.'

Convincing as these statements may seem to be, coming from writers with contacts with the Stoker family, Bram himself made no reference to Transylvania, vampires or even the name of Dracula being mentioned by Vambéry in his highly autobiographical two volumes of *Personal Reminiscences of Henry Irving* in which he devotes a couple of pages to the meeting with Vambéry.

Nor have any letters between Stoker (a prolific letter writer) and Vambéry ever come to light. Further, there is not a single mention of Dracula, vampires or even Vlad the Impaler, the favoured role model for the 'Un-Dead Count', in any of Professor Vambéry's voluminous writings.

This is not to deny the versatile Hungarian at least a small part in the legend of Dracula. For in Chapter Eighteen of the novel, Van Helsing refers to 'my friend Arminius of Buda-Pesth University' and his request to him 'to make his record; and, from all the means there are, he tell me of what he [Dracula] has been.' It appears self-evident to us that Ludlam – and those who have taken his account as gospel – transposed fiction into fact as the basis for the claims regarding 'co-operation' between the two men.

Bram's son, Noel, is also the authority cited for the information that his father began work on *Dracula* 'in 1895 or 1896'. In fact, now that Bram's working papers are available for examination, it is quite clear that he had started on the book at least five years earlier. The documents, which comprise three packages consisting of eighty pages of notes, are part of the Philip H. and A. S. W. Rosenbach Foundation in Philadelphia, and are in excellent condition considering they are now over a hundred years old.

This remarkable collection, which represents the gestation of *Dracula*, consists of a number of typewritten pages and numerous sheets of paper covered in Stoker's scrawling, almost illegible handwriting. Clearly he had used anything to hand when making his preliminary notes, for among the items are pieces of notepaper embossed with the insignia of the Lyceum Theatre and several sheets of hotel stationery including one from a Philadelphia hotel which, as we shall show, has especial significance. The typewritten pages are also significant in indicating that Stoker had made himself familiar with this labour-saving new invention ahead of most of his contemporaries and then used it later to type out the whole manuscript.

The documents include descriptions of people, places and customs in the vicinity of the River Danube, notes on superstitions, animal behaviour, the theories of dreams, certain types of head and neck wounds, plus a number of curious inscriptions from tombstones and some train timetables. Further, there are records of conversations with fishermen and coastguards and details copied from the *Fishery Barometer Manual* (1887) by Robert H. Scott, the secretary of the Meteorological Office, relevant to storms and shipwrecks.

Of particular interest are the sheets of notes about the plot of the novel itself; Stoker was at one time evidently intending to set it in Styria, the home of Le Fanu's 'Carmilla', and to feature a vampire countess. Both of these are scored out and a footnote on another page, similarly deleted, reveals that Bram considered naming his anti-hero 'Count Wampyr'! Completing this Pandora's box is a clipping from the *New York World* of 2 February 1896, headlined 'Vampires in New England', and more typed extracts from three books: *Magyarland: Being the Narrative of our Travels Through the Highlands and Lowlands of Hungary* by 'A Fellow of the Carpathian Society', published by Sampson Low in 1881, which he used for some of his scenic details; *On the Track of the Crescent: Erratic notes from the Piraeus to Pesth* by Major E. C. Johnson, published by Hurst and Blackett in 1885, utilised as a source of history; and, perhaps most interestingly of all, *An Account of the Principalities of Wallachia and Moldavia*, by William Wilkinson, to which we shall return shortly.

Unfortunately, because only a few of these items are dated, it is impossible to put them in the precise order in which Bram Stoker wrote them. However, the date on the earliest document does dispel once and for all the idea that he did not begin work on the novel until the mid-1890s.

The crucial document is a handwritten sheet of paper dated 8 March 1890, which is doubly significant because it is also an outline of the first section of *Dracula* and matches almost precisely the final published version. The notes make it clear that right from the beginning Stoker intended the story to be told in a series of letters and journals.

This literary formula was first attempted by Wilkie Collins in *The Woman in White* (1860). Collins wrote in his preface to the original edition of the novel:

An experiment is attempted in this novel, which has not (so far as I know) been hitherto tried in fiction. The story of the book is told throughout by the characters of the book. They are all placed in different positions along the chain of events; and they all take the chain up in turn, and carry it on to the end.

It is of passing interest that here is another link in the Irish umbilical cord: William Wilkie Collins, author of the first detective mystery novel in English literature, was the grandson of the Irish writer William Collins (*c.* 1740–1812) of Co. Wicklow, known for his rather curious books, the *Memoir of George Morland* and *The Story of a Picture*. Wilkie Collins' father was a well-known landscape painter and became a Royal Academician who named his son after the painter Sir David Wilkie. The name of Wilkie Collins (1824–1889), who was brought up in London and Italy, is now synonymous with the mystery genre not only for *The Woman in White* but for *The Moonstone* (1868).

In his work notes, Stoker summarised what were to be the contents of these letters and diaries in one or two lines. The first thing that catches the eye is that Dracula is unnamed, and there is no reference to vampires beyond a description of a mysterious being living in a castle in Styria described as 'an old dead man made alive . . . waxen colour'.

According to the notes, several of the early letters are to be addressed to the old man by his solicitor concerning his affairs in England. This lawyer is evidently Jonathan Harker, although he is not named. The young man also features in another early scene outlined by Stoker and set in the castle, in which he confronts three voluptuous young women. 'Young man goes out – sees girls – one tries to kiss him not on lips but throat. Old Count interferes – rage and fury diabolical – This man belongs to me – I want him – a prisoner for a time – '

Another set of handwritten papers dated 14 March 1890 specifically outlines the four main sections of the book. It has evidently been reworked by the author at least once and carries several deletions and additions. Aside from the titles of the sections and the names of those involved, Styria has been altered to Transylvania and a location has been decided upon for the opening episode in England: the town of Whitby.

Today, because of the fame of Bram's novel, Whitby, which huddles in a cleft of the River Esk to avoid the full fury of the North Sea gales, draws 'scores of people searching for the non-existent grave of the fictitious vampire', according to a recent *Daily Express* story. Notwithstanding this, it does still have a slightly sinister reputation which was not helped when the national press reprinted a story from the local newspaper, the *Whitby Gazette* of 24 March 1994, while we were conducting our research. In this it was reported that during a soccer match the town's goalkeeper had been taken to hospital suffering from a sudden loss of memory. 'It was really strange,' the club secretary was quoted as saying, 'but there was no sign of injury apart from two small marks on his neck.'

Whitby would prefer to be known as the birthplace of two famous seafarers, Captain James Cook, whose ship the *Endeavour* carried him around the world on three remarkable voyages of exploration, and the less celebrated William Scoresby, a whaler who accounted for 533 whales during his long voyages and invented the first 'crow's nest'; however, it was the visit of Bram Stoker that forever changed its reputation in world opinion.

Bram, Florence and their son Noel, who had been born in London on 29 December 1879, arrived in the town during the second week of August 1890. They took lodgings at 6 Royal Crescent. What made them decide to take a three-week vacation there? It is interesting that also staying in Whitby during that August was George du Maurier (1834–1896), the novelist and illustrator who was the father of actor-director Gerald du Maurier and grandfather of novelist Daphne du Maurier. George certainly knew the Stokers and, indeed, had published a cartoon of them in the 11 September 1886 edition of *Punch* entitled 'A Filial Reproof'. It showed Bram and Florence reclining in wicker chairs at a country house party. Noel stands behind his mother. The caption reads: 'Mamma to Noel, who is inclined to be talkative, "Hush Noel! Haven't I told you often that little Boys should be *Seen* and not *Heard*?" Noel: "Yes, mamma! But you don't Look at me!"' This has been interpreted by the 'psychological school' to fuel their assessment of the Stokers' relationship and Florence's attitude as a parent, but it was surely never intended to be taken so seriously.

Almost as soon as they arrived, the Stokers were invited to tea with the English biographer and novelist Violet Hunt (1866–1942). Her father was the Pre-Raphaelite painter Alfred William Hunt (1830–1896). They went to Broad Ings Farm, between Whitby and Robin Hood's Bay, on 8 August. Violet Hunt noted in her diary for that day that Bram was a 'nice healthy stalwart Irishman, as sweetnatured and gentlemanly as it is possible'. She adds, 'Bram is a dear and Mrs is so pretty and kind'.

Back in Whitby, Florence and Noel went off to local shows while Bram sometimes frequented the upstairs lounge of the adjacent Royal Hotel with its panoramic view of the coast or set off for walks along the cliffs. Once settled, he began the serious plotting of his novel; the landscape, the local history and even the people of Whitby combining to give him inspiration.

And when he wanted facts to support his fiction, there was always the local library to which, according to the evidence of the Rosenbach papers, he paid several visits.

Modern Whitby has not changed a great deal since Bram Stoker came holidaying, as a series of old photographs of the town taken between 1875 and 1910 by a contemporary photographer, Frank Meadow Sutcliffe, reveals. Many of the buildings clinging to the steeply sloping cliffside still have a Victorian look about them, rich with history, and though the washerwomen who once lined the harbour jetties are gone, it is still a working port and in their place are groups of fishermen from lobster boats and Swedish freighters who are not that different in appearance to those seen in Sutcliffe's sepia prints.

Towering over the bay on the eastern side is the noble ruin of Whitby Abbey – the abbey of Streoneshalh, it was called by the Angles – founded by St Hilda in 657. The sanctity of the abbey caused the little port to take the name Witebia (Whitby), the white or (spiritually) pure place. It was here in 664, curiously enough, that the leading Irish theologians of the Celtic Church argued with their opposite numbers from Rome before King Oswy of Northumbria in order that he could decide which doctrine his kingdom would henceforth follow. He opted for Rome. Today the abbey of St Hilda is acknowledged as one of the most spectacular monastic sites in England. The saintly abbess was said to be so formidable that she could turn snakes to stone and local children still believe that if they point their shoes in the direction of her window in the abbey, she will grant a wish. The establishment Hilda ran was a mixed sex monastery, as many Celtic foundations were. It is recorded that Hilda preferred to follow the teachings of the Irish monks who converted Northumbria to Christianity rather than those of Rome and did so in spite of Oswy's decision. The abbey was home to Brother Caedmon (d. 680), the Whitby cowherd turned poet who is regarded as the first English poet. Whitby, like many other monastic foundations, was sacked by marauding Danes. The ghost of the distraught Abbess Hilda is said to appear in the ruins as a ghostly figure all in white. Even without her presence, on winter evenings the whole area has an eerily evocative atmosphere whenever sea mist obscures the landscape and the occasional foghorn can be heard droning somewhere in the gloom.

Just below Whitby Abbey stands St Mary's church, as curious a parish church as any to be found in England; it has no electric lights, wooden pews and services are conducted entirely by candlelight. In the vestry there is a stone memorial to the crew of a fishing boat lost in a terrible storm which also bears the complete text of a letter to *The Times*. Even more curious is the churchyard full of blackened and pitted tombstones rising like gnarled fingers from the earth. It was from these that Bram Stoker copied the inscriptions found among his working papers and which he later transcribed into his novel. The graveyard reaches to the very edge of the East Cliff and Stoker made free use of it for the scene where Dracula sinks his fangs into Lucy Westenra, the 'Un-Dead's' first English victim.

Although some ideas for the novel were evidently in Stoker's mind at this time, another significant moment occurred when he wandered around the harbour and met a local coastguard at the Tate Pier. Among the papers in Philadelphia is a record of their subsequent conversation which is dated 11 August 1890.

Told me of various wrecks [Stoker wrote in black ink in scrawling unpunctuated sentences]. A Russian Schooner 120 tons from Black Sea ran in with all sail main stay foresail jib nearly full tide Put out two anchors in harbour I look and she slewed round – against pier – Another ship got into harbour Never knew how All hands were below praying . . . Above Russian vessel was light ballasted with silver sand.

On another sheet, undated but almost certainly from the same period because of the similarity of the ink, Stoker has added some more information, perhaps from the same source.

On 24 October, 1885 the Russian schooner *Dimetry* about 120 tons was sighted off Whitby about 2 pm. Wind northeast Force 8 (fresh gale) strong sea on coast (cargo silver sand – from mouth of Danube) ran into harbour by pure chance avoiding rocks. The following is extract from the Log Book of the Coast Guard station.

Attached to this piece of paper is a smaller sheet containing the unadorned facts of the incident. The *Whitby Gazette* had reported the incident and Bram rewrote this report to use in his novel as from a fictional newspaper, the *Dailygraph*.

These details were adapted by Stoker as the model for the arrival of Dracula on the ship *Demeter*, complete with its fifty boxes containing Transylvanian soil, which is driven in the teeth of a gale through the harbour entrance and crashes into the long stone jetty flanked by the curve of Tate Hill Sands. The Count then dashes ashore in the shape of an immense dog and disappears among the alleyways of Henrietta Street.

> But, strangest of all, the very instant the shore was touched, an immense dog sprang up on the deck from below, as if shot up by the concussion, and running forward jumped from the bow on the sand. Making straight for the steep cliff, where the churchyard hangs over the laneway to the East Pier so steeply that some of the flat tombstones – 'thruff-steans' or 'through-stones' as they call them in the Whitby vernacular – actually project over where the sustaining cliff has fallen away, it disappeared in the darkness, which seemed intensified just beyond the focus of the searchlight.

Here again Bram chose his route with great care, for Henrietta Street under its earlier name of Haggerlythe was believed to be haunted by a vicious *thost-dog*; a particular Yorkshire monster which is said to attack humans, especially children and young girls.

The power of superstition has, in fact, exercised a strong grip on the minds of Whitby people for centuries, as Stoker discovered. Among the more harmless of these traditions is the idea that any fisherman who sees a pig or a woman as he is walking to the harbour is destined for bad luck and should not go to sea that day. More romantic is a belief among local girls that if they hold a black handkerchief in front of a new moon they will see the face of their future husband in their dreams. On the darker side, the local Whitby jet – fossilised wood that has been subjected to chemical action in stagnant water and then flattened by enormous pressure – is said to be a very potent charm against the powers of witchcraft. And there is still on show in the local museum the wizened hand of a murderer which, after his execution, was severed at the wrist; superstition maintains that it can be used as a charm against burglars because of its power to send victims into a deep sleep.

Bram made good use of the superstitions he came across, relating their influence through his character, the gnarled old seaman, Mr Swales. Local inhabitants still recall their grandparents talking about a George Swales who kept the Granby Hotel on West Cliff during the 1890s and was said to be a fund of stories about local traditions. They believe he was Bram's model for the ancient mariner, although he did not suffer the fate of Bram's Mr Swales who is found with his neck broken in St Mary's churchyard. The real George Swales died peacefully in his bed aged ninety-three.

The pampered teenager Lucy Westenra and her friend Mina Harker (née Murray), who feature so prominently in the Whitby section of *Dracula* and are so central to the plot, were also drawn from life. Two attractive young ladies shared lodgings at 7 The Crescent, now East Crescent, a few steps along from where Bram was staying, and his initial courteous 'Good morning' soon turned to more intimate conversations when the pair returned the red-bearded gentleman's warm smile. This pair became Lucy and Mina of the Crescent, which *Dracula* enthusiasts have now identified as 4 Crescent Terrace. In 1897 it was an apartment house run by a Mrs Strong. Among its distinguished occupants was Russell Bailey, the inventor of the bridge that bears his name.

Bram made 7 The Crescent the residence of Samuel F. Billington, the lawyer, who handled the import of Dracula's 'cargo' from Transylvania.

Neither of the two young ladies Bram meet in Whitby can ever have imagined that they would feature in one of the world's most famous novels. Nor that the more vivacious of the two, who would be Lucy Westenra, would suffer such a terrible experience in St Mary's churchyard on the bench in front of the tall regency Gothic windows of the north transept. If they ever knew of their part in the creation of *Dracula*, there is sadly no indication of this on record.

There is also no trace of the flat slab gravestone, or *thruff-stean*, positioned beneath the bench which is said to be the last resting place of the suicide, George Cannon. It was, of course, in this unhallowed spot that Dracula hid away during his ten-day sojourn in Whitby. This is not to say that such a stone did not exist in St Mary's churchyard for many have disintegrated, subsided or been weathered beyond recognition during the past hundred years.

From the church, the view is uninterrupted across the harbour to the railway station on New Quay Road. At the time of Stoker's visit this was the terminus of the old North Eastern Railway line which ran across the moors to York, and it was from here, aided by his railway timetables, that Bram planned the Count's departure for London in one of his fifty boxes on the 9.30 a.m. goods train to King's Cross. It cost Mr Billington the sum of £8 2s. 3d. for the firm of Carter, Patterson and Co. to transport Dracula's fifty boxes to Carfax near Purfleet.

The location for the first English segment of *Dracula* was not all that Bram Stoker found during his holiday in Whitby. His papers also reveal that it was in the local library that he came across the perfect birthplace for his 'old dead man made alive' . . . and even his name.

The clue to this lies on a typewritten page of notes headed 'Whitby Library O.1097'. The town had, in fact, possessed its own book-lending library for almost half a century when Stoker came to stay, and being an area much concerned with seafaring and travel was particularly well stocked with factual works dealing with the far corners of the world. In the section marked 'O' – for Occidental – were several shelves of titles about Eastern European countries. The book which Stoker borrowed with the number O.1097 was entitled *An Account of the Principalities of Wallachia and Moldavia with Various Political Observations Relating to Them*. The author's name was William Wilkinson (1758–1830) and his 320-page volume had been published in 1820 by Longman, Hurst, Rees, Orme and Brown, another London publishing house, like Constable, keen on travelogues. Wilkinson had been British Consul at Bucharest before his retirement and brought a profound knowledge of the country and its people to his study.

Quite why Bram Stoker should have selected this particular title is now impossible to determine. Perhaps, as we argued earlier, the stories of his brother George were in the back of his mind as he pulled it from the shelf, or perhaps even a reference from his father-in-law who had passed through Varna. It was, of course, from Varna that the *Demeter* set sail for Whitby bearing Dracula and his boxes. Or perhaps it was simply the old coastguard's story of the wreck of the Russian ship *Dimetry* that made him go in search of material about the Black Sea and the Danubian countries. As it transpired he could not have made a more perfect choice. Indeed, he found almost everything he needed when only a few pages into the book and it is tempting to imagine the excitement that he must have felt in his rooms in Whitby when he read and then made notes of the following lines:

P. 19 DRACULA in Wallachian language means DEVIL. Wallachians were accustomed to give it as a surname to any person who rendered himself conspicuous by courage, cruel actions or cunning.

P. 18. 19. The Wallachians joined Hungarians in 1448 and made war on Turkey, being defeated at battle of Cassova in Bulgaria and finding it impossible to make stand against the Turks submitted to annual tribute which they paid until 1460 when Sultan Mahomet II being occupied in completing conquest of island in Archipelago gave opportunity of shaking off yoke. Their VOIVODE (DRACULA) crossed

Danube and attacked Turkish troops. Only momentary success.
Mahomet drove him back to Wallachia where pursued and defeated
him. The VOIVODE escaped into Hungary and the Sultan caused his
brother Bladus to be received in his place. He made treaty with
Bladus binding Wallachians to perpetual tribute and laid the foundations of that slavery not yet abolished.

This was, of course, only the starting point of Bram Stoker's research
into the name Dracula. Another handwritten note among the papers,
which is also undated, reveals that at some point he read an article
'Transylvanian Superstitions' by the historian Emily de Laszowska Gerard
(1867–1928). She was the English wife of a Hungarian army officer who
had lived in the territory for two years while her husband was serving
there. The essay had been first published in the July 1885 issue of
Nineteenth Century magazine, the prestigious monthly journal edited by Sir
James Knowles. Bram had himself recently contributed to the magazine
with 'Actor Managers' (June 1890) and would follow this with a whole
series of topical articles about the arts including 'The Question of a
National Theatre' (May 1908), 'The Censorship of Stage Plays' (December
1909) and 'Irving and Stage Lighting' (May 1911). We believe Stoker had
the relevant issue at home in London and once Transylvania had been
planted in his mind in Whitby he turned to Emily Gerard's essay on his
return.

'Transylvanian Superstitions' is, in fact, replete with information about
Dracula's homeland; its traditions, '*Drakuluji* devils' as they are called and,
best of all, the *nosferatu* or vampires. The invaluable and colourful detail
which it provided Stoker for his novel can be judged quite easily from the
following typical example.

Transylvania might well be termed the land of superstition, for
nowhere else this curious crooked plant of delusion flourishes as
persistently and in such bewildering variety. It would almost seem as
though the whole species of demons, pixies, witches and hobgoblins,
driven from the rest of Europe by the wand of science, had taken
refuge within this mountain rampart, well aware that here they would
find secure lurking-places, whence they might defy their persecutors
yet awhile.

Later she continues:

The spirit of evil (or, not to put too fine a point upon it, the devil) plays a conspicuous part in the Roumanian code of superstitions, and such designations as the *Gregynia Drakuluj* (devil's garden), the *Gania Drakuluj* (devil's mountain), *Yadu Drakuluj* (devil's hell or abyss) &etc. which we frequently find attached to rocks, caverns or heights, attest the fact that these people believe themselves to be surrounded on all sides by a whole legion of evil spirits.

And, finally, perhaps the most influential paragraph of all in Emily Gerard's essay:

More decidedly evil, however, is the vampire, or *nosferatu*, in whom every Roumanian peasant believes as firmly as he does in heaven or hell. There are two sorts of vampire – living and dead. The living vampire is in general the illegitimate offspring of two illegitimate persons, but even a flawless pedigree will not ensure anyone against the intrusions of a vampire into his family vault, and will continue to suck the blood of other innocent people till the spirit has been exorcised, either by opening the grave of the person suspected and driving a stake through the corpse, or firing a pistol, shot into the coffin. In very obstinate cases, it is further recommended to cut off the head and replace it in the coffin with the mouth filled with garlic, or to extract the heart and burn it, strewing the ashes over the grave. That such remedies are often resorted to, even in our enlightened days, is a well attested fact, and there are probably few Roumanian villages where such has not taken place within the memory of the inhabitants.

All other influences apart, it is clear to us that just by reading William Wilkinson's book and the article by Emily Gerard, Bram had more than enough background material on Transylvanian superstitions and vampire lore to make correspondence with Professor Arminius Vambéry, as many have claimed, not only an added chore for a man already overloaded with work but also totally unnecessary.

Bram's working papers have one more piece of evidence to offer from the Whitby period. Either during his stay in the town, or soon afterwards, Bram revised his plans for three of the chapters of the novel. One that he had summarised as 'The Auctioneer' was now deleted and replaced with the words 'Whitby – argument uncanny things'. A second described as

'The Doctor' was crossed through and substituted by 'Whitby – the storm – ship arrives'. Finally, a reference to 'the lawyer's clerk' now became 'Lucy walks in her sleep'.

Here, to all intents and purposes, was Bram's ripening plan for the arrival of the Count in England and the series of events which would set up the rest of the drama. He no doubt returned to London and his duties with Irving at the Lyceum Theatre at the end of August satisfied that he now had quite a few of the important bones of his story in place. Although he had settled on Transylvania as Dracula's homeland, he still had nowhere for his vampire to dwell. This element of the story would present itself to him when he next took a holiday – further to the north still . . . in Scotland.

CHAPTER TEN

The Castle of Dracula

Athough Bram Stoker returned from his holiday in Whitby relaxed, not to mention pleased by the town's inspirational effect and the work he had been able to do on his novel, he had no particular inclination to go back to the Yorkshire coast. Instead, when the demands of his job enabled him to take more time off in August 1893, he headed further north to Aberdeenshire, in Scotland, and found himself modest accommodation in Peterhead, another little seaside town clustered around a busy harbour which had once been famous as a whaling port.

At first sight, there are curious similarities between Peterhead and Whitby which might well have been one of the reasons for Bram's choice. Here, once again, he discovered a thriving fishing industry; extensive renovation had been started on the harbour in 1886, which would earn it the epithet of the 'national Harbour of Refuge'. Above the town, there towered the ruins of a pre-Reformation church, St Peter's, surrounded by blackened and deeply scarred tombstones. And in the town itself was a museum devoted to local history. The impression of Peterhead was one of bustling activity, a feature that has continued to the present day. The herring fleet is now augmented by supply vessels which ply backwards and forwards to the offshore oil rigs in the North Sea.

Bram had come to Peterhead not only for the rest but also to research background material for one of Irving's planned future productions, *Cymbeline*. Shakespeare had derived his play from Ralph Holinshed's *The Chronicles of England, Scotland and Ireland* (1577) and it had been based partly on a local tradition. Irving was anxious to get some 'local colour' for his production. Bram also hoped to find some time for his own current project. So, each morning, he set out from Peterhead to walk along the coast, occasionally stopping to make jottings in his notebook; some for the Shakespearean production and some for his novel. Bram's working notes, dating from 1892, confirm that by this time he was already referring to his 'waxen old man' as Dracula; and he had decided upon Bistritz and the Borgo Pass in Transylvania as his vampire's home territory. What he needed now was a suitable model for Dracula's castle and the right kind of scenic colour. In August 1893 he discovered both.

Thanks to his daily walks, Bram soon found all his old vigour returning. It was not long, either, before he was exploring ever further southwards along the wild sweep of coast in the direction of Aberdeen. First, he passed round Buchan Ness with its magnificent lighthouse built in 1827 by Robert Stevenson (1772–1850), the grandfather of the novelist Robert Louis Stevenson. Next he went on past the tiny village of Bullers o' Buchan with its famous inlet created by the 'boiling sea' which is, according to James Boswell, the origin of the name Bullers – 'boilers'. The sight impressed Bram as much as it had done an earlier visitor – Dr Samuel Johnson, who referred to it as a 'monstrous cauldron'. The learned doctor observed: 'No man can see it with indifference who has either sense of danger or delight in rarity.' But it was what Stoker found around the next promontory which really captured his interest and was ultimately to have such a profound impact on him and his writing.

Just about eight miles south of Peterhead, he entered the Bay of Cruden, with its sweep of wide, firm sands and dunes covered in bent grass and moss. Professor Belford imaginatively says that Cruden means 'blood of the Danes'. In fact, it comes from the Scottish Gaelic *crùdan*, a gurnard, so it was the Bay of Gurnards. And there looming above him, visible through a cleft in the great rocks of red granite, he saw the battlements, arched roofs and tower of a castle. Even from where he stood on the beach, it was impossible not to be impressed by the building. And although he did not yet know its name, Bram had found Slains Castle and the inspiration for Castle Dracula.

Ahead of him lay Port Erroll (renamed Cruden Bay in 1924) and, on the far side of the bay, Whinnyford, a huddle of small cottages perched on the edge of a grassy cliff with a footpath winding down to a shingle beach. Further off inland, faint in the blue mist of early afternoon, was the distant outline of the Grampian mountains. The scene instantly captured his imagination and made him determined to stay. Although Whinnyfold has

retained much of its charm to the present day, it is now the point at which
a North Sea oil pipeline comes ashore, albeit underground, while a short
distance inland stand the unmistakable grey shapes of an oil processing
plant.

That the spot entranced Bram is clear from what he wrote in one of his
later books, *The Mystery of the Sea* (1902), a stirring tale of one man's
search for a lost hoard of Spanish treasure in a vessel which had sunk just
off the point known as St Catherine's Dub. In the very opening chapter of
this work, the narrator describes his first impressions of Cruden Bay in
lines which are clearly taken from life.

When first I saw the place I fell in love with it. Had it been possible I
should have spent my summer there, in a house of my own, but the
want of any place in which to live forbade such an opportunity. So I
stayed in the little hotel, the Kilmarnock Arms.

The next year I came again, and the next, and the next.

Just as Whitby has not changed a great deal since Stoker's day, so
Cruden Bay has avoided the worst excesses of 'progress', and it is not
difficult to retrace the author's footsteps along the shore where he
wandered, lost in his thoughts, a century ago. Bram again evocatively
describes the bay in the opening of *The Mystery of the Sea*.

The curved shore of Cruden Bay, Aberdeenshire, is backed by a
waste of sandhills in whose hollow seagrass and moss and wild violets,
together with the pretty 'grass of Parnassus' form a green carpet. The
surface of the hills is held together by bent grass and is eternally
shifting as the wind takes the fine sand and drifts it to and fro. All
behind is green, from the meadows that mark the southern edge of
the bay to the swelling uplands that stretch away and away far in the
distance, till the blue mist of the mountains at Braemar sets a kind of
barrier. In the centre of the bay the highest point of land that runs
downward to the sea looks like a miniature hill known as the Hawklaw;
from this point onward to the extreme south, the land runs high with
a gentle trend downwards.

Cruden sands are wide and firm and the sea runs out a considerable
distance. When there is a storm with the wind on shore the whole
bay is a mass of leaping waves and broken water that threatens every
instant to annihilate the stake-nets which stretch out here and there

along the shore. More than a few vessels have been lost on these wide
stretching sands, and it was perhaps the roaring of the shallow seas
and the terror they inspired which sent the crews to the spirit room
and the bodies of them which came to shore later on, to the
churchyard on the hill.

The Kilmarnock Arms, then a twelve-bedroom establishment with two
bathrooms, is still there on the western bank of the Water of Cruden; a
sunken garden fringed by willows helps to retain its essentially Victorian
character, no matter whether the place is busy with summer holiday-
makers or, in the winter, local folk. Named in recognition of the 17th Earl
of Erroll being created a peer of the United Kingdom with the title Baron
Kilmarnock, the establishment was, in the 1890s, trying to attract holiday-
makers with the appeal of the beach and 'bathing houses' just a seven-
minute walk away, trout and sea fishing, game shooting ('guns and dogs
readily available for hire') and a nearby golf course. In the old leather-
bound visitors' book, Bram's entry is still there for all to see: further
confirmation of his emotional attachment to the place.

'Delighted with everything and everybody,' it reads in his familiar
scrawl, 'and hope to come again.'

James Cruikshank, who ran the Kilmarnock Arms with his wife, found
his own little piece of immortality thanks to the Irish visitor. For the
couple feature in *The Watter's Mou'* (1895), a novel Stoker completed prior
to *Dracula*, which was also published by Constable. This story, which
takes its name from the course of the Waters of Cruden, deals with
smuggling and the heroic efforts of a young coastguard, Willie Barrow, to
curtail the illicit trade – even though he knows his sweetheart is the
daughter of one of the worst offenders. In this first composition inspired
by the Aberdeenshire coast, the Cruikshanks' inn is the setting for a couple
of early scenes in the melodrama which ends in double tragedy for young
Barrow and his lover.

Mrs Cruikshank, who lived to be almost a hundred and died less than
twenty years ago, retained the fondest memories of Bram Stoker.

'He was one of the nicest men I ever knew,' she told a visitor in 1976.
'A big, cheery, handsome Irishman. Mr Stoker told me that he got all his
ideas for his stories when he was holidaying in Cruden Bay, walking the
sands to Whinnyford or scrambling over the rocks north to the castle and
the Bullers.'

In his subsequent visits, Bram was accompanied by Florrie, who, it seems preferred to play golf while Bram was off on his walks.

Apart from the novel's authentic portrait of the coast and its people, *The Watter's Mou'* is interesting to students of the *Dracula* legend because it is the first of Bram Stoker's books to reveal his very real interest in, and vivid way of describing, strange geographical formations: the selfsame kind of grotesque rock formations that are depicted around Castle Dracula in the Transylvanian mountains. In one memorable episode in *Dracula*, when Van Helsing is describing the empathy between the Count and his environment, he says in a speech that was, in fact, written in Cruden and reflects almost exactly the wild coastline:

'All the centuries of the world aid him; all the forces of nature that are occult and deep and strong must have worked together in some wondrous way. The very place where he has been alive Un-Dead for all these centuries, is full of strangeness of the geological and chemical world.'

'Un-Dead' is a word with apt connotations for Cruden Bay, too, for it is similarly steeped in ancient superstitions, as we have discovered.

Although Bram was comfortable enough in the Kilmarnock Arms, he was anxious for a place on his own and when the opportunity arose he decided to rent one of the cottages across the bay at Whinnyfold. He chose a slate-roofed, white-walled building known as 'The Crookit Lum', after the ten-degree list of its chimney; this, too, is still standing although it has changed somewhat in the interim, gaining an extra window and front entrance. Although there are no physical traces of Bram's occupancy to be found in the house, a previous owner did discover, while digging in the garden, a number of Victorian ink bottles bearing the familiar manufactur-er's name of Stephens which can have only belonged to the author and bear silent witness to his productivity.

From the front of this cottage there is an uninterrupted view across the bay over the notorious reef known as the Skares Reef to Slains Castle. According to local legend, Bram spent hours lying in a hammock watching the sea; especially the great jagged rocks which rose through the surface like huge fangs. Indeed, standing in this same spot today, it is not difficult to appreciate how the whole scene must have impinged itself on Bram's mind. In *The Mystery of the Sea*, he describes them thus:

It is here, where the little promontory called Whinnyfold juts out, that the two great geological features of the Aberdeen coast meet, the red sienite of the north joins the black gneiss of the south. That union must have been originally a wild one; there are evidences of an upheaval which must have shaken the earth at its centre. Here and there are great masses of either species of rock hurled upwards in every conceivable variety of form, sometimes fused or pressed together so that it is impossible to say exactly where gneiss ends or sienite begins; but broadly speaking here is an irregular line of separation. This line runs seaward to the east and its strength is shown in its outcrop. For a half mile or more the rocks rise through the sea singly or in broken masses ending in a dangerous cluster known as 'The Skares' and which has had for centuries its full toll of wreck and disaster. Did the sea hold its dead where they fell, its floor around the Skares would be whitened with their bones, and new islands could build themselves with the piling wreckage. At times one may see here the ocean in her fiercest mood; for it is when the tempest drives from the south-east that the sea is fretted amongst the rugged rocks and sends its spume landwards. The rocks that at calmer times rise dark from the briny deep are lost to sight for moments in the grand onrush of the waves. The seagulls which usually whitened them, now flutter around screaming, and the sound of their shrieks comes in on the gale almost in a continuous note, for the single cries are merged in the multitudinous roar of sea and air.

In these surroundings, Dracula's Castle in faraway Transylvania, which Bram had never visited, came alive in his imagination.

On some days, Bram would stride out along the beach, walking-stick in hand, passing the boats of the local fisherman laid up on the shore with their nets alongside. They, too, are still to be seen today, looking much as they must have done in his time. And there is something about their sturdiness which serves as an ever-present reminder that no matter how tranquil the sea may seem, this is a dangerous stretch of coast with a fearsome reputation for shipwrecks. Bram also discovered this fact and first noted it in *The Watter's Mou'*.

Just as he had done at Whitby, Bram struck up conversations with the local people, getting them to confide their local traditions and folklore. He heard stories about Mary Finlay, the oldest inhabitant, who, as a sickly child, had been subjected to a bizarre ritual to prevent the spirits known as the '*guidmannies*' from stealing her life-blood. Another woman, Bella Allen, told him how on Lammas night the ghosts of those who had been drowned in the bay during the past twelve months rose up and made their way to St Olave's Well as a dreadful warning to those who did not treat the sea with respect. But perhaps most curious of all was the sight of the old 19th Earl of Erroll, who lived in Slains Castle above the bay, walking down the street of Cruden each day dressed in an ancient tweed suit, insisting that all the villagers tip their hats or curtsey to him as he passed by.

Although none of these people found their way directly into *Dracula*, their dialects did. For the expressions that Stoker attributes to a number of his characters in Whitby are more the dialect of Scots folk than Yorkshire people. 'Hafflin', 'scunner', 'death-sark', and 'dinna fash yersel' were as familiar then in Cruden Bay as they are today.

Someone who did find his way into the novel in the guise of a Scottish seaman was Bram's old friend, the lawyer, Thomas Donaldson of Philadelphia, to whom he would later give the manuscript. He appears as 'Captain Donelson', the skipper of the *Czarina Catherine* who describes the memorable journey of his ship from London to the Black Sea with Dracula in his coffin on board, as recounted in Jonathan Harker's *Journal* of 30 October. Donelson's lines about the reactions of some of his crew to the ship's cargo are among the most evocative in the book.

'The Roumanians were wild, and wanted me right or wrong to take out the box and fling it in the river. I had to argy wi' them aboot it wi' a handspike; an' when the last of them rose off the deck, wi' his head in his hand, I had convinced them that, evil eye or no evil eye, the property and the trust of my owners were better in my hands than in the river Danube. They had, mind ye, taken the box on the deck ready to fling it in, and as it was marked Galatz via Varna, I thocht I'd let it lie till we discharged in the port an' get rid o't athegither. We didn't do much clearin' that day, an' had to remained the nicht at anchor; but in the mornin', braw an' airly, an hour before sun-up, a man came aboard wi' an order, written to him from England, to receive a box marked for one Count Dracula. Sure enuch the matter was one ready to his hand. He had his papers a'reet, an' glad I was to be rid o' the dam thing, for I was beginnin' masel' to feel uneasy at it. If the Deil did have any luggage aboord the ship, I'm thinkin' it was nane other than that same!'

As Bram had found in Whitby, the Cruden Bay coastguard was also an excellent source of information, especially about the smuggling which had been rife on the coast for years, many of the caves having made ideal hiding places for contraband. However, no matter where he went around the bay, his eyes were constantly being drawn back to Slains Castle, perched on the edge of the cliffs known as Bowness, at almost precisely the point on the coast where the red granite of the north meets the volcanic gneiss, or metamorphic rock, of the south. He knew that the old Earl of Erroll lived in the building and so, one morning, when his curiosity finally got the better of him, he climbed up the pathway to investigate.

Today, any visitor to Cruden Bay will find themselves drawn to the castle in much the same way. And because it now lies ruined and desolate, the first impression is that it looks much as Castle Dracula has always looked in popular imagination. But that was not the building that confronted Bram Stoker when he climbed up to the promontory for the first time in August 1893. What he saw was the impressive castle of the Lord High Constable of Scotland which had been a source of admiration to visitors for over two centuries.

Interestingly, these ruins are not the original Slains Castle. That stood some five miles to the south-west at Mains of Salins where it had been the ancestral home of the Earls of Erroll for generations. Fortune had indeed favoured Bram Stoker when he stumbled upon its location, for the history of the Errolls is as full of dark rituals, rumours of fertility cults and blood sacrifice as anything that he might have dreamed up for Count Dracula.

The Hay family, who became the Earls of Erroll, were Normans who had settled in Scotland in 1160 under the patronage of King Malcolm IV ('The Maiden'). William Hay married the daughter of the clan chieftain of the Mac Garadh sept. A Hay commanded the bodyguard of Robert I ('The Bruce') as Constable of Scotland. The office ranks as the senior subject of Scotland after the Blood Royal. The office was made an hereditary right of the Hay family in 1314 by Robert I. Hay's successors became barons in 1429, and in 1452 the 2nd Lord Hay became Earl of Erroll. Today, Merlin Hay, the 24th Earl of Erroll, still holds the hereditary titles of Lord Hay, Baron of Slain, The Mac Garadh Mòr and 33rd Chief of the Clan Hay. He also holds the office of 28th Lord High Constable of Scotland.

It is argued that the story of the origin of the family fortunes was used by Shakespeare in *Cymbeline* although he changed the time of the events to the days prior to the Roman occupation of Britain; Cymbeline is an Anglicisation of the name of the great Celtic king Cunobelinus (the hound of Belinus) who died c.AD40. The historical source for the play, as we have pointed out, was Holinshed's *Chronicles* but several themes, such as Iachimo's wager, are taken from Boccaccio's *Decameron*.

The result of the Hay family's service to the Scottish kings caused them to become a power in the land, although local gossip soon began to envelop them and their estates in superstition. Because Cruden Bay faces out towards the rising sun, sun worship was said to take place there; a number of ancient standing stones reinforce this idea. And fear of the dead was widespread, special precautions being taken at the time of death to ensure that the departed did not return to trouble the living. The spirit world was a living thing to the people of Cruden Bay and the 'Un-Dead' were either to be appeased with gifts of food or prevented from entering buildings by the use of onions laid on window sills. All these pagan beliefs came to Bram Stoker's attention – fuelling his imagination which was already alight with his vampire theme.

Of special interest, too, were the tales of a great oak tree that grew on the Errolls' land and was said to be associated with the ancient fertility cult of the goddess Diana. Whereas Diana is the Roman goddess of the hunt and the moon, her cult was invoked among the Celts of Gaul and Britain and mingled with indigenous beliefs. The legend connecting her with the Erroll land, and a prophecy associated with it, had already caught the interest of the great social anthropologist and folklorist, Sir James Frazer (1854–1941) who wrote about it in his classic work *The Golden Bough*, published in 1890.

In this book Sir James explained that the 'golden bough' was another term for mistletoe, which, according to Pliny, was used by the ancient Celts in their fertility rituals. This was particularly relevant to the Errolls whose family emblem was a piece of mistletoe, linking them to the god of Norse mythology, Balder, the son of Odin and Frigg, who was killed by Hoder with a stake of mistletoe. Sir James wrote:

> The view that the mistletoe was not merely the instrument of Balder's death, but that it contained his life, is countenanced by the analogy of a Scottish superstition. Tradition ran that the fate of the Hays of Erroll was bound up with the mistletoe that grew on a certain great oak. A member of the Hay family has recorded the old belief as follows: 'Among the low country families the badges are now almost generally forgotten; but it appears by an ancient MS. and the tradition of a few old people in Perthshire, that the badge of the Hays was the

mistletoe. There was formerly in the neighbourhood of Erroll, and not far from the Falcon stone, a vast oak of an unknown age, and upon which grew a profusion of the plant; many charms and legends were considered to be connected with the tree, and the duration of the family of Hay was said to be united with its existence. It was believed that a sprig of the mistletoe cut by a Hay on All Hallow Mass eve, with a new dirk, and after surrounding the tree three times sunwise, and pronouncing a certain spell, was sure charm against all clamour or witchery, and an infallible guard on the day of battle. A spray gathered in the same manner was placed in the cradle of infants, and thought to defend them from being changed for elf-bairns by the fairies. Finally, it was affirmed, that when the root of the oak had perished, 'the grass should grow in the hearth of Erroll, and a raven should sit in the falcon's nest'. The two most unlucky deeds which could be done by one of the name of Hay was, to kill a white falcon, and to cut down a limb from the oak of Erroll. When the old tree was destroyed I could never learn.

Although there is no direct evidence to support the fact, it seems highly probable that Bram Stoker had read *The Golden Bough* – or would do so as part of his research for *Dracula*. The book was one of the publishing sensations of its time, not dissimilar in its impact to Stephen Hawking's *A Brief History of Time* (1992). It contained a lot of detail relevant to primitive superstitions and, specifically, a section on protection against vampires.

Despite their association with the darker arts, the Earls of Erroll had great power within their domains. They could levy taxes on their tenants, raise an army and dispense justice on wrongdoers. In 1594, however, Francis Hay, the 9th Earl of Erroll (1564–1631), fell out of step with his forebears and plotted a rebellion against James IV with George Gordon, 6th Earl of Huntley of Aberdeen. It appeared that both Erroll and Huntley were Catholics and disagreed with the Reformist zeal of the king. They sought assistance from Spain. A battle was fought at Glenlivet on 3 October 1594. The King's army was commanded by the 7th Earl of Argyll. While they seem to have had the better of the engagement, Erroll and Huntley fled before the reinforcements of the King. James VI bombarded Huntley Castle and then turned on Slains Castle (at Mains of Salins), razing it to the ground. All that remains today of Old Slains Castle is a gaunt ruined tower overlooking a gravelly beach. Both Erroll and Huntley fled abroad. In 1596 Huntley was allowed to return after he had offered to prove his loyalty by 'extirpating the barbarous peoples' of Gaelic Scotland. Already Anglicised Scotland was embarking upon its policy of destroying the Scottish Gaelic language and culture. For this King James VI made Huntley a Marquis.

Erroll spent some time in France but was also eventually granted a pardon by James and allowed back to Scotland. Suitably chastened, he decided to sever all links with his former residence and build a new castle behind Port Erroll. He did, though, retain the original name. Slains comes from the Gaelic *slaine* meaning 'fullness' or 'health'. There is also a Slane Castle, taking its name from the same word, in Co. Meath, Ireland, which is the scene of the tale of the hapless Jemmy Nowlan, as we have discussed in Chapter Five. One wonders whether Bram recognised the connection. In the seventeenth century, Slains Castle was considerably extended and in subsequent years the Errolls played host to many distinguished visitors, not the least of them being the great English lexicographer, essayist, poet and moralist, Dr Samuel Johnson (1709–1784) who stayed there with his friend James Boswell (1740–1795), and gave this graphic description in his *Journey to the Western Isles* (1775):

> We came in the afternoon to Slains Castle, built upon the margin of the sea so that the walls of one of the towers seem only a continuation of a perpendicular rock, the foot of which is beaten by waves. To walk round the house seemed impracticable. From the windows, the eye wanders over the sea that separates Scotland from Norway, and when the wind beats with violence must enjoy all the terrible grandeur of the tempestuous ocean. I would not, for my amusement, wish for a storm; but as storms, whether wished for or not, sometimes happen, I must say, without violation of humanity, that I should willing look out upon them from Slains Castle.

James Boswell also adds his more reserved but nonetheless interesting impressions of the castle in his *Journal of a Tour to the Hebrides with Samuel Johnson* written at the same time:

> Slains is an excellent house. The noble owner has built of brick, along the square in the inside, a gallery, both on the first and second story, the house being no higher; so that he has always a dry walk, and the rooms, to which formerly there was no approach but through each

other, have now all separate entries from the gallery which is hung
with Hogarth's works and other prints.

In the interim, however, tragedy had continued to haunt the Errolls. Sir
William Hay, who had supported Charles I during the Civil War, was
beheaded for his loyalty. Then financial ruin engulfed James Hay, the 15th
Earl, after he was given the unenviable task of organising the enormously
expensive wedding of George III to Charlotte of Mecklenberg-Strelitz.
The 19th Earl, William Hay, only just escaped with his life during the
Crimean War and returned battle-weary to Scotland to face the daunting
task of keeping the estate from bankruptcy. An air of doom seemed to have
settled over the family seat by the closing years of the nineteenth century.
The malevolent spirits that had pursued the Errolls down the centuries
may have seemed almost tangible to Bram Stoker as he stared up at the
Gothic edifice on the edge of the cliffs that August day.

His curiosity excited, Bram determined to find out more about Slains
Castle. The enquiries he made among the local people did not disappoint
him. In addition to the family's chequered history, he learned about the
building's awesome architectural style – it was designed by John Smith,
Aberdeen City Architect, for the 17th Earl in 1836–7 and incorporated
parts of earlier castles including that visited by Johnson and Boswell – its
collection of excellent paintings and furniture, and a dining-room which
had for years been regarded as one of the most beautiful in any Scottish
stately home. These facts later appeared, almost word for word, in *Dracula*.
Of Castle Dracula, Bram wrote that its 'broken battlements showed a
jagged line against the sky'; and of the interior that 'the curtains and
upholstery of the chairs and sofas and the hangings are of the costliest and
most beautiful fabrics and must have been of fabulous value when they
were made'.

Of the present occupants of Slains Castle, Bram learned that word had
it that the Earl's eldest son, Victor, was the hope for the future with plans
for a career in the diplomatic service. What Stoker had no inkling of then
– and indeed may never have heard about at all – was that Victor Hay
wanted to write and had plans for a novel also inspired by the castle: a
novel in which elements of vampirism would play a significant part.

If Victor Alexander Sereld Hay (1876–1928), later 20th Earl of Erroll,
is remembered today, it is as a pillar of the diplomatic service, who was
the British High Commissioner in Germany in the 1920s and a prominent
member of the House of Lords. Few know that he was also a dramatist –

he wrote two plays, *The Chalk Line*, a three-act drama about an eternal triangle produced in Cologne in 1922, and *The Dream Kiss*, a farce about somnambulism put on in Wimbledon in 1924 – and even fewer know that he was the author of a novel about the 'Un-Dead' entitled *Ferelith* published in 1903.

Like his forebears, Victor Hay was a staunch monarchist. Queen Victoria was his godmother and there never seemed any doubt that he would serve the Crown in one way or another. He was nearing the end of his teens when Bram Stoker first came to Cruden Bay, and although the diplomatic service was already beckoning, he nursed literary aspirations and would often slip away to write in the library of Slains Castle. It is, however, doubtful whether the two men ever cast eyes on each other during any of Bram's visits; and though it is tempting to imagine Victor Hay at work in the castle while Bram Stoker walked beneath musing over his novel, it is impossible to substantiate.

Ferelith, the young nobleman's novel, is now an exceedingly rare book. It was described in a solitary review in *The Times* as 'a weird and rather gruesome ghost story', though this does scant justice to the ingenious plot and macabre style of the work. Set in 'Glamrie Castle' – immediately recognisable as Slains – and drawing on the Erroll family's long associations with the supernatural, it is the tale of the castle's new *nouveau riche* owner, William Brambles, and his beautiful wife Ferelith. Ferelith soon falls under the spell of a mysterious night-time visitor. In another curious coincidence that links Victor Hay's book to *Dracula*, it too is told in diary form.

In these entries, Ferelith describes her conversations with the castle's unearthly occupant who speaks of himself as 'a dead man who cannot sleep'. He has fallen in love with her, he says, and hopes to gain salvation through his love being reciprocated. Each night, trembling with emotions, Ferelith lies awake awaiting the stranger's return and the following day sets down in her diary what happens.

March 3rd – For the third time I found him standing beside me. He assured me I had nothing to fear from his presence and then dashed off into a torrent of words. 'Ah! the torture I have suffered this hundred years. A hundred years! And it is but a drop in the aeons of time to come. I have told you of my career in the world of men. I have told you of my crimes, of my sins. I cannot scientifically explain to you the state in which I am in. I am dead, yet I may not sleep. And all the time my passion growing, my longing increasing. Fear me not; if only you could love me in return.' At this, I thought I should die for very bliss. And my lips just murmured, 'I *do* love you.'

March 4th – I am under the spell of a great happiness. I can scarcely write for thinking of it. Yet surely no love before was like my love? My lover is a dream, a myth, a fantasy . . .

March 17th – He has come to me twice again. And nothing has occurred to ruffle our passionate communion. I become intoxicated with the magic touch of his filmy arms, I drink red nectar from his gossamer lips. It is all so faint and fairy-like, yet so deliciously delirious as well.

But this mysterious being is not intent on draining Ferelith of her blood. He has more carnal pleasures in mind and makes her pregnant. Ferelith is left to face her husband – and the dilemma as to whether the father of her child is man or ghost.

Despite the originality of its plot, not to mention the illicit relationship – which may well have offended some readers of the period – *Ferelith* was not a commercial success and any thoughts Victor Hay may have nursed of restoring the family fortune through his writing quickly dissolved. Instead, he employed his ability and undoubted personal charm to forge a career in the diplomatic service which prospered until his premature death on 20 February 1928, at the age of fifty-one. By that time, Bram Stoker, the man who had walked along the beach below his castle a quarter of a century earlier, was a household name.

At the time of Victor Hay's death, Slains Castle had suffered a fate not unlike that of its predecessor down the coast. After the death of his father in 1916, the new 20th Earl had been forced to sell off the building to a wealthy shipowner, Sir John Ellerman, in order to settle death duties. Ellerman himself disposed of the estate in 1923 and in 1926 the new owner auctioned Slains: the lead was stripped from the roof to be sold as scrap, a vast amount of fittings were removed and the building was partially demolished. Today all that remains of the once great pile with its palatial lawns and gardens are the granite walls and an iron staircase in one of the towers which leads to the once famous dining-room. Weeds have run riot over the lawns and gardens and forced their way into most parts of the wind-blown ruin. On the wall beside one window, in this hollow shell, a graffiti artist, perhaps mistaking the building's associations with another horror classic, has carved the word 'Frankenstein'.

The evidence of the manuscript of *Dracula* suggests that Jonathan Harker's experiences in Castle Dracula, which comprise the opening chapters of the novel, were actually written by Stoker while staying in Cruden Bay; which further underlines the effect Slains had upon his imagination. The castle itself makes a brief appearance in Stoker's first 'Cruden Bay novel', *The Watter's Mou'* where Maggie talks of being unnerved by 'a glimpse of the lighted windows of the castle on the cliff'. It is only mentioned in passing in *The Mystery of the Sea*.

Bram Stoker's discovery of Cruden Bay and Slains Castle was another defining moment in the creation of *Dracula*. His visits to the east coast of Scotland had not only helped him to add several more important elements to his plot but provided him with a model for his vampire's environment – and, perhaps most important of all, for Count Dracula's mountain stronghold.

Although much of the rest of the story would be written in London and on tour with Irving in America, Bram Stoker returned to Cruden Bay in the late summer of 1900 for one final act in the history of the novel. Following the publication of the hardcover edition of *Dracula*, Constable had decided to issue a sixpenny paperback version. But in order to make it viable, Otto Kyllmann asked Bram to delete 25,000 words from the text. He chose to do this in the same spot where he had looked out across the bay to Slains Castle and found his inspiration. It could not have been more fitting.

CHAPTER ELEVEN

The Count in London

WHEN BRAM RETURNED TO LONDON after his 1893 holiday, the plot of *Dracula* was clear in his mind. Cruden Bay had provided the setting for the Count's castle; Whitby had given him the vampire's point of arrival in the country; now he merely needed the focal point of the 'Un-Dead's' activities in Britain. It seemed obvious to him that the most natural place was London and the bits of it which formed part of his everyday life; especially those between his home in Chelsea and the Lyceum Theatre in the Strand. Both of these landmarks – and the other localities which Bram chose for his background and which can easily be found on any map – still exist today.

The distance between Bram's home at 18 St Leonard's Terrace, near the Royal Hospital, which is famous for its venerable pensioners in their scarlet uniforms, and the theatre on Wellington Street, at the junction of the Strand with the Aldwych, is less than three miles; little more than a brisk stroll for a man who had been a champion walker in Dublin – although the demands of theatrical life probably meant that Stoker took a hansom cab between the two places on most days.

When he first moved to Chelsea, Bram often travelled on the river ferry from the Chelsea Embankment to Waterloo Bridge. Family tradition, according to Professor Belford, was that this was a preferred method of travel; he would breakfast late and then catch the ferry at 11 a.m. Professor Belford should have known, however, that this route would not have allowed him to pass under London Bridge (p. 129). While on such a journey, on the ferry *Twilight*, about 6 p.m., presumably going to the Lyceum for the evening performance, on Thursday, 14 September 1882,

Bram saw an elderly man jump overboard. Bram did not hesitate but jumped in to save the man, who was attempting suicide. Bram managed to drag the man to the bank and carry him to his own house where his brother George, who was staying with Florrie and himself, tried to revive him. It was too late. The unknown old man was dead. The newspapers seized on the drama of the rescue attempt and an artist's impression of 'Mr Bram Stoker's Gallant Act' appeared in *The Penny Illustrated* of 4 November. A cartoon showing Henry Irving praising him appeared in *The Entr'acte*, 23 September. Bram later received the Bronze Medal of the Royal Humane Society for his attempt. An old friend of his Dublin days, the Irish comedian J. J. Toole, telegraphed from a Manchester theatre, where he was appearing: 'Bravo Bram, splendid – shall drink to your good health all night!'

In later years Bram varied his route, depending on the availability of time, and did occasionally enjoy the exercise that the pedestrian journey offered by way of Buckingham Palace and up the Mall or along Piccadilly to the Strand. Small wonder that he should have made use of spots along the way with which he was familiar for crucial scenes in *Dracula*; nor that he chose to locate the Count's London residence at one of the capital's most prestigious addresses in Mayfair. Although this building within sight of Hyde Park is actually given a non-existent number in the novel, we are in no doubt as to the actual property which Bram Stoker had in mind.

St Leonard's Terrace, where the Stokers lived during the final year he was writing *Dracula*, is a row of Georgian houses overlooking the green sward of Burton's Court. It is a short walk from Stoker's previous house at 27 Cheyne Walk. Burton's Court was the original forecourt of the Chelsea Royal Hospital, and has been used for recreation ever since the 1880s when it became a sports ground for the Brigade of Guards. At the end of the terrace are the impressive buildings of the old Duke of York's Headquarters. The little block of terraced houses numbered 26–30 dates from the latter half of the eighteenth century and is shown on *Thompson's Map of Chelsea* (1836) as 'Green's Row' after the important Green family of brewers who carried on a flourishing business in Westminster.

The most famous resident of St Leonard's Terrace in Stoker's time was Professor Graham Wallas (1858–1932) who lived at No. 38 and was one of the founders of the Fabian Society as well as exercising a profound influence upon the young political thinkers of his day. After a spell of schoolmastering and university lecturing, for which he developed a formidable reputation, Wallas helped to found the London School of

Economics and later became its Professor of Political Science. His influential teaching and writings in social psychology, including *Human Nature in Politics* (1908) and *The Great Society* (1914), emphasised the role of irrational forces which determined public opinion and political attitudes. A man of colloquial eloquence, he was part of Chelsea and London society in the years around the turn of the century; as he was a keen theatre-goer, it is tempting to believe that he met his neighbour, Bram Stoker, although there is no evidence to support this suggestion.

According to London historian John East, Bram's first residence in Chelsea was at 4 Durham Place, another terraced property on the right-hand side of Burton's Court. But, certainly, the Stokers were settled for over ten years at Cheyne Walk before they moved, in 1896, into 18 St Leonard's Terrace during the writing of *Dracula*. The latter property has changed very little since Stoker's day; it is a handsome, four-storey dwelling, with an iron balcony on the second floor and decorated in white. One of the traditional Blue Plaques commemorating the fact that the author of *Dracula* lived there is the only noticeable change. Despite Chelsea's reputation as the home of the 'Sloane Rangers' and frequent displays of ostentatious wealth, Bram's little corner of London is still a haven of peace and quiet with picturesque views across the well-manicured turf of Burton's Court towards the Thames. Only the tall chimneys of the Battersea Power Station, just visible over the roof of the Royal Hospital, indicate the advent of the twentieth century.

The nearest location to his home that Bram chose to use in *Dracula* was Hyde Park, which he passed on his way to and from the Lyceum. In yet another example of the way his fiction is derived from fact, he describes the return of Mina Harker to London from Whitby in a *Journal* entry of 22 September which might almost be the author himself writing.

> We came back to town quietly, taking a 'bus to Hyde Park Corner. Jonathan thought it would interest me to go into the Row for a while, so we sat down; but there were very few people there, and it was sad-looking and desolate to see so many empty chairs. It made us think of the empty chair at home; so we got up and walked down Piccadilly.

As the couple walk along the famous three-quarters of a mile road towards Piccadilly Circus dwelling on the recent death of Lucy Westenra, Jonathan suddenly turns very pale and stares at a tall, thin man with a beaky nose, black moustache and pointed beard who is intently watching a pretty young girl. 'His face was not a good face,' Stoker's narrative tells us, 'it was hard, and cruel, and sensual, and his big white teeth that looked all the whiter because his lips were so red, were pointed like an animal's.' When this mysterious stranger hails a hansom and drives off, Jonathan gasps out that the man was Dracula – but a Dracula who has grown younger. This encounter, incidentally, happens in broad daylight, a continuity problem for those who follow the rule that the vampire has to return to his grave between sunrise and sunset. The pair sit down in Green Park; 'it was a hot day for autumn, and there was a comfortable seat in a shady place'. Here the shaken Jonathan falls into a twenty-minute slumber.

Almost opposite the leafy enclave of Green Park is Berkeley Street which links Piccadilly to beautiful Berkeley Square. The Berkeley Hotel standing at the corner of this junction was already a fashionable meeting place in Bram's day as well as being considered an extremely comfortable hotel with an excellent restaurant that had earned a favourable entry in *Baedeker's Guide to London*. Stoker chose it as Van Helsing's hotel – a good choice for a man of the professor's fastidious and traditional habits because it was well established and could trace its origins back to the early days of the mail coaches when it was the starting point of journeys to the West of England. There does appear, however, to be a slight discrepancy in Bram's meticulous planning. Van Helsing, in his letter to Seward of 2 September, asks him to book rooms in the Great Eastern Hotel in Liverpool Street, whose rail terminal was where the boat trains from Holland via Harwich would have come in. When he arrives in London, he is staying at the Berkeley. What had caused the move? It seems unlikely that the exacting Bram would have forgotten Van Helsing's request. Had he meant to proffer his readers a reason for the change?

Two roads further along from the Berkeley stands the Hotel Albemarle in the street which bears its name. Here stayed Arthur Holmwood who enlists the aid of Dr Jack Seward to try to save his doomed fiancée, Lucy Westenra, in another of the early London scenes of *Dracula*. It was an even more obvious establishment for Bram Stoker to have featured in his stories, for in the 1890s the mottled pink building with its high gables had been rebuilt. The rebuilding was complete in 1889 and it was generally acknowledged to be the smartest hotel in London's West End. The Albemarle was patronised by royalty, the aristocracy, statesmen and members of Parliament as well as the leading figures in the arts. Byron and Horatio Nelson had stayed there; Whistler had used a room to make

sketches from; Lillie Langtry was a regular visitor, and according to
popular gossip had a permanent suite to entertain her admirers, including
the future Edward VII. Oscar Wilde, too, was often in the hotel during
the height of his fame and there seems no reason to doubt that Bram, and
perhaps even Sir Henry Irving on a few occasions, met him there.

The last thoroughfare off Piccadilly which Stoker utilised was narrow
Sackville Street which provides a short-cut to Regent Street just before it
reaches Piccadilly Circus. Here he places the offices of the 'house agents'
Mitchell, Sons and Candy, who arranged the sale of the Mayfair residence
to a foreign nobleman. Jonathan Harker has to use his wits to extract from
the company's priggish member of staff the name of the new owner – one
'Count de Ville'. Harker has no doubt that de Ville is, in fact, Dracula.

The whereabouts of the Count's home are, perhaps not surprisingly,
rather more veiled in Stoker's narrative than any of the other London
locations. In Jonathan Harker's *Journal* for the evening of 2 October, the
young solicitor describes how he found the property:

At Piccadilly Circus I discharged my cab and walked westward;
beyond the Junior Constitutional I came across the house described,
and was satisfied that this was the next of the lairs arranged by
Dracula. The house looked as though it had been long untenanted.
The windows were encrusted with dust, and the shutters were up.
All the framework was black with time, and from the iron the paint
had mostly scaled away. It was evident that up to lately there had
been a large notice-board in front of the balcony; it had, however,
been roughly torn away, the uprights which supported it still
remaining. Behind the rails of the balcony I saw there were some
loose boards, whose raw edges looked white. I would have given a
good deal to have been able to see the notice-board intact, as it would,
perhaps, have given some clue to the ownership of the house.

Harker also goes round to the rear of the property. 'The mews were
active,' he adds, 'the Piccadilly houses being mostly in occupation. I asked
one or two of the grooms and helpers whom I saw round if they could tell
me anything about the empty house. One of them said that he heard it had
lately been taken, but he couldn't say from whom.'

Jonathan is not to be easily distracted from his quest and the following
day learns that the property – which Stoker numbers as 347 Piccadilly –
was formerly the home of the late Mr Archibald Winter-Suffield and had

been sold to the mysterious Count de Ville by his executors. Unfortunately, from the point of view of identifying the building today, there is no No. 347 Piccadilly, nor any record of a property in the vicinity which belonged to a man of that name in the late Victorian era. But nevertheless Bram, continuing to base his fiction on real places, as always has laid his clues for the keen literary detective to follow.

The Junior Constitutional to which Harker refers was located at 101 Piccadilly and behind it run several little mews precisely like those mentioned by Jonathan Harker. Another of the young man's informants, a carrier named Sam Bloxam, who took a number of 'heavy boxes' to No. 347, describes it as a tall building 'with a stone front with a bow on it, an 'oigh steps up to the door'. He adds equally significantly, 'I forgets the number but it was only a few doors from a big white church or somethink of the kind'. In Down Street, less than a hundred yards from the Junior Constitutional, stands just such a big white building – Christ Church.

Our study of the area has led us to the conclusion that Dracula's London residence was here, just a few yards from where Piccadilly meets Park Lane at Hyde Park Corner – No. 137 Piccadilly to be precise. The property occupying this site has recently been refurbished but the previous building matched Stoker's description of a tall, impressive building complete with a balcony and iron railings along the front. It is not hard to imagine it catching Bram's eye as he passed by, giving him the impression that here was just the sort of residence a foreign nobleman would have chosen for himself. Today, 137 Piccadilly serves – appropriately – as the offices of Universal Pictures, makers of the first *Dracula* movie, and is easily spotted next door to the popular Hard Rock Café.

The Lyceum Theatre to which Bram commuted each day is, of course, quite unmistakable. The sixth theatre to stand on the site – although the porticoed front was only added in 1834 – it began life as a musical hall, but later proved even more successful as the venue for staging Shakespeare and other classic plays. Following its closure and rapid deterioration in recent years, the building was finally restored and reopened as a theatre in the autumn of 1996. Its history has of late, though, been a rather chequered one.

Back in 1939, when the curtain came down on the last performance of *Hamlet* starring John Gielgud, the Lyceum had been compulsorily purchased for a road-building scheme to ease traffic congestion and looked certain to be demolished. But with the advent of the Second World War, the building was given a stay of execution and instead became a very

popular dance hall and, subsequently, a venue for pop music concerts. In
the mid-1980s, it was again used for some outstanding productions by the
National Theatre Company, but these did nothing to ensure its future and
once again its doors were closed. Finally, in 1996, the beginning of a £14.5
million refurbishment by the Apollo Leisure Group ensured that the
Lyceum is once again able to stage the kind of spectaculars that Bram
Stoker helped to organise, and Henry Irving starred in, a century ago.
Curiously, although Stoker in *Dracula* refers to Ellen Terry (1847–1928),
regarded by many as the greatest English actress of the nineteenth century
and Irving's co-star for twenty years at the Lyceum, there is no mention
of his employer or the Lyceum Theatre. Instead, Bram refers to the rival
Adelphi Theatre just a few yards along the Strand!

Among the other familiar London landmarks mentioned in the novel are
Hampstead Heath and its environs – the population of which is thrown
into a state of turmoil by the activities of the 'bloofer lady' who attacks and
bites the throats of young children; and Whitechapel, where Dracula stores
several more of his heavy boxes in what is the heart of 'Jack the Ripper'
territory. Bram may well have thought that the association with the serial
killer's murders in 1888, which were still very much in the public mind,
would add an extra *frisson* to his narrative.

Perhaps more intriguing – and certainly more puzzling – are the
extraordinary events which occur in a churchyard on the outskirts of the
city which Bram refers to simply as 'Kingstead'. There is, in fact, no such
burial ground within the vicinity of the city; but once again we believe we
have found the original location utilised by the author.

The events at 'Kingstead' are recounted in Dr Seward's *Diary* of 29
September when Van Helsing enlists the aid of the doctor and Arthur
Holmwood to go to the grave of Holmwood's late fiancée Lucy Westenra,
who he believes has become one of Dracula's Un-Dead. The professor is
also convinced that she is the 'bloofer lady' preying on children on
Hampstead Heath. Although horrified at Van Helsing's suggestion, the
men accompany him to Kingstead and there in the Westenra tomb – in
one of the most gruesome episodes in the entire book – Holmwood is
encouraged to drive a stake through Lucy's quivering body, cut off her
head and fill the mouth with garlic.

Because of the proximity of Hampstead Heath to the famous Highgate
Cemetery, it has long been assumed that this was Bram Stoker's model for
Kingstead. The authors have attended guided tours of the cemetery in
which enthusiastic guides have recounted the story, entirely without

foundation, of how Bram would come on a Sunday afternoon to Highgate to take tea (a peculiar Victorian weekend pastime), and have even pointed to a particular mausoleum as the Westenra tomb. This legend was also given substance by the fact that the catacombs at Highgate Cemetery have often been used by film-makers in their vampire movies, from Hammer *Dracula* movies to one of the best renditions of the story made for BBC Television with Louis Jordan as Dracula in 1976. But, in fact, Highgate Cemetery could not have been the model for Kingstead. One of the first researchers to dispute the generally held view was Philip Temple, writing in the *Times Literary Supplement* of 4 November 1983:

As Dr Seward refers to Jack Straw's Castle and later to the Spaniards Inn familiarly enough, it is obvious that they were not going to Highgate; the road would have taken them past the Spaniards, in which case Seward would have known the way. Nor can they have been crossing the Heath to Highgate because of the description of street lamps on the way. Nor can they have been going to Hampstead churchyard . . . as this would have meant going further into Hampstead village. The inference is that they were going along the North End Road, through Golders Green and along Brent Street to Hendon parish church. The route was straightforward, once the right directions had been taken at the inn. The area was largely countryside.

Although Philip Temple seems slightly confused about locating Jack Straw's Castle and the Spaniards Inn, it does not detract from his main argument. The fact is that if one left Jack Straw's Castle in the direction of the Spaniards Inn one would be journeying along Spaniards Road, across the northern rim of Hampstead Heath, swinging round on the only road leading to Highgate village. Dr Seward's *Diary*, 26 September, recounts how Van Helsing and Seward make a preliminary visit to the Westenra tomb.

[They] dined at Jack Straw's Castle [still a very popular inn] along with a little crowd of bicyclists and others who were genially noisy. About ten o'clock we started from the inn. It was then very dark and the scattered lamps made the darkness greater when we were once outside their individual radius. The Professor had evidently noted the road we were to go, for he went on unhesitatingly; but, as for me, I was in quite a mix-up as to locality. As we went further and further, we met fewer and fewer people, till at last we were somewhat surprised when we met even the patrol of horse police going their usual suburban round. At last we reached the wall of the churchyard, which we climbed over.

A distant clock was striking twelve when Seward began his vigil in the churchyard. Here is an indication of the distance travelled: it does not take two hours to walk from Jack Straw's Castle to Highgate. However, when Seward and Van Helsing rescue a small child they take it back to the edge of Hampstead Heath, leave it for a policeman to find and go silently away. 'By good chance we got a cab near the "Spaniards" and drove to town.'

Philip Temple re-emphasises the point which we have been making throughout this book that Bram Stoker drew unfailingly on actual places for his fictional settings. 'Factual accuracy – of geography and even train timetables – characterises *Dracula*,' he writes, 'a device which makes the story more credible to the reader.' Indeed, the length of the journey, the mention of street lamps (the journey along the Spaniards Road across the Heath and countryside was unlit in the 1890s) could, as Philip Temple suggests, only lead the intrepid pair in one direction, towards Golders Green along North End Road, allowing them to meet 'the patrol of horse police going their usual suburban round'. Mr Temple goes on:

Stoker goes to some lengths to pinpoint Kingstead, and the place he evidently had in mind was Hendon. It would have taken only about an hour to reach Hendon from the inn, a distance of about three miles. This fits in well with Stoker's times, for it was just midnight when Seward and van Helsing, having opened Lucy's coffin and found it empty, took up their hiding places in the churchyard to await the return of the Un-Dead.

As any London map shows, Hendon lies between *Kings*bury and Hamp*stead* and in the 1890s was still only considered to be a 'large village', albeit one that was developing rapidly. A prominent feature then – as today – was the churchyard of St Mary's which, we believe, was Bram's model for his setting, and where can still be found a tomb that matches the description of Lucy Westenra's mausoleum. Although modern Hendon, dominated by the ceaseless traffic entering and leaving the M1 motorway, not to mention the presence of the huge Brent Reservoir, has been swallowed up in the maw of London, in St Mary's churchyard the atmosphere of Victorian times still largely survives among the rows of dissimilar graves and the clusters of overhanging evergreen trees.

At the eastern end of the churchyard stands an imposing stone tomb as high as a single-storey building with a porticoed entrance surrounding a huge, embossed door. Such mausoleums are rare in any churchyard, and this one dominates its surroundings in eerie splendour. It is, in fact, the last resting place of a distinguished Hendon resident, Philip Rundell, who had the tomb specially built years before his demise in 1827. As with so many other artifacts described by Bram in *Dracula*, the tomb matches precisely the Westenra vault that is opened by Van Helsing in Dr Seward's *Diary* account: 'a lordly death-house in a lonely churchyard, away from teeming London.'

There are two possible explanations as to why Bram may have chosen this particular grave for one of the most sensational scenes in his book. Firstly, he may have been told about it by one of his friends – to whom he would later dedicate *Dracula* – and secondly, he may have read about a vampire-like outrage which occurred at St Mary's churchyard in a newspaper report which appeared at the time when, as we know, he was already mapping out the plot for his novel.

Bram's friend was Hall Caine, himself a highly successful Victorian novelist, who from time to time visited the poet-sculptor Thomas Woolner (1826–1892), a long-time resident of Hendon living in Brent Street. Woolner, who came to public attention with his first major work, 'Eleanor sucking the Poison from Prince Edward's Wound', was a conspicuous member of the Pre-Raphaelite movement, and apart from making busts of many of his famous contemporaries – his sculpture of Tennyson is in Westminster Abbey – he wrote poetry for *The Germ* and essays on architecture. The graveyard of St Mary's was one of his favourite places and he conveyed this enthusiasm to all he met. It seems probable that Hall Caine, who was equally close to Bram Stoker, passed on to his friend information about St Mary's when he was seeking inspiration for such a setting. Certainly, no one can doubt the influence Hall Caine had upon the creation of *Dracula*.

For many years, a mystery which intrigued readers of *Dracula* was Bram's dedication of his famous work 'To my dear friend Hommy-Beg'. All manner of solutions were suggested to the question, Who was 'Hommy-Beg'?, including the idea that it must be some Turk who had supplied information to the author. In fact, the epithet disguised the identity of the Manx novelist Sir Thomas Hall Caine KBE (1853–1931). He was the son of Sarah and John Hall Caine from Ballaugh, between Peel and Ramsey, and his grandparents and uncle had farmed on the edge of the Curragh in Ballaugh. In a short memoir in the *Manx Quarterly*, October 1921, Hall Caine recalled that his paternal grandmother spoke no English. She was entirely literate in her native tongue Manx, which is a sister tongue to Irish and Scottish Gaelic. 'I recall the skill with which she could turn up a favourite text in her Manx Bible at the proper page,' Hall Caine wrote, adding: 'She called me Hommy Beg, which was Manx for Little Tommy.'

In both Irish and Manx, when addressing someone called Thomas in the vocative form, the 'T' is aspirated. *A Thomais* is pronounced 'ah homash'. *Beg/Beag* is both the Irish and Manx word for 'little'. In Hall Caine's Manx-speaking family, he was known by the endearment 'Hommy-Beg' or 'Little Tommy'. It is apparent that some of his close friends, of whom Bram was one, used this nickname also. Hall Caine admitted that while he could speak Manx, his prononunication sounded like 'hard swearing'.

Hall Caine had originally left the Isle of Man to become a journalist on the Liverpool *Town Crier* where he impressed Henry Irving with his critique of his production of *Hamlet*. Irving became a close friend of Hall Caine and later introduced Bram Stoker to him, as a result of which they, too, became intimates, often sharing information and giving advice about their literary works. One rumour that persisted before the discovery of the manuscript of *Dracula* in America suggested that Hall Caine had actually written the final draft of the novel for Bram. The first of Hall Caine's own books appeared in 1885 but it was with novels such as *The Deemster* (1887), *The Bondman* (1890) and *The Manxman* (1894) that he became a bestselling writer. In the latter years of his life Hall Caine returned to the Isle of Man and was elected to the House of Keys in the Manx Parliament. He had certainly shared Bram's enthusiasm for the supernatural and dedicated his novel *Capt'n Davy's Honeymoon* (1892) to Bram. It has also been argued that, following Bram's success with *Dracula*, it was Hall Caine who suggested he desert Constable and take his work to William Heinemann Ltd who were Hall Caine's own publishers.

The newspaper article which also could well have brought St Mary's church to Bram's attention appeared in the issue of *Lloyd's Weekly Newspaper* for 10 November 1892. It concerned an incident which had occurred just over sixty years before in November 1828, when a man named Holm had asked the vicar's permission to open up his family vault to allow his medical student son, Henry, to have the opportunity to examine some bones as part of his study. Somewhat reluctantly, the clergyman agreed – but decided to keep a watch on the two men when they entered the vault the following day. What he saw confirmed his worst fears. For once inside, the young Henry Holm proceeded to cut off the head of one of the corpses and place it in a bag. It later transpired that the body had been that of his own mother who had died in 1809.

The furious clergyman alerted the law and father and son were soon charged and found guilty of committing 'an outrage to public decency'. Only the fact that Henry Holm was a *bona fide* student – he said in court that he had removed the head because he wanted to study it in order to trace an hereditary disorder – saved him from a prison sentence. Instead he was fined £50, his father £5, and the case quickly earned a place in local folklore. In retelling the grisly events *Lloyd's Weekly Newspaper* informed its readers that the Holm vault could still be located only a few yards away from the churchyard's most famous tomb – the Rundell mausoleum.

Such a story might be dismissed as a coincidence if there was not strong evidence that Bram saw the newspaper account. In fact, it appeared on exactly the same page as a lengthy and laudatory review of Henry Irving's new production of *King Lear* which had just opened at the Lyceum. Part of Bram's duties was to collect all newspaper items about his employer and the theatre and it is inconceivable that he would have missed this critique complete with several illustrations from the play in what was then a very popular London weekly newspaper. Or that his interest in the macabre – especially anything to do with the dead, considering his then current project – would not have drawn his attention to the bizarre story of Henry Holm. The similarity between the medical student's severing of his mother's head from her body and the actions of his character Arthur Holmwood in *Dracula*, in cutting off Lucy Westenra's head, requires no further comment. Philip Temple in his researches into the locality of 'Kingstead' has added that Bram could well have taken the name for his heart-broken lover turned vampire hunter from the same source. Certainly, on the evidence of the rediscovered manuscript, the name Holmwood was only inserted after it had been typed, lending weight to this theory.

It is one of the more curious aspects of the *Dracula* legend that, although Bram ranged far and wide in his search for authentic background material, and consulted many newspapers as well as books and documents, only one press cutting was found among his papers, a report from the *New York World* of 2 February 1896. It was headlined 'Vampires in New England'.

Subtitled 'The Old Belief Was that Ghostly Monsters Suckled the Blood of Their Living Relatives', the two-column feature reported on the discovery of vampirism made by 'an ethnologist of repute', George R. Stotson, in the scattered Rhode Island hamlets of Exeter, Foster, Kingstown and east Greenwich. As a result of his research, Stotson had concluded that 'the ancient vampire superstition still survives in the States, and within the last few years many people have been digging up dead bodies for the purpose of burning their hearts'. By way of comparison, the ethnologist added that 'in some parts of Europe the belief still has a hold on the popular mind' and cited cases in Greece, Armenia and Hungary.

As Bram was in America in February 1896, masterminding Irving's sixth tour of the USA, it seems probable that he clipped the article from *The New York World*, which had always been prominent among US papers in warmly receiving any new production by the English actor. If it was not actually torn from the paper by his own hand, it could just as easily have been supplied by Thomas Donaldson whom he saw again in Philadelphia and who was fully *au fait* with the theme of the novel which his friend was working on.

Bram, in fact, made full use of Irving's two US tours in 1895 and 1896 to continue working on *Dracula* between engagements, as the evidence of the scraps of hotel notepaper from the time substantiates. The second of these tours, which lasted for seven months and included 240 performances, was one of the actor's most successful visits to America and undoubtedly added to the glow of pleasure he was already feeling from the knighthood he had been awarded on 24 May 1895 – by coincidence the same day Oscar Wilde was convicted at the Old Bailey. It was also in the spring of 1896 that the work Bram had put into researching *Cymbeline* at Cruden Bay, while also gathering material for *Dracula*, came into its own when Irving decided to stage the play in the autumn. *Cymbeline* opened at the Lyceum on 22 September 1896, with Irving as the 'subtle, tenebrous, deadly creature', Iachimo, and although the acerbic critic, George Bernard Shaw, condemned it as 'stagey trash', it ran until just before Christmas to full houses.

The American trips also convinced Bram about his model for Count Dracula in the form of the newly ennobled thespian. Bram had already decided that his vampire would change from an old man into a younger one and vice versa after each infusion of blood; and Irving just as easily slipped into any age depending on what part he was playing. In April 1894 – a crucial period in the development of *Dracula* – he had begun a four-month run in *Faust* at the Lyceum and repeated his coldly majestic interpretation of Mephistopheles, a part he played in all almost 700 times, in the States during the following year.

Reviews of Irving in *Faust* speak of his 'Satanic qualities' with J. F. Nisbet of *The Times* referring to the actor's personality as being 'peculiarly rich in the elements of the weird, the sinister, the sardonic, the grimly humorous, the keenly intellectual'. Indeed, the character of Mephistopheles is still widely regarded as one of the actor's finest achievements, 'remaining indelibly stamped upon the mind as a great creation'. What better model could Bram have for his Un-Dead Count than this figure who prowled and raged before his eyes on the stage every night, and of whom the critic of the *Toronto News* wrote: 'We have had *Faust* sung to us and *Faust* played to us, but never have we had Goethe's immortal work presented as it was at the Grand Opera House last night.'

We have no doubt that Irving was Stoker's model for Dracula. Just as Lord Byron is acknowledged to have inspired the vampire character in the novel by his physician John Polidori, *The Vampyre* (1819), so Sir Henry inspired Dracula. The similarities in physique and looks are striking and obvious; and it is not beyond the realms of possibility that Bram would have liked his employer to play the role of the vampire on stage – Irving's hissing, metallic voice and saturnine air as seen in *Faust* would have made him ideal and certainly a precursor to the enduring interpretation given by Bela Lugosi on the screen. The only problem, of course, was that Irving witnessed the free performance of *Dracula or The Un-Dead – In a Prologue and Five Acts* at the Lyceum on the morning of Tuesday, 18 May 1897, just before the publication of the book. He pronounced on it in one word: 'Dreadful!'

If this verdict hurt Bram Stoker he gave no indication. Probably at the time he had no more ambition for his novel than that it would pay a few domestic bills. He certainly had no idea that the book he had worked upon while travelling in two continents, and finally delivered to Otto Kyllman at Constable, would later be hailed as a masterpiece of horror fiction and still be avidly read a hundred years later. Nor that *Dracula* would promote more research, study and rumours concerning its origins and composition than he could possibly have imagined.

CHAPTER TWELVE

The Mystery of Stoker's Death

Dracula WAS PUBLISHED on Thursday, 24 June 1897, in a first printing of 3000 copies. Bound in pale yellow cloth with the title and author embossed in red – there was no dust jacket – the book was priced at six shillings. The first copies to leave Constable's offices in Whitehall were destined for the literary editors of the major national newspapers and magazines. The reviews which the novel gathered were numerous, mostly enthusiastic, but not always from expected quarters.

The *Daily Mail* for example, found the book 'weird, powerful and horrible', accurately comparing its impact to *Frankenstein, Wuthering Heights* and *The Fall of the House of Usher*. But, the critic said, '*Dracula* is even more appalling in its gloomy fascination than any of these!' The *Pall Mall Gazette* considered it 'horrid and creepy to the last degree and one of the best things in the supernatural line that we have been lucky enough to hit upon'. The *Punch* reviewer, who signed himself enigmatically as 'The Baron de B-W', recommended the work unreservedly to 'all who enjoy the very weirdest of weird tales'. *The Bookman* 'read nearly the whole with rapt attention. It is something of a triumph for the writer . . .'

Bram's literary friends were just as enthusiastic. Anthony Hope, the author of *The Prisoner of Zenda* (1894), wrote on 27 June 1897: 'Your vampires robbed me of sleep for nights.' On 20 August 1897, Conan Doyle wrote: 'I think it is the very best story of diablerie which I have read for many years. It is really wonderful with so much exciting interest over so long a book there is never an anticlimax.'

Surprisingly, the normally genteel magazine, *The Lady*, also found room for a mention, allowing itself to become quite overwhelmed by the story which was 'so fascinating that it is impossible to lay it aside.'

In fact, Bram's biggest female fan was to prove his mother who, after receiving a copy, wrote to her son from Rathgar:

> My dear, it is splendid, a thousand miles beyond anything you have written before, and I feel certain will place you very high in the writers of the day – the story and style being deeply sensational, exciting and interesting.

She added, a few days afterwards:

> I have seen a great review of *Dracula* in a London paper. They have not said one word too much of it. No book since Mrs Shelley's *Frankenstein* or indeed any other at all has come near yours in originality, or terror – Poe is nowhere. I have read much but I never met a book like it at all. In its terrible excitment it should make a widespread reputation and much money for you.

Whether the elderly Charlotte Stoker realised the influence that her own stories, and the family's Irish background, had exerted upon the creation of *Dracula* will never be known. But she was undoubtedly the first reader to appreciate the genuine importance of the book and the fame that it would bring to Bram. Her only error was in thinking that the book would make him wealthy. For the sad fact remains that the greatest sales of *Dracula*, its enormous popularity as a subject for movies, and the use of the central character in countless sequels and every form of merchandising, were only to come long after Stoker's death when the work was in the public domain and free for anyone to reprint or adapt for the screen.

There is another Irish tie with *Dracula* in that the first commercial dramatisation of the novel as a three-act play was written by the actor Hamilton Deane. He was from Dublin and had joined Irving's Lyceum company in 1899. In 1923, at the height of his stage fame, Deane turned to the idea of a dramatisation. *Dracula* was put on at the Grand Theatre, Derby, in June 1924. Dracula was played by Edmund Blake. Dora May Patrick, Deane's wife, played Mina Harker. G. Malcolm Russell portrayed Van Helsing. When the play, a success in the provinces, opened at the Little Theatre in London, on 14 February 1927, Raymond Huntley, only twenty-two years old, took the role of Dracula. The play was a commercial success in spite of adverse reviews and went on to the Duke of York's and Prince of Wales Theatres. In spite of the jeers of critics, it ran for 391 performances. Huntley went on to become a well-known character actor, usually as a self-satisfied businessman or a supercilious type, in films.

In 1927 an American producer, Horace Liveright, purchased the play and made Deane collaborate with writer John Lloyd Balderston on a new draft. It opened at the New York Fulton Theatre in October 1927 and starred the unknown Bela Lugosi, who was to make the role of the 'Un-Dead' his own. The theatre was booked solidly for a year. By 1931 the first major 'talkie' *Dracula* film was released to the public and Lugosi took the role from stage to film. Film sequel followed film sequel.

These years made up for the three long years when Florence fought to get compensation from the German film company Prana-Films who, in 1921, issued an unauthorised silent screen version under the title *Nosferatu: Eine Symphonie des Gravens* written by Henrik Galeen, directed by Friedrich Wilhelm Galeen and starring Max Schreck. Florence demanded £5000 and the destruction of the film. Prana-Films declared themselves bankrupt and claimed the film had been incinerated. Universal, however, paid Florence $40,000 for the film rights in 1931.

The Deane and Balderston play was published as *Dracula* by Samuel French of New York in 1933. In 1939 Hamilton Deane finally brought his play to the very stage where Bram had put on his first reading to protect his copyright. The Lyceum production ended with a memorable meeting on stage between Bela Lugosi, now firmly associated in the public's minds with Dracula due to the films, and Hamilton Deane. Deane's final portrayal of Dracula was in 1941. By that time five 'Dracula' films had been made. Within the next fifty years a further thirty-six major 'Dracula' films were to appear.

It was the fifth 'Dracula' movie which suddenly created widespread publicity for the Un-Dead Count although, ironically, the character of Dracula did not appear in it. The film which suddenly gained the attention of the press was based on Bram's short story 'Dracula's Guest', the deleted first chapter of his novel. It had been retitled for the screen *Dracula's Daughter* by Universal Pictures in 1936. The controversy arose when it was banned as 'too horrific' by the Entertainments Committees of the London, Surrey and Middlesex County Councils.

The film, which credited its origin to Bram's short story, was directed by Lambert Hillyer, with a screenplay by Garrett Fort and Oliver Jeffries. Gloria Holden played the Un-Dead 'Countess Marya Zaleska'. The film is also notable for the appearance of Hedda Hopper (1890–1966) in her acting days before she rose to become Hollywood's most powerful gossip columnist. *The Times*, of 11 July and 21 July 1936, in an article headlined 'Ban on "Horrific" Film', reported that in spite of an announcement by Lord Tyrrell, President of the British Board of Film Censors, that 'the horrific category of films had now ceased to exist', it had been decided that in the London area the film could only be shown under the conditions applicable to the 'horrific' category. *The Times* observed:

> A decision to place a film in the horrific category may easily affect the takings of cinemas showing it, but the licensing authorities' view is that children should not be frightened by the exhibition of such films and a previous warning should be given to parents. The horrific category was introduced in 1934 after a large meeting at Caxton Hall, which was attended by delegates from the London Morality Council and the National Council of Women and similar bodies.

Rather than reducing the takings at cinema box-offices, the reverse was true. Audiences flocked to see the film, encouraged by the 'ban'. It was the start of the amazing Dracula film industry.

Dracula had been Bram's fourth novel. He was to write seven more novels as well as works of non-fiction and a posthumous collection of short stories. His literary output began to increase after the death of his friend, mentor and employer, Henry Irving, who collapsed and died after a performance of *Beckett* in Bradford on 13 October 1905. Bram now needed to rely more on his literary work for an income. But all his work was to be dwarfed by *Dracula*. He wrote four more novels with weird themes – *The Mystery of the Sea* (1902), *The Jewel of Seven Stars* (1903), *The Lady of the Shroud* (1909) and *The Lair of the White Worm* (1911) – but all fall far short of the standards he had set in his vampire novel. It is true that *The Jewel of the Seven Stars* helped to give birth to the subsequent Egyptian 'mummy' horror cult and that it has been filmed twice to date, and that *The Lair of the White Worm* has also been filmed by Ken Russell, but the sheer scalp-crawling terrors of *Dracula* are missing. Only in some of his short stories, collected in *Dracula's Guest and Other Weird Stories* (1914), did he even begin to approach the standard set by his own success.

Daniel Farson presents Stoker dying in poverty and failure. Certainly, as he was no longer able to rely on an income from the Lyceum, an income from his literary output was essential. Daniel Farson appears to censure

Bram's brother Sir William Thornley for not helping him out of the financial difficulties of his latter years. We are told that 'Bram was applying desperately for £100 from a literary fund'. It is true that Bram did petition for a grant from the Royal Literary Society in February 1911. But one questions just how financially 'desperate' he was. In making the claim he states that his earnings for 1910 were £166. This is just over the average wage which was £150 per annum. Of this £166, Bram had confessed (in December 1910) to his brother Thornley that his income from royalties had only been £86 that year. 'Not much for a living wage,' he comments, 'but there is hope that we can manage and pull through.' Professor Belford agrees that things were in a bad way and that the Stokers were forced out of their Chelsea house in 1911 to a smaller apartment at 26 St George's Square, Belgravia.

Farson goes so far as to claim that a rift had taken place between Bram and William Thornley. 'His [Bram's] only child was named after Thornley but perhaps Thornley had become too "posh" to care much about Bram's misfortune.' Even if Bram was in the dire straits depicted by Farson, he had not been ostracised by his brother, as the biographer claims. During this very period, William Thornley had sat down to make out a new will in which he left £1000 to Bram and £200 to Bram's son, Noel. The sum of £200 also went to another nephew, Thomas Thornley Stoker. The probate on William Thornley's will was granted in June 1912, just after Bram's own death, with the £1000 going to Bram's heir and executor, his widow Florence.

Bram's own will was made on 19 March 1912, just a month before he died. His estate was valued at £5640 5s. 7d., according to the probate on his will. This was before the receipt of the £1000 legacy from Bram's brother, who died some weeks after him, which was paid to Florence. Yet all previous biographies give £4723 as the sum left by Bram. The only explanation is that someone has deducted the £1000 instead of adding it on. Even so, one would hardly claim, comparing this to the average income of the day, that Bram had died in poverty. Therefore Bram's 'desperate finances' would seem rather relative. Daniel Farson's graphic picture, given in *The Mail on Sunday* 3 January 1993, of the Stokers being so poor that Florrie had to go out to work, reading aloud to Thackeray's daughter for the sum of 3s.6d. an hour, seems hard to accept in view of the financial position revealed by Bram's will.

Bram's books continued to sell after his death and monies now began to come in from motion picture rights to *Dracula*. Yet when Florence died at her home in Knightsbridge in 1937, her estate was only valued at £6913 9s. 1d. after she had made certain bequests. The London Library was the recipient of her collection of books by the Irish writer Maria Edgeworth (1767–1849). The London Museum received a portrait of Henry Irving by Sir Bernard Partridge, an Irving statuette by Onslow Ford and Irving's hand in bronze, all items once treasured by Bram. To the Victoria and Albert Museum went Florrie's Sheffield toast rack in the form of a lyre, some Nailsea glass, including a window stop in the form of an animal, and a blue Bristol glass roller. To her niece Phillippa Margey Adams went some family portraits, Rockingham china, work boxes, needle-point and other items. Apart from some other small financial bequests, her son Noel was chief beneficiary. He had married in July 1910 and, uninspired by his father's love of the theatre and literature, had become an accountant.

The last great mystery that surrounds Bram Stoker and the *Dracula* legend is his death. For just as myth and rumour have enveloped the writing of his famous novel, so the actual cause of his end has been the subject of a great deal of controversy and argument and legend-making.

Bram Stoker's first biopgrapher, Harry Ludlam, in recounting Bram's death at 26 St George's Square, Belgravia, on 20 April 1912, doubtless thought he was being diplomatic when he reported that the death certificate recorded that Bram had died from 'exhaustion'. Bram's great-nephew, Daniel Farson, became the first biographer to reveal the full wording of the cause of death given on his death certificate – 'Locomotor Ataxy 6 months Granular Contracted Kidney. Exhaustion. Certified by James Browne MD'. Locomotor ataxy means an inability to co-ordinate the voluntary movements, and the granular, or roughened, contracted kidneys point to kidney failure.

Daniel Farson believed that this was the equivalent to the medical conditions *tabes dorsalis* and *general paresis*, otherwise General Paralysis of the Insane, usually the result of tertiary syphilis. Certainly, Boyd's *Textbook of Pathology* (1943), a standard work for students of its day, says: '*Tabes dorsalis* or *locomotor ataxia* is a syphilitic disease of the [spinal] cord ...' Farson comments: 'My doctor was astonished that Dr Browne had not used a customary subterfuge, such as "specific disease".'

If we accept that Farson's interpretation is correct, then any lack of subterfuge, as noted by him, may be put down to the conscientious and ethical character of Bram's doctor, Dr James Browne, who has been overlooked in this story. Perhaps this was because the name seems at first glance, so nondescript that other biographers thought there would be nothing of interest about Dr Browne. But he was linked with a unique piece of Irish literary history. James Browne MD was born in 1869 in Sunday's Well, Cork, the eldest son of a local business family, many of whom had entered the service of the Catholic Church. His uncle was Bishop of Cloyne; his maternal grandfather was a Lord Mayor of the city. After studying medicine in Ireland, James Browne went to work at Southwark Hospital, London. James had the difficult experience of having to sign his own father's death certificate in 1898 when his father died in a swimming accident at Crosshaven, Co. Cork. James, though not a writer, was also a member of the Irish Literary Society and therefore may well have been a friend of Bram through this connection as well as being his doctor.

It was James' brother, Father Francis Browne, who became immortalised in James Joyce's *Finnegans Wake* as 'Mr Browne the Jesuit'. Frank, a Jesuit priest, was the exact contemporary and friend of James Joyce at what was then the Royal University of Ireland at St Stephen's Green in Dublin, from 1899 to 1902. Both Frank Browne and James Joyce had parents from Cork, both had been to school at Belvedere College, where their friendship began, and both were keen photographers. Whereas Joyce was to open Dublin's first cinema, The Volta, on Mary Street in 1909, Father Browne was to spend a lifetime with his camera. His collection of 42,000 photographs, taken all over the world, has made him acknowledged as one of the great photographers of the century. His most famous series of pictures was taken on the maiden voyage of the ill-fated *Titanic* in 1912. Frank had sailed on the *Titanic* from Southampton to Cherbourg and then to Queenstown (Cobh). His stateroom was next to that of the designer of the *Titanic*, Thomas Andrews from Comber, Co. Down, the managing director of Harland and Wolff of Belfast, which had built the liner. Andrews was to go down with the ship.

Father Browne took many photographs while the *Titanic* was at sea. He was scheduled to continue on the last leg of the voyage to New York but at Queenstown he received a telegraph from the Provincial Superior of the Jesuits in Dublin telling him succinctly 'to get off that ship'. His last photo, taken on 11 April from the tender at Queenstown, was of Captain Edward J. Smith almost prophetically gazing into a life-boat.

On the day Frank's brother James was writing the death certificate of Bram Stoker, 20 April, Frank was returning to Queenstown from Dublin to attend a memorial service conducted by their uncle Robert, the Bishop of Cloyne, for the *Titanic* victims at St Colman's Cathedral. It was also the day when the official inquiry into the sinking was due to start. Frank's *Titanic* photographs are now world famous. *Father Browne: A Life in Pictures* by E. E. O'Donnell mentions his brother's link with Bram Stoker.

One could point out that there is yet another link between the Browne, Joyce and Stoker families. While the parents of both Browne and Joyce were from Cork, both families originated in Co. Galway. And it was in Kilsheagh, Co. Galway, that a Stoker married a Browne linking the two families by marriage in the early nineteenth century.

But to return to Farson's claims. We have to question whether the medical advice he received about the meaning of the certificate was entirely correct, and whether there can be any other explanation for the condition which brought about Bram's death. We sought several medical opinions, one of which resulted in a very different explanation.

It is by no means certain, says one of the pathologists we consulted, that tertiary syphilis lay behind the words on the death certificate as they stand. In modern times, the words '*locomotor ataxia*' would not even be used on a certificate as they describe a symptom, not a cause, and such a symptom could be due to any number of causes. What immediately sprang to this doctor's mind was Parkinson's disease, a degenerative brain disorder sometimes connected with encephalitis and sometimes caused by mumps, rabies or herpes viruses. Another cause could be multiple sclerosis, although the onset of this chronic degenerative disease of the central nervous system usually appears between the ages of twenty and forty.

As to the 'granular contracted kidney', what immediately came to the mind of the expert was tuberculosis, identified by Robert Koch in 1882 and formerly known as consumption. But the condition could also come about through any urinary infection. This is significant. Farson reports that his mother believed Bram had Bright's disease, a disease of the kidneys now known as acute glomerulonephritis, and that he suffered from gout in his last years, which is a form of arthritis. Bright's disease alone could have led to the granular contracted kidney. Bram had, in fact, suffered a stroke in 1906. He had been unconscious for twenty-four hours on that occasion. He suffered a second stroke in May 1909.

Professor Belford's biography became the first study to refute the claims of Daniel Farson, quoting two leading medical authorities. One of them states clearly: 'If Stoker had *locomotor ataxia* for only six months before his death, then it is unlikely it was due to syphilis.' Professor Belford's advice was that the *locomotor ataxia* was more likely to be a residual symptom from the two strokes that Bram had suffered.

We consulted the retired eminent pathologist, Professor Denis Baron, who concurs with the medical advice given to Daniel Farson. 'I believe that in former times the terms [*locomotor ataxia* and *tabes dorsalis*] were synonymous, though this does not mean the diagnosis was correct.' However, Professor Baron pursued the matter by consulting contemporary textbooks of medicine, such as *A System of Medicine VII*, 1910, by Osler and Macrae. '*Tabes dorsalis* is also known as *locomotor ataxia*,' it states. It also says: 'We are safe in saying that syphilitic infection is by far the most common cause of *tabes dorsalis* . . . A person who has not had syphilis was not likely to have *tabes dorsalis*.' Professor Baron points out that the Wasserman test, a reliable laboratory diagnostic procedure, was introduced in 1906. However, we do not know whether this was done in Bram's case nor whether there was an autopsy. It seems unlikely. Professor Baron's comment on the matter is: 'Syphilis till proved otherwise: after all, this was a common disease amongst a section of the literati of the nineteenth century. I am surprised that Dickens was not affected with his Parisian brothel crawls with Wilkie Collins. AIDS has now taken its place.'

Yet, in the interests of total accuracy, we can only conclude that the modern legend that Bram Stoker died from syphilis is, as yet, 'unproven' in Scottish legal terms.

Nevertheless, the theory that Bram Stoker died of syphilis has opened up a new 'Dracula industry'. Articles and books have flooded forth, fast and furious, each adding to the legend, so that no one now doubts the veracity of the syphilis legend. Speculations as to how Bram Stoker contracted syphilis have occupied many scribes. Farson mentions a theory that 'possibly the disease was contracted in Paris, where so many "faithful husbands" such as Charles Dickens and Wilkie Collins had gone for discreet pleasure before him'. It was known that Bram had visited Paris, says Farson. This then gave birth to another story that Bram contracted syphilis while he was visiting Oscar Wilde in exile in Paris, the result of an indiscretion while bringing money from Willie Wilde to his brother.

Daniel Farson's positive assertion as to the cause of his great-uncle's death has allowed a new outpouring of bizarre hypotheses to be churned out in both journals and books. Farson himself has led the way with his own articles which have appeared in various publications from *Penthouse* to *The Mail on Sunday*. These psychoanalytical dissertations, attempting to prove that Bram suffered from various sexual frustrations, have become legion. Freudian analysis has been conjured to show that Bram was 'full of sexual rage'. Maurice Richardson, one of the earliest to write an article on 'The Psychoanalysis of Ghost Stories', says of *Dracula*:

> Guilt is everywhere and deep ... A blatant demonstration of the Oedipus complex. From a Freudian standpoint – and from no other does the story really make sense – it is seen as a kind of incestuous, necrophilous, oral-anal-sadistic all-in wrestling match.

The author who wrote in an article in *Nineteenth Century* (1908) on contemporary fiction, criticising its promiscuity, might well have been astounded. Bram wrote that 'the only emotions which in the long run harm, are those arising from sex impulses'. Yet it could be argued that Bram's moralising was made from a position of guilt. He certainly argued for censorship. While saying that 'it is as natural for man to sin as to live' he goes on to say that 'women are the worst offenders in this form of breach of moral law'. Naturally, this has also been seized upon as Bram blaming his sexual downfall on women.

The point is, once it was accepted that Bram had contracted syphilis, and died from it, all manner of interpretations of his work were then conjectured. Farson himself admits (in *Penthouse*): 'I would hardly recognise a Freudian symbol myself if I fell over one, but in *The Lair of the White Worm* they are inescapable. It is such a weird book that it may well become a cult, and it is significant that it is next in popularity to *Dracula* as far as sales are concerned, though virtually unknown. It is rampant with sexual symbolism and hallucination.' Later, Farson would say of his great-uncle: 'He was a walking casebook of sexual confusion.'

But why would the personable, handsome young Irishman, who had married one of the great beauties of the day, and who had a healthy son, eventually turn into a sexually repressed figure of tragedy; a figure presented by Farson as ending his days as a terminally ill, half-blind, worn-out shell of a man who considered himself a failure in life? Indeed, Farson himself is the only source to provide any arguments to support this image. It must be said that Bram's immediate descendants disagree not only with their biographer cousin's interpretation of the death certificate but with his various stories of Bram's sexual frustrations. However, in support of his arguments, Farson says that from his researches and from what his grandmother, Enid Stoker, told him, Florrie was an emotionally cold woman who was not really capable of love. Farson says it was probable that Florrie refused to have a sexual relationship with Bram after the birth of their son Noel; this would have led to Bram's frustrations and explain his obsession with the ideal woman. It is claimed that the 'ideal woman' is an image which is presented in most of Bram's works.

Certainly many signs and symbols may be read into Bram's work for those who wish to seek out such signs and symbols. This much can surely be said for every writer's work. For example, Freudians and Jungians have had a field day analysing Henry Rider Haggard's novel *She* (1887), imputing all manner of psychological problems to one who was, in essence, simply an excellent storyteller. So it may be argued with Bram Stoker. It does not alter the fact that we are merely in the realms of speculation; speculation that still continues to give a living momentum to the legend of Bram Stoker and *Dracula*. The arguments will undoubtedly continue to rage over the interpretation of the cause of death as given on Bram's medical certificate. Indeed, arguments will also undoubtedly continue to rage over the influences leading to the creation of Bram Stoker's classic work. That is merely proof of the enduring quality of the novel, of the emotions that it has aroused and continues to arouse. It does not detract from the fact that *Dracula* is one of the most terrifying and best-known books ever written.

ACKNOWLEDGEMENTS AND
SELECTED BIBLIOGRAPHY

We would like to particularly acknowledge the invaluable advice and assistance from the following (in alphabetical order) in helping us prepare this study: Jack Adrian, Mike Ashley, Professor Denis N. Baron, Jim Buchan, Tony and Muriel Coughlan of Trinity College, Dublin, Richard Dalby, Richard Noel Dobbs, Daniel Farson, Bruce Francis, Alan R. Fulton, Brian Inglis, Dick Le Fanu, Mark Le Fanu, Dennis MacIntyre of the Bram Stoker Summer School and Dan O'Donoghue. Special thanks must go to an indefatigable researcher – Elizabeth Murray. We also express our appreciation to Dr Jeanne Youngson, *Dracula* fan and expert, for her enthusiasm over the years.

LIBRARIES AND REPOSITORIES

Aberdeen Central Library
Aberdeen Evening Express Ltd
Bram Stoker Society Library, Dublin
British Library, London
William Andrews Clarke Library (for letters of Oscar Wilde to Florence Balcombe (Stoker) see 'Books' under Rupert Hart-Davis)
Department of Irish Folklore, University College, Dublin
General Register Office, Dublin
General Register Office, London
The Brotherton Collection, Leeds University Library (thousands of items mostly directed to Bram as business manager of the Lyceum and replies)
London Library
National Library of Ireland, Dublin
Public Record Office, London (for Army service records such as James Balcombe service record WO 31/995, WO 25/431, etc.)
The Philip H. and A. S. W. Rosenbach Foundation Library, Philadelphia (Bram Stoker's working papers and notes for *Dracula*)

Shakespeare Memorial Theatre Library, Straford-upon-Avon (Bram Stoker's collection
   of papers relating to Sir Henry Irving)
Trinity College Library, Dublin
Whitby Public Library
Whitby Express Ltd

GUIDES/REFERENCE BOOKS

A List of the Officers of the Army and Royal Marines on Full and Half Pay (War Office)
   1814, 1815, 1816, 1817, 1818.
Dictionary of National Biography.
Dublin Historical Record, Vols XIV and XXX (material on Harcourt Street, Ely Place
   and 'hanging judges').
Ellis's Irish Education Directory and Scholastic Guide, ed. William Edward Ellis, Dublin
   1885.
The Clergy Lists (Lists of Clergy for Ireland), 1863, 1870, 1877 etc.
The New Annual Army List, 1853, etc., ed. Colonel H. G. Hart, John Murray, London.
Thom's Official Directory etc, *Thom's Trade Directory*, *Thom's Law Directory* etc., Alex
   Thom and Co. Ltd, Middle Abbey Street, Dublin (1846–1912).
Twentieth Century Authors, Kunitz and Haycraft, 1st edition.
20th Century Literary Manuscripts, D. I. Masson (for listings of Bram Stoker's letters
   and locations).
Who Was Who, 1897 onwards.

UNPUBLISHED PAPERS FROM THE BRAM STOKER SUMMER SCHOOL
(Bram Stoker Society Library, Dublin)

'Bram Stoker's *Dracula* – the Clontarf, Dublin and Irish Influences', Dennis McIntyre.
'Bram Stoker and Irish Gothic', R. J. McNally.
'Bram Stoker and the Irish Supernatural Tradition', Leslie Shepard.

UNPUBLISHED THESIS

'Bram Stoker and the Irish Supernatural Tradition', Freddie Burns.

ARTICLES

Anon. 'Irishmen in the Balkans', *Irish Sword*, Vol. IX, No. 34.
Anderson, W. M. E. 'Battle of Ballinamuck, 1798', *Irish Sword*, Vol. I, No. 2 (See also
   Vol. I, No. 3.)
Bierman, Joseph S. 'The Genesis and Dating of *Dracula* from Bram Stoker's Working
   Notes', *Notes and Queries* 24 (1977).
Bierman, Joseph S. '*Dracula*: Prolonged Childhood Illness and the Oral Triad',
   American Imago 29 (1972).
Copson-Niecko, Maria J. E. 'Irish-Polish Correspondence – concerning plans to enlist
   in the Service of the Porte in 1850 and 1855', *Irish Sword*, Vol. XI, No. 44.

Craft, Christopher. 'Kiss me with Those Red Lips: Gender and Inversion in Bram Stoker's *Dracula*', *Representations* 8 (1984).

Cranny-Francis, Anne. 'Sexual Politics and Political Repression in Bram Stoker's *Dracula*', in *Nineteenth Century Suspense: From Poe to Conan Doyle*, ed. Clive Bloom, Macmillan, London, 1988.

Crotty, Francis, 'A Letter from Varna, 1854', *Irish Sword*, Vol. XIV, No. 57.

Dalby, Richard. 'Bram Stoker', *Book and Magazine Collector*, London, October 1991.

Demetrakopoulos, Stephanie. 'Feminism, Sex Roles, Exchanges and Other Subliminal Fantasies in Bram Stoker's *Dracula*', *Frontiers: A Journal of Women's Studies* 2 (1977).

Drummond, James. 'Bram Stoker's Cruden Bay', *Scots Magazine*, April 1976.

Drummond, James. 'Dracula's Castle', *The Weekend Scotsman*, 26 June 1976.

Farson, Daniel. 'The Cult of *Dracula*', *Penthouse*, 1975.

Farson, Daniel. 'The Sexual Torment of the Man who Created *Dracula*', *The Mail on Sunday*, 3 January 1993.

Fry, Carroll. 'Fictional Conventions and Sexuality in Dracula', *Victorian Newsletter*, 42 (1972).

Griffin, Gail B. 'Your Girls That You All Love Are Mine; *Dracula* and the Victorian Male Sexual Imagination', *International Journal of Women's Studies* 5 (1980).

Hamilton, Alan. 'The Port of Whitby', *The Times*, 26 October 1991.

Howes, Marjorie. 'The Mediation of the Feminine: Bisexuality, Homoerotic desire, and Self-Expression in Bram Stoker's *Dracula*', *Texas Studies in Literature and Language* 30 (Spring 1988).

Johnson, Alan. 'Dual Life: The Status of Women in Stoker's *Dracula*', *Tennessee Studies in Literature* 27 (1984).

Johnson, Alan. 'Bent and Broken Necks: Signs of design in Stoker's *Dracula*', *Victorian Newsletter* 72 (1987).

MacGillivray, Royce. '*Dracula*: Bram Stoker's Spoiled Masterpiece', *Queen's Quarterly* 79 (1972).

McGrath, Kevin. 'Count Maximilian Ulysses Brown(e) (1705–57): An Irish Field Marshal in the Austrian Service', *Irish Sword*, Vol. 1, No. 3.

Martin, Philip. 'The Vampire in the Looking-Glass; Reflection and Projection in Bram Stoker's *Dracula*', in *Nineteenth Century Suspense: From Poe to Conan Doyle*, ed. Clive Bloom, Macmillan, London, 1988.

Ó Sandáir, Cathal. 'Dracula Domharfa', *Irish Times*, 18 May 1993.

Pope, Rebecca A. 'Writing and Biting in *Dracula*', *LIT – Literature Interpretation Theory*, Vol. 1 (March 1990).

Richardson, Maurice. 'The Psychoanalysis of Ghost Stories', *Twentieth Century* No. 166 (1959).

Ronay, Gabriel. 'Exploding the Bloody Myths of *Dracula* and Vampires', *The Times*, 4 December 1971.

Senf, Carol A. '*Dracula*: Stoker's response to the New Woman', *Victorian Studies* 26 (1982).

Senf, Carol A. '*Dracula*: The Unseen Face in the Mirror', *Journal of Narrative Technique* 9 (1979).

Temple, Philip. *Times Literary Supplement*, 4 November 1983.

Turner, Francesa. 'Whitby Experience', *Yorkshire Life*, September 1986.
Von Allendorfer, F. 'Irish Officers in the Turkish Service', *Irish Sword*, Vol. II, No. 9 and J. L. Garland, *Irish Sword*, Vol. III, No. 11.
Weissman, Judith. 'Woman and Vampires: *Dracula* as a Victorian Novel', *Midwest Quarterly* 18 (1977).
Note: a source for the literary endeavours at Trinity College, Dublin, during Bram's time is the pages of the magazine *Kottabos*, published William McGee, Nassau Street, Dublin, 1861–1895, *passim*.

BOOKS

Alder, Lory, and Dalby, Richard. *The Dervish of Windsor Castle* (a biography of Arminius Vambéry), Bachman and Turner, London, 1979.
Bailey, Kenneth C. *A History of Trinity College, Dublin 1892–1945*, The University Press, Dublin, (Trinity College) and Hodges, Figgis and Co. Ltd, Dublin, 1947.
Belford, Barbara. *Bram Stoker: A biography of the author of Dracula*, Weidenfeld and Nicholson, London, 1996.
Brereton, Austin. *The Life of Henry Irving*, Longman, Green and Co. London, 1908.
Browne, Nelson. *Sheridan Le Fanu*, Arthur Baker Ltd, London, 1951.
Buchan, Jim. *Bygone Buchan*, The Buchan Field Club, 1987.
Buchan, Jim. *Peterhead and District*, European Library, Zaltbommel, The Netherlands, 1995.
Cameron, Sir Charles. *History of the Royal College of Surgeons in Ireland and of the Irish schools of medicine*, Fannin and Co. Dublin, 1916.
Carter, Margaret L., ed. *Dracula: The Vampire and the Critics*, UMI Research Press, Ann Arbor, USA, 1988.
Copper, Basil. *The Vampire in Legend, Fact and Art*, Robert Hale, London, 1973.
Cox, Montagu H. and Norman, Philip. *London County Council Survey of London* (Vol. XIII), B. T. Batsford, London, 1930.
Crofton Croker, T. and Clifford, Sigerson, *Legends of Kerry*, Geraldine Press, Kerry, Ireland, 1972.
Dalby, Richard. *Bram Stoker: A Bibliography of First Editions*, Dracula Press, London, 1983.
Dalby, Richard. *Dracula's Brood*, Crucible, an imprint of Aquarian Press, London, 1987.
Danaher, Kevin. *In Ireland Long Ago*, Mercier, Cork, 1964.
Danaher, Kevin, *Irish Country People*, Mercier, Cork, 1966.
De Blacam, Aodh. *A First Book of Irish Literature*, The Talbot Press, Dublin, 1925.
de Vere White, Terence. *The Parents of Oscar Wilde – Sir William and Lady Wilde*, Hodder and Stoughton, London, 1967.
Donaldson, Thomas. *Walt Whitman: The Man*, Gay and Bird, London, 1897.
Dunne, John. *Haunted Ireland*, Blackstaff, Belfast, 1977.
Ellis, Peter Berresford. *A Dictionary of Irish Mythology*, Constable, London, 1987.
Ellmann, Richard. *Oscar Wilde*, Hamish Hamilton, London, 1987.
Farson, Daniel. *The Man Who Wrote Dracula: A biography of Bram Stoker*, Michael Joseph, London, 1975.

Frazer, J. G. *The Golden Bough: A Study in Magic and Religion*, Macmillan and Co., London (1957 ed.).

Glut, Donald F. *The Dracula Book*, The Scarecrow Press Inc, New Jersey, USA, 1975.

Gogarty, Oliver St John. *As I Was Going Down Sackville Street*, 1937.

Graves, Alfred Perceval. *To Return to All That*, Jonathan Cape, London, 1930.

Grogan, Ellinore. *The Life Of J. D. Bourchier*, Hurst and Blackett, London and Dublin, 1926.

Haining, Peter. *The Dracula Scrapbook*, New English Library, 1976.

Haining, Peter, ed. *Shades of Dracula: The Uncollected Stories of Bram Stoker*, Kimber, London, 1982.

Haining, Peter. *The Dracula Centenary Book*, Souvenir Press, London, 1987.

Haining, Peter. *Great Irish Stories of the Supernatural*, Souvenir Press, London, 1992.

Haining, Peter. *Great Irish Stories of the Unimaginable*, Souvenir Press, 1994.

Haining, Peter. *The Vampire Omnibus*, Orion, London, 1995.

Harmon, Maurice. *Modern Irish Literature – A Reader's Guide 1800–1967*, Gill, Dublin 1967.

Hart-Davis, Rupert ed. *The Letters of Oscar Wilde*, R. Hart-Davis, London, 1962.

Hyde, Douglas. *A Literary History of Ireland*, T. Fisher Unwin, London, 1899.

Ingram, John H. *Edgar Allan Poe: His Life, Letters and Opinions*, Ward, Lock, Bowden and Co., London, 1891.

Irving, Laurence. *Henry Irving: The Actor and his World*, Faber and Faber, London, 1951.

Joyce, P. W. *A Social History of Ancient Ireland*, Longman, Green and Co., London (2 vols), 1903.

Larminie, William. *West Irish Folk-tales and Romances*, London, 1893.

Leatherdale, Clive. *Dracula: The Novel and the Legend*, Aquarian Press, London, 1985.

Leatherdale, Clive. *The Origins of Dracula*, William Kimber, London, 1987.

Lougy, Robert E. *Charles Robert Maturin*, Bucknell University Press, USA, 1975.

Lovecraft, H. P. *Supernatural Horror in Literature*, Dover Books, New York, 1973.

Ludlam, Harry. *A Biography of Dracula: The Life Story of Bram Stoker*, published for the Fireside Press by W. Foulsham and Co., London, 1962.

McCormack, W. J. *Sheridan Le Fanu and Victorian Ireland*, The Lilliput Press, Dublin, 1991.

Mackenzie, Andrew. *Dracula Country*, Arthur Baker Ltd, London, 1977.

MacMahon, Gerald. *The Origins of the Irish Literary Society, London, with some notes on the early years*. A paper read to the Society, 1 June 1993, printed by Paper Press, London, 1993.

McNally, Raymond T. and Florescu, Radu. *In Search of Dracula*, Warner Brothers, New York, 1973.

Marcus, Phillip L. *Standish O'Grady*, Bucknell University Press, New Jersey, USA, 1970.

Masters, Anthony. *The Natural History of the Vampire*, Rupert Hart-Davis, London, 1972.

O'Curry, Eugene. *On the Manners and Customs of the Ancient Irish*, 3 vols, London, 1873.

O'Donnell, E. E. *Father Browne: A Life in Pictures*, Wolfhound Press, 1994.

O'Donoghue, David J. *Life and Writings of William Carleton* (2 vols), Dublin, 1896.

O'Donoghue, David J. *Life and Writings of James Clarence Mangan*, Dublin, 1897.

Ó hÓgáin, Dáithi. *Myth, Legend and Romance: An Encyclopaedia of the Irish Folk Tradition*, Ryan Publishing, London, 1990.

Ó Súilleabháin, Seán. *A Handbook of Irish Folklore*, M. H. Gill, Dublin, 1942.

Ó Súilleabháin, Seán. *Caitheamh Aimsire ar Thórraimh*, An Clóchomhar Teo., BAC, Éire, 1961.

Poe, Edgar Allan. *Tales of Mystery and Imagination*, with introduction by Pádraic Colum, J. M. Dent and Son, London, 1908.

Pozzuoli, Alain. *Bram Stoker: Prince des Ténèbres*, Librairie Séguier, Paris, 1989.

Ronay, Gabriel. *The Dracula Myth*, W. H. Allen, London, 1972.

Roth, Phyllis, A. *Bram Stoker*, Twayne Publishers, Boston, 1982.

Ryan, W. P. *The Irish Literary Revival: Its History, Pioneers and Possibilities*. Lemma Publishing Corporation, reprint ed., New York, 1970, Facsimile reprint of first edition published London, 1894.

St Claire, Sheila. *Folklore of the Ulster People*, Mercier, Cork, 1971.

Stoker, George. *With the Unspeakables & etc*, John Falconer, Dublin, 1878.

Traubel, Horace. *With Walt Whitman in Camden*, University of Pennsylvania Press, 1953.

Tremayne, Peter. *Irish Masters of Fantasy*, Wolfhound Press, Dublin, 1979.

Twitchell, James. *The Living Dead: A Study of the Vampire in Romantic Literature*, Duke University Press, Durham, 1981.

Tyrrell, R. Y. and Sullivan, Edward. *Echoes from Kottabos*, E. Grant Richard, London, 1906.

Walford, Edward. *Old and New London*, Vol. III (Westminster and Western Suburbs), Cassell, Petter, Galpin and Co., n.d. *c*.1890s.

Whitman, Sarah H. *Edgar Poe and His Critics*, (privately printed) New York, 1859.

Wilde, Lady. *Ancient Legends, Mystic Charmes and Superstitions of Ireland*, Ward and Downey, London, 1888.

Wilde, William. *Irish Popular Superstitions*, Orr and Co., Dublin, 1852.

Wolf, Leonard. *A Dream of Dracula: in Search of the Living Dead*, Little Brown, Boston, 1972.

Wolf, Leonard. *The Annotated Dracula by Bram Stoker*, New English Library, London, 1975.

Woodward, Ian. *The Werewolf Delusion*, Paddington Press, London and New York, 1979.

CHRONOLOGY OF BRAM STOKER'S BOOKS
(UK first editions; US title given where retitled)

The Duties of Clerks of Petty Sessions in Ireland, John Falconer, Dublin, 1879. (non-fiction)

Under the Sunset, Sampson Low, Marston, Searle and Rivington, London, 1882. (short stories)

The Snake's Pass, Sampson Low, Marston, Searle and Rivington, London, 1891.

The Watter's Mou', Archibald Constable and Co., London, 1895.

The Shoulder of Shasta, Archibald Constable and Co., London, 1895.

Dracula, Archibald Constable and Co., London, 1897. (This was originally entitled 'The Un-Dead' on the MS, now in private hands.)

Miss Betty, C. Arthur Pearson, London, 1898. (This was originally written as 'Seven Golden Buttons', original MS in Brotherton Library, Leeds.)

The Mystery of the Sea, William Heinemann, London, 1902.

The Jewel of Seven Stars, William Heinemann, London, 1903.

The Man, William Heinemann, London, 1905. (published in the USA as *The Gates of Life*, Cupples and Leon, New York, 1908.)

Personal Reminiscences of Henry Irving, 2 vols., William Heinemann, London, 1906. (non-fiction)

Lady Athlyne, William Heinemann, London, 1908.

Snowbound, Collier and Co., London, 1908. (short stories)

The Lady of the Shroud, William Heinemann, London, 1909.

Famous Imposters, Sidgwick and Jackson, London, 1910. (non-fiction)

The Lair of the White Worm, William Rider and Son, London, 1911.

Dracula's Guest and other weird stories, George Routledge and Son, London, 1914. (short stories)

INDEX